D0410713

Just Words

Just Words

On Speech and Hidden Harm

Mary Kate McGowan

Great Clarendon Street, Oxford, OX2 6DP,
United Kingdom

Oxford University Press is a department of the University of Oxford. It furthers the University's objective of excellence in research, scholarship, and education by publishing worldwide. Oxford is a registered trade mark of Oxford University Press in the UK and in certain other countries

© Mary Kate McGowan 2019

The moral rights of the author have been asserted

First Edition published in 2019

Impression: 1

All rights reserved. No part of this publication may be reproduced, stored in a retrieval system, or transmitted, in any form or by any means, without the prior permission in writing of Oxford University Press, or as expressly permitted by law, by licence or under terms agreed with the appropriate reprographics rights organization. Enquiries concerning reproduction outside the scope of the above should be sent to the Rights Department, Oxford University Press, at the address above

You must not circulate this work in any other form
and you must impose this same condition on any acquirer

Published in the United States of America by Oxford University Press
198 Madison Avenue, New York, NY 10016, United States of America

British Library Cataloguing in Publication Data

Data available

Library of Congress Control Number: 2018958114

ISBN 978–0–19–882970–6

Printed and bound in Great Britain by
Clays Ltd, Elcograf S.p.A.

Links to third party websites are provided by Oxford in good faith and for information only. Oxford disclaims any responsibility for the materials contained in any third party website referenced in this work.

To Mike, Shea, and Nora
who heal me

Contents

Acknowledgments

This book has been a long time coming. I began thinking about these issues when preparing to teach a Philosophy of Language course for the first time when I started teaching at Wellesley College in the fall of 1998. I wanted to make the technical issues come alive for students so I read Rae Langton's "Speech Acts and Unspeakable Acts." I got hooked. I thank Rae for her beautiful work and for paving the way. I also thank David Lewis for his beautiful work, his encouragement of this use of his scorekeeping framework, and his decency.

Although it is just a collection of words, it has taken me a very long time to figure out which words and which order to put them in. They have been re-arranged many times. The manuscript has undergone several complete overhauls. Each time, I benefited from the careful and thoughtful feedback of a brilliant and patient Wellesley student. They are Sara Helmers, Bianka Takaoka, and Edilia Foster. I am extremely grateful to them for their suggestions. For help compiling the index, I thank the brilliant and intrepid Audrey Powers.

This project has been supported by the Suzy Newhouse Center for the Humanities at Wellesley College and the American Council of Learned Societies. These sources of support were not just financial; they also helped to motivate me. In the winter of 2014, the Newhouse Center also sponsored a day-long seminar on the manuscript. As a result, this book has benefited from thoughtful suggestions from Carol Dougherty, Bianka Takaoka, Catherine Elgin, Sally Haslanger, Elisabeth Camp, Lynne Tirrell, Luvell Anderson, Catherine Wearing, and Marion Smiley. I am extremely thankful to the Newhouse Center and all of the participants for the time, consideration, and feedback. The current version is greatly improved in both clarity and detail, thanks to their probing questions.

The material in this book has been presented to many different audiences. They include: Panel on Feminist Applications of Speech Act Theory for the 2001 Independent Activities Period at M.I.T., the 2001 Society for Philosophy in the Contemporary World 2001 Annual Conference, Bryn Mawr College, Boston Area Reading Group in Ethics at

Boston University, The Fellowship of Women: The Work of the AAUW Education Foundation Annual Meeting, the Workshop on Gender and Philosophy at M.I.T., Brandeis University, Wellesley Club of Houston, University of Massachusetts, Boston, The Language and Law Roundtable at the Center for the Study of Mind in Nature at the University of Oslo, PHIL 252 at Washington and Lee University, the philosophy department at Washington and Lee University, 2010 Eastern Division Meeting of the American Philosophical Association, Minnesota Wellesley Alumna Association, the philosophy department at Georgetown University, 2012 Central Division Meeting of the American Philosophical Association, PHIL 24.S40 at M.I.T., PHIL 248 at Harvard University, the philosophy department at the University of Oklahoma, 2012 World Congress Meeting of the International Political Science Association, U.S. Embassies in Aberbaijan, Armenia, and Georgia (sponsored by the U.S. Department of State through the Virtual Student Foreign Service Program), Feminist Philosophy and Pornography Conference at Humboldt University, 2014 Southern Society for Philosophy and Psychology Meeting, 2015 Wintersession for the Freedom Project at Wellesley College, the philosophy department at the University of Connecticut, Philosophy and Law Seminar at the University of Chicago Law School, Workshop on Global Expressive Rights and the Internet at the Gender Research Institute at Dartmouth College, the philosophy department at the University of Missouri, Minorities and Philosophy talk at Yale University, 2016 Language and Law Seminar at Dartmouth College, the 2016 Wintersession for the Freedom Project at Wellesley College, PHIL 9840 class at the University of Missouri, PHIL 473 class at Amherst College, Forry and Micken Lecture Series at Amherst College, Republique des Savoirs Seminar on Free Speech at the Ecole Normale Superieure, Voicing Dissent Workshop at the Humanities Institute at the University of Connecticut, Free Speech and its Discontents Workshop at the Center for Human Values at Princeton University, 2018 Eastern Division Meeting of the American Philosophical Association, the 2018 Wintersession for the Freedom Project at Wellesley College, Wellesley Neighbors, and the Ethics Program at Agnes Scott College. I thank each of these entities and audiences for helping to improve this project through their critical engagement. All remaining defects are, of course, on me.

Many have helped in various ways. For their feedback, engagement, and/or support, I thank: Luvell Anderson, Robert Brooks, Susan Brison,

Helena de Bres, Catherine Z. Elgin, Edilia Foster, Deirdre Galway, Helen Ann Patricia Shea McGowan Gardner, Corinne Gartner, Katherine Gelber, Sandy Goldberg, David Miguel Gray, Mitchell Green, Jack Greichen, Maureen Greichen, Daniel Harris, Sally Haslanger, Hep Cat II, Claire Horisk, Robin Jeshion, Casey Johnson, Rae Langton, David Lewis, Steffi Lewis, Shen-Yi Liao, Catharine MacKinnon, James Mahon, Ishani Maitra, Erich Matthes, Alison McIntyre, Paul McGowan, Susan McGowan, Tim McGowan, Rachel McKinnon, Mari Mikkola, Matthew Moss, Mihaela Popa, Hilary Putnam, Ruth Anna Putnam, Nikki Ramsoomair, Frederick Schauer, Jessica Shlasko, Robert Mark Simpson, Marion Smiley, Sarah Sorial, Jason Stanley, Lindsey Stewart, Natalie Stoljar, Tanya Sullivan, Asta Sveinsdottir, Bianka Takaoka, Lynne Tirrell, Whitney Tully, Julie Walsh, Catherine Wearing, Caroline West, and Claudia Yau.

I thank my editor, Peter Momtchiloff, and the reviewers for Oxford University Press.

I also benefited from several other layers of professional support. My home department, at Wellesley College, is a truly collegial environment and I am daily grateful to work in it. Wellesley students are so smart, motivated, politically engaged, and thoughtful; teaching them keeps philosophy fun. I am also fortunate to be at an institution that values feminist scholarship. This ought to be true everywhere but it is not. Last, I count myself lucky to be in the Boston area where there is a critical mass of scholars working on social issues with philosophical tools. In particular, I thank Sally Haslanger and M.I.T.'s Workshop on Gender and Philosophy. Being a part of this group made this project possible.

Finally, I thank my entire extended family. I thank every single sibling, cousin, aunt, uncle, parent, grandparent, and even ancestor. The zaniness attracted me to the rigor of philosophy and kept me grounded. I thank that spot of turnips in Spunkane and the shellfish in Faha West. Last but certainly not least, I thank Mike, Shea, and Nora; they inspire and recharge me. I could not have done this without them.

Introduction

An employee brags about his sexual conquest to a co-worker while they are on break in the employee lounge.

This offhand remark oppresses. Moreover, it does so even when the speaker does not intend to do so and even when the speaker is utterly unaware of doing so. What words do is not a simple function of either speaker intention or speaker awareness. This remark can oppress even in cases where the speaker has no special authority. Ordinary people under ordinary circumstances can unwittingly oppress others with their everyday comments. The power to verbally oppress comes from the social context; it need not reside in the speaker.

A white man spews racist vitriol at the only African American passenger on a public bus.

In the United States, this utterance is treated as the expression of a political viewpoint and it is thus highly protected political speech. It should not be. Even within the heightened free speech commitments of the United States, there are sufficient grounds for regulating this utterance and others like it. Furthermore, the reasons for regulating it are exactly the same reasons that justify the regulation of other uncontroversially regulable categories of speech. Racist speech in public places is harmful enough to warrant legal intervention.

A worker hangs a sexually explicit poster in his personal locker at work.

This action can subordinate and this is so even if the person who hangs the poster does not have any communicative intentions whatsoever when doing so. It can subordinate even if that person does not *mean* anything at all by hanging the poster. A subordinating action need not be a communicative one.

Just Words: On Speech and Hidden Harm argues for these surprising results and it does so by identifying a previously overlooked manner in which speech is harmful. Although the potential harmfulness of speech is now widely recognized, we nevertheless need to be as clear as possible about what the harms are and how the speech in question brings those harms about. Clarity on these two points is important for social, political, moral, and jurisprudential reasons.

This book identifies a previously overlooked mechanism by which ordinary speech by ordinary speakers under ordinary circumstances enacts harmful norms and thus constitutes, rather than merely causes, harm. Harm constitution is a technical notion; it is a distinct way of causing harm. Harm is constituted when the harm is brought about via adherence to norms enacted.

Standard examples of utterances that constitute harm involve authoritative speech. Suppose, for example, that the C.E.O. of a company enacts a new hiring policy by declaring that women are no longer eligible for employment. Suppose further that the employees adhere to this policy so a discriminatory hiring practice ensues. Because the harm of discrimination is brought about via adherence to the hiring policy (which is a norm) enacted by the C.E.O.'s utterance, the C.E.O.'s utterance constitutes rather than merely causes the harm of discrimination.

In this book, I argue that there is another way for speech to enact norms and thus to enact harmful norms but this other way does *not* require an exercise of speaker authority. In fact, ordinary utterances routinely enact norms without the speaker having or exercising any special authority. Because our utterances (and our actions more generally) are contributions to norm-governed social practices, they enact norms in those practices. Moreover, sometimes the enacted norms are harmful and, when they are, harm is constituted, rather than merely caused.

This mechanism of norm-enactment is ubiquitous but overlooked; it is subtle and obscured. The covert nature of this phenomenon thus conceals the harm constituted and masks our complicity in it. Drawing attention to this mechanism therefore identifies further harms and highlights our role in bringing those harms about.

The vast majority of scholars (in law, political theory, feminism, philosophy) who work on the harmfulness of speech focus exclusively on the harms caused. The few scholars who focus on a constitutive connection between speech and harm treat norm-enacting speech as an exercise of speaker authority so that only authoritative speakers are able to verbally enact harmful norms and thus verbally constitute harm. *Just Words: On Speech and Hidden Harm* demonstrates that non-authoritative speakers can and do verbally constitute harm. In fact, we do so unwittingly and often.

That harm is constituted rather than merely caused is important for many reasons. First, bringing further instances of verbal harm constitution to light shows that speech is more harmful than we thought. Moreover, the clearer we are on the connection between speech and its associated harms, the better positioned we are to prevent, minimize, or redress those harms.

This difference between causing harm and constituting it also matters to the law. In any jurisdiction embracing a free speech principle, the harmfulness of speech is the only legitimate justification for its regulation. The type of harm, the amount of harm, and the *connection* between the speech and harm all matter when assessing whether some category of speech is harmful enough to warrant its regulation. Because speech that constitutes harm is distinct in the eyes of the law, identifying additional instances of it opens up potential justifications for further speech regulation.

Furthermore, identifying this subtle mechanism of norm enactment shows how the specific everyday actions of ordinary individuals contribute to broader social structures. Since those structures just are collections of norms and practices, enacting norms actually *extends* these structures. It also brings them to bear in the micro context of utterance and personal interaction. We are thus not mere passive cogs; we are active perpetuators and extenders of social structures and practices.

Finally, highlighting the role that speech plays in extending and enlivening unjust social structures shows that speech is no mere symptom of the social problem; it is a crucial mechanism through which these unjust hierarchies are enacted and perpetuated.

Overview and highlights

The first half of *Just Words: On Speech and Hidden Harm* argues for this previously overlooked mechanism of norm-enactment. The investigation begins in the kinematics of conversation where I argue that conversational contributions routinely enact norms for the conversation to which they contribute. Then, I argue that the phenomenon generalizes. I argue that moves in other norm-governed activities (and not just conversational moves) enact norms for those activities too.

The second half of the book applies this insight to a series of examples: sexist remarks (Chapter 5), actions involving pornography (Chapter 6), and racist utterances in public spaces (Chapter 7). These examples demonstrate that speech can constitute a variety of different harms. It can oppress, subordinate, silence, and discriminate. These types of harm are characterized and instances of speech that constitute them are explored.

Some surprising results are generated. An offhand sexist remark can oppress even when the speaker has no intention of doing so, even when the speaker has no special authority for doing so, and even when the remark is not even addressed to the person oppressed by it. Because the remark is a contribution to broader social practices, it taps into normative features of those larger social structures. The oppressive power comes from those structures but they are brought to bear on that microenvironment by that single remark by that individual.

Other results are provocative and will no doubt be controversial. In Chapter 7, for example, I argue that there are sufficient grounds to justify the legal actionability of racist utterances in public places. In particular, I argue that racist statements by a mere passenger on a bus can constitute a hostile and thus discriminatory environment. Since a public bus is a public accommodation, equal access and protection under law require a change to current U.S. free speech law and practice.

Other results are explanatory. One might wonder how speech can be really harmful when a speaker has neither the intention nor the awareness of harming. A claim that an utterance or type of speech is harmful might seem to require positing either a malevolent speaker or an oversensitive audience member. Such false dilemmas plague our public discussions about social issues. Once we see, however, that language use routinely functions in socially important but barely conscious ways, we are able to recognize unintended but real connections between speech and harm.

The terrain

This book contributes to what might be called the linguistic approach to group-based injustice.[1] On this view, speech plays a central role in enacting and perpetuating unjust social hierarchies. Although most now

[1] Others include: MacKinnon 1993 and Langton 2009. The title of this book is also a nod to MacKinnon 1993.

recognize that speech can be harmful, many nevertheless regard speech as playing a rather minor role in bringing about the various harms associated with group-based injustice. On this view, things like racist hate speech are a mere symptom or side effect of racism; they play no real role in establishing or perpetuating racist ideologies or practices. Racist utterances and their toleration are an indicator of racism but they are not constitutive of it.[2] As we shall see, though, this view overlooks the fact that speech routinely (and covertly) enacts norms and norms prescribe who can do what. Speech is thus paramount in signaling, enacting, and maintaining unfair distributions of social power and it does so along group lines.

Of course, that speech plays a central role in group-based social injustice does not mean that speech is the *only* thing that matters.[3] Plenty of other things (e.g. poverty, violence, and incarceration rates to name just a few) are also urgent. Rather, the central claim of the linguistic approach is that speech is *one* of the things that crucially matter. It has an enormous power to shape and reshape the social world and we cannot afford to overlook that.

Just Words: On Speech and Hidden Harm engages multiple audiences, literatures, and subfields of philosophy simultaneously. The first half of the book is primarily philosophy of language and pragmatics of conversation. The relevant background is offered for those readers not already familiar with it. The second half of the book involves social and political philosophy, feminist philosophy, and philosophy of law. Again, the requisite background is offered for the uninitiated.

This is a book in philosophy. Since the issues addressed are so complex and multi-faceted, there are inevitably pieces of the puzzle that are not philosophical in nature. As a result, some issues—even some very important issues—are left to experts outside of philosophy. Although I rely on the existence and normative force of social norms, for example, I do not identify the precise content of those norms. This is an empirical

[2] In fact, this is the official position of the American Civil Liberties Union on campus speech codes. https://www.aclu.org/other/speech-campus.

[3] Some argue that attention on speech is misplaced and distracts from the *real* problems, like poverty, violence, *de facto* segregation, and discrimination. See, for example, Gates 1993.

matter for others to settle.[4] Although I argue that there is sufficient theoretical justification, in terms of harm prevention, for treating certain sorts of public racist utterances as legally actionable, I leave it to others to determine exactly how to regulate such utterances. This is a matter best left to those with expertise in law and the criminal justice system. Even within philosophy (broadly understood), some relevant and important details are here left open for others to fill in and I am explicit about this when it is helpful to the reader to be so.

Potential applications of the mechanism identified here are wide open. In this book, the sneaky mechanism of norm-enactment is applied to expressions of sexual bravado, actions involving pornography, and racist utterances. Others have applied the framework (relying on previously published work) to topics not explored here: sedition law,[5] racial figleaves,[6] acts of slurring,[7] political dog whistles,[8] the responsibility of overhearers,[9] defining a regulable class of hate speech,[10] issues in disability studies,[11] and even the basis for empirical work in socio-drama.[12] Elsewhere, I have applied it to microaggressions.[13] Clearly, potential applications of the framework are not exhausted by those explicitly developed in this book. It is my hope that the details, extensions, and clarifications developed here both facilitate these further applications and dispel misunderstandings in the extant literature.

Chapter summaries

Chapter 1 presents the required background in the philosophy of language and it clarifies the nature of enactment, harm constitution, and social norms.

Chapter 2 argues that conversational contributions routinely enact norms for the conversation to which they contribute. Such conversational exercitives involve an important but overlooked mechanism of verbal norm enactment.

[4] In earlier work, I was less clear about this reliance on empirical matters. For this criticism, see Schauer 2014.

[5] See Sorial 2010 and 2015.

[6] See Saul 2017.

[7] See Bianchi 2014; Lenehan 2014; Popa-Wyatt and Wyatt 2017; Soon, "On Slurring," unpublished manuscript; Cousens 2014.

[8] See Saul 2018.

[9] See Ayala and Vasilyeva 2016.

[10] See Gelber 2017.

[11] See Aas 2016.

[12] See Codatos, Testoni, and Ronzani 2012.

[13] See my 2018a; 2018b.

Chapter 3 explores differences between conversational exercitives and standard exercitives. Although both enact norms, standard exercitives do so via an exercise of speaker authority but conversational exercitives work differently. Other similarities and differences are also explored.

Chapter 4 argues that the phenomenon of conversational exercitives generalizes. It is not just verbal contributions to conversations that enact norms; verbal contributions to other norm-governed activities also do so. Such covert exercitives are presented and explored.

Chapter 5 applies our understanding of covert exercitives to an example of sexist speech. An offhand sexist remark is shown to be oppressive even though the speaker does not intend to oppress, the speaker does not have any particular authority, and the remark is not aimed at the persons oppressed by it.

Chapter 6 uses the framework of covert exercitives to explore the potential harms of actions involving certain types of pornography. The nature of pornography, the crucial role of context, and the harms of both subordination and silencing are discussed.

Chapter 7 applies the phenomenon of covert exercitives to free speech issues. The philosophical foundations of a free speech principle are presented and different sorts of arguments for speech regulation are discussed. It is shown that because racist speech in public places enacts discriminatory norms, there is a harm prevention justification for its legal actionability.

Finally, in the Conclusion, we explore how the sneaky mechanism of norm enactment identified in this book can enact positive (rather than harmful) norms. Just as our speech acts can enact harmful norms by tapping into pernicious social practices, so too can they enact more egalitarian norms by tapping into different and more just social practices. This highlights ways in which even relatively powerless individuals can bring about positive, even if highly localized, social change.

1

Preliminaries

1.1 Introduction

Before we can delve into the main arguments of this book, some preliminaries are required. First, the requisite background in the philosophy of language is presented. Then, some complexities about enacting are made explicit. Finally, the distinction between causing and constituting harm is clarified. Because this material is presented in order to be as widely accessible as possible, some selectivity and simplification are involved.

1.2 Language use

Here is a certain naïve and outdated picture of how language works. When a speaker wants to communicate some proposition or claim p, the speaker says something that (literally) means p. A hearer accesses p by simply decoding the literal meaning of what the speaker actually says.[1] In this picture, communication is just a matter of coding and decoding the content of what the speaker wants to communicate. This picture of language use is highly intuitive. After all, we use language to communicate what we mean and we say (or write) things that have meaning, so it makes sense that what we say (or write) should match the meaning we intend to convey.

As intuitive as this picture may be, it has been effectively refuted and abandoned. It cannot deal with a wide variety of familiar linguistic phenomena. As a matter of fact, we rarely say what we mean. Instead, we say something else that enables the hearer to figure out what we mean.[2]

[1] Here and throughout the book I use the term 'hearer' to refer to those persons interpreting an occasion of language use, thereby including persons unable to hear. Although I acknowledge and regret the ableist assumptions, I here reluctantly abide by prevailing practice.

[2] See, for example, Grice 1989: 26–31.

To see an example of this, consider the following. Suppose that Paul and Matt are talking about how strangely Peter has been behaving lately and Paul says, "Anyone who loses a wife and mother in the same day would have a tough time of it." Matt takes Paul to be telling him that Peter lost his wife and mom in the same day and that these losses explain why Peter is behaving so strangely lately. Although this is precisely what Paul intends to communicate to Matt, it is not what Paul actually says. What Paul actually says is a general claim about people who lose a wife and mother in the same day; it is not a claim about Peter at all. Despite this, Matt is able to infer Paul's intended meaning (that claim about Peter) from the conventional meaning of what Paul actually says along with facts about the context and the cooperative nature of conversation. The point for us now is that what Paul means and what Paul says are distinct. As one can see then, communication is not a mere matter of decoding the meaning of the language used.

That we often mean something different from what we say draws our attention to an important distinction between conventional meaning, on the one hand, and speaker meaning, on the other. What Paul means by what he says (his speaker meaning) is clearly distinct from the conventional meaning of what he actually says. Irony provides another illustration of this contrast. Suppose that my beloved husband Mike enters the room, trips on an ottoman and then lands on my dinner plate and, as I wipe pasta sauce from my face, I say: "Mike you sure are graceful!"[3] What I mean here (among other things) is that Mike is extremely clumsy. What my words actually mean (that is, the conventional, as opposed to the speaker, meaning of my utterance) is that Mike sure is graceful. Again, speaker meaning, or what the speaker means by what she says, is distinct from the conventional meaning of the words actually used.[4]

[3] This example is fictional. I thank Albert Michael Booth for suggesting that I make this explicit.

[4] As we shall see in further detail later in this section, speaker meaning is sometimes used in a narrow sense to refer only to the content the speaker intends to communicate. A hearer might, for example, correctly identify the content of my order while mistaking that order for a mere suggestion. In such a case, speaker meaning in the narrow sense is recognized but speaker meaning in the broad sense is not. Unless otherwise indicated, I shall use speaker meaning in the broad sense. There are controversies regarding the correct account of speaker meaning. Grice's (1989) account has been very influential but it has also been (widely) criticized for being too audience-based (or focused on communication as opposed to expression). For an example of this sort of criticism of Grice's account, see Davis 1992.

Another important distinction concerns the difference between sentences or sentence-types (that is, punctuated strings of words) and utterances (fully contextualized uses of words on particular occasions). Consider the sentence, 'She went home.' There are many instances of that sentence-type; 'She went home' is written or said in many different places and contexts. Moreover, what that sentence means (even conventionally) clearly varies from use to use. On one occasion, it might mean that Sheila went to 13 Elm Street. On another it might mean that Jeanne went back to the Middle East and, on yet another, it might mean that Lori left the party. For this reason, many deny that sentences (qua sentence-types) are the bearers of meaning. On this view, a sentence independent of a context of use fails to have a determinate meaning. What bears meaning are particular uses of sentences on particular occasions. In what follows, I will not be concerned with sentences or sentence-types. Rather, I shall focus on sentence-uses on particular occasions and I will often refer to them as 'utterances'.

As mentioned above, the decoding picture of language has been rejected. Language theorists now agree that language use is highly inferential. In fact, even direct literal language use involves complex inferential reasoning. Suppose, for example, that I say, 'Peter is tall' and I mean what I say. I am not being ironic or insinuating that something else is true of Peter because he is tall. Even here, however, hearers must make rather complex inferences to correctly interpret my utterance. For starters, they need to figure out which Peter I am talking about. Furthermore, they also need to figure out what constitutes being tall for someone like Peter. If he is a professional basketball player, for example, then saying that he is tall probably means that he is over seven feet. If, however, Peter is a preschooler, then it means no such thing.[5]

Finally, it is helpful to think of language use in terms of solving a certain sort of coordination problem. Coordination problems are situations involving more than one agent, where what one ought to do depends on what others decide to do and where there is a shared goal. Suppose, for example, that my husband and I get separated while we are

[5] There is considerable controversy in the literature regarding the role of context in fixing the conventional meaning of (or the proposition expressed by) the sentence uttered. For a sampling of positions, see Stanley 2000; Carston 2002; Lepore and Cappellen 2005; and MacFarlane 2009.

leaving a concert. In this situation, we have a common goal; we each want to find the other. It doesn't really matter where we meet so long as we do meet somewhere. Our decisions are also mutually dependent. That is, where I should go depends on where he decides to go and vice versa. As one can see, this is a coordination problem. In this case, I decide to walk to the car because I figure that Mike will do the same. I figure that he'll do the same because I figure that he'll figure that I'll walk to the car. We routinely face such decision situations and we often manage to successfully solve them.

How does language use involve the solution to a coordination problem? Well, the common goal is successful communication and what participants ought to do depends on what other participants do. In particular, speakers say what they think will enable hearers to figure out what they mean (appealing to the conventional meaning of what is said, along with common knowledge and context). Hearers interpret the speaker in terms of what the hearer thinks the speaker means. Both speakers and hearers must coordinate in this way in order to successfully communicate.[6]

In sum then, I work within a conception of language use according to which our use of language is highly inferential, context-sensitive, and focused on the communication of linguistic intentions. This is a broadly Gricean framework.[7] There are, of course, alternative frameworks. Habermas's theory of communication and Robert Brandom's inferential role semantics might serve my purposes just as well. Although there are multiple and important similarities between these frameworks and the

[6] See Lewis (1969) 2002 and Sperber and Wilson 1986.

[7] There is an important division today within the Gricean framework, between Griceans and relevance theorists but they are both Gricean in this broad sense. They both regard language use as highly inferential and context-sensitive. They both view language use as involving the solution of a communication coordination problem. And both are primarily concerned with the interpretation end (that is, with explaining how hearers manage to figure out what a speaker means and what the speaker means to do with her words). The main difference between them concerns what they use to do the explaining. While Griceans appeal to the cooperative nature of conversation and to Grice's four maxims (of quality, quantity, relevance, and manner), relevance theorists appeal only to relevance in their special technical sense (of maximizing cognitive effect while minimizing cognitive effort). See Grice 1989 and Sperber and Wilson 1986.

aspects of language use stressed here, these alternative frameworks are not explored in any great detail in this book.[8]

1.3 Speech acts

Here is another naïve and outdated view of how language functions: Language use is merely in the business of expressing claims. In his *How to Do Things with Words*, J. L. Austin drew our philosophical attention to the inadequacy of this view by highlighting a range of other functions of language use.[9] Austin demonstrates that, in addition to making true or false claims about the world, speech can constitute action. Promises, bets, and apologies are all actions that can be performed by saying certain words under certain circumstances.[10]

Austin also distinguished amongst three different forces of speech. First, the *locutionary* force of an utterance is its sense (meaning) and reference (things referred to). When I tell John, "Officer Jones is using his radar gun on Rt. 24," my utterance has locutionary force. 'Officer Jones' refers to Officer Jones, 'radar gun' refers to radar guns, 'Rt. 24' refers to Rt. 24 and the sentence expresses the claim that Officer Jones is using his radar gun on Rt. 24. My utterance has locutionary force since I uttered words that have meaning and reference.[11] Locution fixes the (conventional) content. It resolves ambiguities and fixes indexicals.[12] There may be many people in the universe called 'Officer Jones' but this particular use of this expression refers to a particular person.

It is important to notice that locution concerns content and is not the same as assertion. Assertion, by contrast, concerns the *speaker's commitment to the truth of* that content. To see this difference more clearly, note that when I said, 'Mike, you sure are graceful' I expressed the claim that Mike sure is graceful but I did not commit to (the truth or the probable truth of) the claim that Mike sure is graceful. I said something with a

[8] See Habermas 1984. For work within that framework, see Gelber 2002. There is also Brandom's inferential role semantics. See Brandom 1994. For work within that framework, see Kukla and Lance 2009 and Tirrell 2012.

[9] See Austin 1975. [10] See also Green 2017a.

[11] This is sometimes called a rhetic act. See Austin 1975: 93. Neither the meaning nor the extension (referent) needs to be fully determinate.

[12] There are controversies regarding how this content is fixed. Specifically, there are controversies over the role of context in fixing content. For additional information, see note 5.

particular content (and thereby performed a locutionary act) but I did not thereby assert (or commit to) that content. As one can see then, locution is conceptually distinct from assertion.

Second, the *illocutionary* force of an utterance is the action constituted by the utterance in virtue of the utterance functioning as speech. Although the physical production of speech (whether written, verbal, or signed) is an action, it is not an illocutionary act. The illocutionary act is performed by means of the locutionary act of expressing content. When I said, "Officer Jones is using his radar gun on Rt. 24" I thereby asserted (and thus committed myself to the truth of) the claim that Officer Jones is using his radar gun on Rt. 24. In addition to asserting, other illocutionary acts include ordering (e.g. "I order you to shut the door") and promising (e.g. "Yes, Father, I promise to go to Mass each week").

Third and finally, the *perlocutionary* force of an utterance is a certain sort of causal effect on the audience. In order for a causal effect to be a perlocutionary effect, it must be brought about by means of the linguistic functioning of the utterance.[13] In other words, non-linguistic causal effects of speech (such as a shrill voice breaking glass or a loud announcement waking someone) are not perlocutionary effects since these causal effects are not brought about by means of the hearer's recognition of the conventional meaning of the words uttered. Perlocutionary effects are thus a subset of causal effects. Typically, there is a particular perlocutionary effect that the speaker hopes to bring about via her utterance. When I said that Officer Jones is using his radar gun on Rt. 24, I aimed to warn John that he should drive within the speed limit; I aimed to cause him to believe that Officer Jones would catch him if he did not.

Of course, an utterance might not bring about its intended perlocutionary effect. John might think that I am mistaken or he might not realize that I aim to warn rather than merely to inform him. When this happens, the utterance in question has failed to bring about its intended (perlocutionary) effect and the utterance is thus unsuccessful in an

[13] When characterizing perlocution, many repeat part of what Austin said about it: the perlocutionary act is the act performed *by* saying something whereas the illocutionary act is the act performed *in* saying something. See Austin 1975: 91–103. Notice that this is not really a characterization of perlocution; it is a test to distinguish between perlocution and illocution. Theorists disagree about how useful this criterion is.

important respect. Besides warning, other perlocutionary effects include convincing, alarming, persuading, scaring, amusing, and inspiring.

These distinctions (amongst locutionary, perlocutionary, and illocutionary force) show how complex and multi-faceted utterances really are. It also illuminates a variety of ways that communication can fail. Consider the following. Suppose that I say to my son, "Mommy wants you to clean your room now," and he takes it as a suggestion as opposed to the order that it was intended to be. Now, there is a sense in which my son recognizes my meaning. He correctly identifies the meaning and the referents of the words I utter. In this case, communication succeeds at the locutionary level. Understanding meaning in this narrow (strictly locutionary) sense, he got it right. That said, there is an important sense in which my son fails to recognize my meaning. After all, he mistakes my order for a mere suggestion. Speaker meaning is sometimes used in a narrow sense to include only the (intended) locutionary content. In the broad sense, however, speaker meaning also includes the intended perlocutionary and illocutionary acts.[14] If I say something with the perlocutionary intention to amuse you but you do not realize this, then you have missed part of my speaker meaning in this broad sense (even if you correctly identify the locutionary content of my utterance). In what follows, I shall use speaker meaning in the broad sense unless otherwise indicated.

One final point before we proceed. The way most philosophers (linguists and psychologists) talk about speech acts is really quite broad. On this conception, speech acts are communicative or expressive acts that do not need to involve the use of words.[15] Waving to greet a friend is a speech act. Nodding in consent is a speech act. Rolling one's eyes to express disdain is a speech act. According to Clark, even a chess move is a speech act.[16] Visual images can also be speech acts. Drawing a line across someone's face on a poster is a speech act. Although I here work with this broader conception of a speech act, I am nevertheless usually interested in utterances that do involve the use of words.

[14] See note 4.

[15] Rod Bertolet (1994), however, works with a much narrower conception of a speech act. He assumes that words must be used.

[16] See Clark 1996.

1.4 Felicity conditions

Different illocutionary acts have different conditions of success. Although one cannot bequeath money one does not have, for example, one can bet money one is without. Similarly, although it takes a special kind of authority to order or command someone, in general no special authority is required to request, suggest, or assert. That said, most speech acts are maximally felicitous only when the speaker has the appropriate standing to perform that speech act. It would be odd to ask a total stranger to clean your gas grille for you. It seems that one must have the appropriate sort of relationship (or standing) with someone in order to felicitously make such a request. I shall have more to say about speaker authority and standing in Section 3.4.

A speech act can be infelicitous or non-ideal even though it constitutes (or performs) the intended illocutionary act. Suppose I say to John, "I apologize for using your nail gun without your permission," but I actually used Dan's nail gun, not John's. Although my apology is non-ideal because it is offered to the wrong person, it is still true that I apologized (to John). (Austin sometimes called such infelicitous illocutions abuses.[17]) As one can see then, not all infelicities or imperfections are fatal ones.

An illocution with a fatal defect, on the other hand, fails, and the illocutionary act attempted is not performed. (Austin calls such failed illocutions misfires.[18]) Suppose that I try to verbally enact higher speed limits in order to avoid paying a fine for speeding. Try as I might, my utterance will misfire; I will fail to enact new speed limits exactly because I do not have the authority to do so and no one thinks that I do.

In what follows, I shall sometimes leave it open whether a particular infelicity is fatal or not. While the precise status of some of these felicity conditions is a bit controversial, certain conditions appear to be especially important for any speech act.

Consider, for instance, speaker intention. When Rebecca said to Simon, "I promise to share my bag of candy with you," she intended that her utterance count as the undertaking of an obligation on her part (to share her bag of candy with Simon). Notice that this *illocutionary* intention (to promise) is distinct from the *sincerity* condition (that she intend to keep that promise and actually share the bag of candy with

[17] See Austin 1975: 16. [18] See Austin 1975: 16.

Simon). After all, Rebecca might well intend that her words be a promise without also intending to keep that promise. Notice further that the failure of this sincerity condition does not disqualify her utterance from being a promise (that is, from constituting the illocutionary act of promising). If it did, insincere promises would be impossible. So would insincere assertions! If, however, Rebecca does not intend for her words to undertake an obligation at all, then it is unclear whether her utterance is a promise.[19] At the very least, it seems that the speaker ought to actually intend to perform the illocutionary act in question; this speaker illocutionary intention condition appears to be an especially important felicity condition for any speech act.

Hearer recognition also seems to be an important condition for most speech acts. Speakers ought to have reasonable expectations regarding what the hearers are likely to be able to recognize. Although there are a variety of different kinds of hearer recognition, the hearer's recognition of the speaker's intended *illocutionary* act seems to be especially important. Suppose that, intending to warn her son (about the possibility of his slipping on ice), Claudia says, "Hayden, it's getting cold and the playground is getting slippery. Let's get inside before you fall and crack your head." Suppose further that Hayden does not recognize her intention to warn him. In such a case, whether he goes inside or not, there is a failure of the hearer's recognition of the speaker's intended illocutionary act. Some, for example Austin, would maintain that the utterance fails to have the intended illocutionary force (of a warning) exactly because the speaker's illocutionary intention went unrecognized.[20] One might instead maintain that the success of our speech acts should not depend on hearer recognition in this way.[21] After all, why should Claudia be unable to warn her son just because he is occasionally dense regarding her illocutionary intentions? I am inclined to say that Claudia performs

[19] Note that there is a difference between not intending to promise and not intending to undertake an obligation at all. I chose the latter in order to exclude possible cases of illocutionary implication. Suppose that verbal contracts are just like promises except that the obligations enacted are stronger. It may be that a person may intend to enact a verbal contract (and not intend to promise) but by enacting that contract one thereby automatically also promises. For an exploration of these sorts of possibilities, see Searle and Vanderveken 1985.

[20] See Austin 1975: 22, 116, 139.

[21] See, for example, Strawson 1964. For a presentation of this position within feminist debates, see Jacobson 1995.

the illocutionary act of warning but she fails to communicate that warning to her son (exactly because he fails to recognize her intention to do so).[22] Despite this controversy regarding the precise role of uptake (that is, the hearer's recognition of the speaker's intended illocutionary act), it does seem to be an especially important felicity condition for most speech acts. That is, whenever that condition fails, the utterance in question is at least infelicitous even if the utterance nevertheless manages to constitute the intended illocutionary act.

Finally, there seems to be an important difference (even if it is only a matter of degree) between formal, ceremonial, institutionalized speech acts, on the one hand, and more ordinary speech acts on the other. Consider first an example of the former. A speaker, during a formal ship-naming ceremony, crashes a bottle of champagne against the hull and says, "I hereby name this ship The Wanderer." This utterance succeeds in naming the ship because several conditions are met. There is a convention operative according to which ships can be named by a speaker saying certain words under certain circumstances. Moreover, there is an explicit procedure to be followed in order to invoke this convention and this procedure is completely and correctly followed in this case. This includes the fact that this speaker has been formally designated as the only person licensed to name this ship in this way.[23]

Consider now an example of a less ceremonial (or more ordinary) sort of speech act. I make a promise to my daughter Nora by saying, "I promise to bring you to the movies next week." There is a sense in which there is a convention according to which one can undertake an obligation simply by saying certain words under the right circumstances and there is (a perhaps thin sense in which there is) an associated procedure for doing so and I am the only person licensed to promise on my behalf. Despite all this, it nevertheless seems fair to say that what is doing the real work in this case is the communication of speaker intention. Ordinary speech acts seem less dependent on convention (and associated procedures) and more dependent on the communication of intention.[24] Formal speech acts, by

[22] See my 2009a.

[23] These conditions follow Austin's (1975: 14–15) analysis of speech acts.

[24] There is controversy regarding the role of convention in speech acts. Austin (1975) and Searle (1969) require that a speech act conform with the associated convention. Strawson (1964) denies that this is necessary and stresses the importance of the communication of intention. For ordinary speech acts, I side with Strawson.

contrast, seem more dependent on convention (and associated procedures) and less dependent on the communication of intention.[25] Another option would be to say that all speech acts are dependent on convention (or practice) but that the conventions (or practices) in question are more or less formal.

1.5 Exercitives

As mentioned in the Introduction, I am, in this book, primarily interested in ways that speech can constitute harm; I am interested in ways that speech can enact norms that prescribe harmful practices. Illocution is one way for speech to enact norms and thus it is one way for speech to enact harmful norms. Since exercitive speech acts are the sort of speech act that enact norms, I now focus on them.

The term 'exercitive' comes from Austin but Austin's taxonomy of speech acts has been criticized.[26] Although Austin's terminology is still used in some literatures, the term 'exercitive' is not used in the mainstream philosophy of language, linguistics, or pragmatics literatures. Despite this, I do use the term and I have two reasons for doing so. First, my work has arisen out of a separate literature that does use the term.[27] Thus, in keeping with, and contributing to, that literature, it makes good sense to maintain terminology. Second, and more important, I find the category of exercitive to be both illuminating and fruitful, as I hope this book will demonstrate.

For our purposes, *exercitive* speech acts enact facts about what is permissible in a certain realm. In Austin's own words, an exercitive speech act is the "exercising of powers, rights or influence."[28] Suppose, for example, that while enacting college policies, the President of Wellesley College declares: "Smoking is no longer permitted in any college building." This utterance is an exercitive because it takes away certain (in this case, smoking) privileges and thereby changes what is permissible on the Wellesley College campus.

[25] Bach and Harnish (1979) distinguish between conventional acts and communicative acts.

[26] See Austin 1975: 151–2. For a classic criticism of Austin's taxonomy, see Searle 1979b.

[27] This literature is sometimes called the speech act approach to free speech; it is also sometimes called (feminist) applied philosophy of language. It has its roots in Langton 1993.

[28] See Austin 1975: 151.

There are several things worth noting about exercitive speech acts. First, exercitives *enact* permissibility facts; they do not merely cause such facts to obtain. When the president declared that smoking is no longer permissible in any college building, a new permissibility fact (that it is impermissible to smoke inside a college building) thereby sprang into existence. Her saying so made it so. Her utterance did not (merely) cause the rules to change.

Second, exercitive speech acts are *authoritative* speech acts since the speaker must have the requisite authority over the appropriate domain.[29] Had a persnickety student uttered the very same words as the president, her utterance would not have had the same exercitive force. This is so even if the student has all of the same intentions as the president. The student's utterance would nevertheless fail to enact new college policy exactly because the student does not have the authority to do so. Note further that the sort of authority in question is restricted to a particular domain. Although the president of Wellesley College has the authority to enact (some) rules for Wellesley College, she does not thereby have the authority to enact rules for other institutions of higher learning or to set the bedtime for my children.

Third, the kind of permissibility facts enacted by exercitive speech acts are quite complex. As we shall see, this notion of permissibility includes what is required (that is, what it is not permissible not to do); it is also often a matter of degree and may function along more than one axis. When my boss says, "You must submit all such requests on-line" she thereby changes what I am required to do. What was permissible before her utterance (submitting a request in writing or in person) is no longer permissible. Thus by verbally enacting this requirement, her utterance thereby enacts new permissibility facts for our workplace. Moreover, permissibility need not be an all or nothing affair. While it may be inappropriate to draw attention to yourself while reading the songbook during Mass, it would be far more inappropriate to do so while reading a novel and it would be worse still to do so while reading anything written by Friedrich Nietzsche! As one can see, permissibility can be a matter of degree. Finally, permissibility is multi-faceted. When Tim drew attention to the fact that he was reading *Thus Spake Zarathustra* during Mass, his

[29] I shall later argue that this is true of only standard exercitives. As we shall see in Chapter 2, there are non-authoritative exercitives.

actions were inappropriate in a variety of ways. His actions were religiously inappropriate since the Catholic Church expects participants to be properly attending to the miracle of the Mass; it was spiritually inappropriate since he ought to have been praying; it was socially inappropriate since he distracted other attendees and insulted their beliefs; and it was personally unkind since he did it in order to wound his religious mother who insisted that he attend Mass in the first place. As one can see, permissibility is multi-dimensional.[30]

Fourth, not all cases of exercitive speech acts are as ceremonial as the sorts of cases discussed by Austin. The case of the college president's utterance is a fairly ceremonial example of an exercitive speech act. The role of college president and the authority of that office are fairly well delineated. Like a judgeship, for example, there is an official procedure for inducting college presidents. Moreover, both what a college president has the authority to do and the circumstances under which she is permitted to do it are explicitly defined. Not all cases of exercitive speech acts, though, involve the formal exercising of the powers of an official office. Parenthood, for example, is not an official office, but parents nevertheless manage to verbally set the rules (i.e. permissibility facts) for their children.[31] Thus, there are less ceremonial cases of exercitive speech acts and they are common enough in everyday life.

Both the ceremonial sorts of cases discussed by Austin and the less ceremonial cases just mentioned are instances of what I call *standard exercitives*.[32] Standard exercitives enact permissibility facts *via an exercise of speaker authority*. Consider again the college president's utterance. Since this utterance enacts permissibility facts (e.g. college smoking policy) and since it enacts those permissibility facts via an exercise of speaker authority (i.e. the president's authority over college policy), it is a standard exercitive speech act.

[30] Tim's action is simultaneously a contribution to several different norm-governed activities and this partially accounts for the multi-faceted nature of the impermissibility of his action. Starting in Chapter 5, we will explore actions that simultaneously constitute contributions to multiple norm-governed activities.

[31] Although parenthood is not an official office, it does nevertheless have a certain legal standing. For instance, parents have certain legal obligations towards and rights over their children. As we shall see (in 3.4), there are various types and degrees of both authority and standing.

[32] Elsewhere, I called them Austinian exercitives. See my 2003 and 2004.

Standard exercitives typically express the content of the permissibility fact being enacted. When the college president said, "I hereby declare that smoking is no longer permitted in any college building," for example, she explicitly expressed the content of the permissibility fact she was enacting. That said, the content can be expressed in other ways (e.g. by presupposition or conversational implicature).[33] Standard exercitives can also be implicit. That is, they need not make it explicit that a permissibility fact is being enacted. I may say "no gum in public," for example, without being explicit about the fact that I am thereby enacting a new rule for my children. Such an implicit exercitive is nevertheless a standard exercitive since it enacts the permissibility fact in question via an exercise of speaker authority.[34]

As one can see, utterances can enact permissibility facts. Standard exercitives do so via an exercise of speaker authority (over the realm in question). As I shall argue in the next chapter, there is another—quite different—way that our utterances enact permissibility facts. As we shall see, what is permissible in any particular conversation is constantly changed by what we say in the conversation. Thus, adding to a conversation enacts conversational permissibility facts and the manner in which such conversational permissibility facts are enacted is quite different from the way in which standard exercitives work.

This concludes the requisite background in the philosophy of language. I turn now to a consideration of some complexities regarding enactment and the constitution of harm.

1.6 On enacting

Some forms of enacting are really easy to do. In fact, we do it all the time. Simply by being and doing things, we thereby routinely affect what is true of the world and thereby enact these truths about it. Very roughly, enacting is a fairly direct way to make something true.[35] When I skip to

[33] For an analysis of implicature, see Grice 1989: 26–31. For a discussion of presupposition, see Stalnaker 1973.

[34] Exercitives can also be indirect. For a discussion of indirect speech acts, see Searle 1979a and Lycan 1986.

[35] Although enacting involves an immediate way of making truths true and it is thus "truth-making" in this minimal sense, I am here entirely agnostic about the underlying metaphysics. What truth-makers are ontologically (states of affairs, tropes, . . .), which sorts

work, for example, I change what is true about the world; I make it the case that I skipped to work. That I skipped to work is enacted by my skipping. Although my skipping involves causal processes of various sorts, my skipping does not cause the truth that I skipped to work; it enacts it. This is a case of simple *direct enacting*. It is direct enacting because the enacted truth (that I skipped to work) does not depend (in any obvious way) on human institutions or practices.[36] It depends only on my skipping actions.

Consider another slightly different example. Sue and Leo are married; Leo dies while far away on a business trip. Leo's death directly enacts the truth that Leo is deceased but that truth in turn enacts the truth that Sue is a widow. Sue's widowhood depends on the fact that Sue and Leo were married to one another at the time of Leo's death and thus it depends on the institution of marriage. As a result, Sue's widowhood is *dependently enacted*.[37]

Although conceptually distinct from being a widow, legally counting as a widow is also dependently enacted. First, one can be a widow even though one does not legally count as one if, for example, one's deceased husband does not legally count as deceased. The two states are thus distinct. As soon as one's legal husband legally counts as deceased, however, one legally counts as a widow. Note that it is not the death of the husband that makes the wife legally count as a widow. Rather, it is the act of making the husband legally count as deceased that does so. Moreover, this act of making the husband legally count as deceased is itself an enacted fact. As this example demonstrates, enactments can be nested and piggyback on one another.[38]

of things bear truth-value (sentences, propositions, . . .), which relation obtains between truth-makers and truth-bearers (necessitation, entailment, grounding, . . .) and even which truths, if any, require their own truth-maker are here left entirely open. For a helpful discussion of the various issues involved with truth-makers, see MacBride 2014.

[36] According to metaphysical non-realism, for example, *all* facts depend on human practices in so far as we privilege only some properties (or conceptual schemes) as eligible to fix facts. I here remain agnostic on this issue. Metaphysical non-realists include Goodman (1978), Putnam (1987), Elgin and Goodman (1988), and Elgin (1996).

[37] In some societies, widowhood is also a subordinate social position. In such societies, widows are deprived of various legal and political rights and they are denied many forms of social support. This social status is dependently enacted. For a discussion of the social norms at play, see Lessig 1995.

[38] Compare this example with Searle's (1995) discussion of nested promises.

Illocution is one way that speech can enact facts. When Dave said, "You deserved better, Mary Kate. I am sorry and I apologize," Dave enacted the fact that he apologized to me. Since this act of apology depends on normative practices, the apology is dependently enacted. Dave's apology also directly enacts other facts. The fact that he spoke and the fact that he uttered certain words are each directly enacted by his utterance. Thus, not every fact enacted by an utterance is an illocutionary act.[39]

Illocution also involves talk of constitution. Utterances with illocutionary force are said to *constitute* the illocutionary act in question. On this way of speaking then, Dave's utterance constitutes an apology: His saying what he said (under the circumstances under which he said it) *just is* an apology. Nothing further needs to happen. I do not need to accept his apology for it to be one. I do not need to believe it to be sincere either. Although illocution involves this sort of constitution talk, it would be a mistake to think that Dave's utterance constitutes an apology only if his utterance in isolation is strictly sufficient for that apology. Other conditions are definitely required.[40] It is prudent to keep in mind then that constitution talk means different things in different philosophical contexts. As we are about to see, the constitution of harm is another case in point.

1.7 On constituting harm

To say that speech constitutes harm is to say that it causes harm *via* the enacting of a norm prescribing that harm. Constituting harm then is really just a very specific way of causing it; it is to cause it via adherence to norms enacted.[41] To say that speech causes harm, by contrast, is to say that it causes harm without also constituting it. That is, the speech is harmful but the harm is not the result of following norms enacted by that speech. An example will help to illustrate this difference.

Suppose that I convince my friends that red-headed people are genetically inferior, disposed to evil, and a threat to all things decent and, as a

[39] These are not illocutionary acts because they do not depend on the recognition of communicative intentions.

[40] One cannot apologize to a toaster. One cannot apologize for what is obviously not one's responsibility. One cannot apologize for what is obviously not wrong. That further conditions are required is nevertheless compatible with this sort of talk of constitution.

[41] Harm constitution relies on causal mechanisms. So does successful illocution. Some mistakenly take reliance on causal mechanisms as evidence that a relation is neither constitutive nor illocutionary. For a particularly clear example of this, see Sumner 2013.

result of coming to believe these things, my friends discriminate against red-headed persons. In this case, my utterances cause discrimination against those red-headed persons. My words cause my friends' beliefs to change and those beliefs in turn cause my friends' harmful discriminatory behavior. The connection between the speech and the harm in this case is (merely) causal.

Contrast that with a different case. Suppose instead that I am an employer and I implement a company hiring policy when I say, "From now on, we no longer hire anyone with red hair." This utterance will cause discriminatory conduct on the part of my employees but it does so via the prescriptive force of the hiring policy enacted by my utterance. Since that discriminatory conduct is brought about by my employees' adherence to a policy that I put into place (i.e. dependently enacted) with my utterance, my utterance (dependently) enacts the norm (that is; the policy) that prescribes the harmful discriminatory practice in question. As a result, my utterance constitutes (and does not merely cause) the harm of discrimination.

Clearly 'constitution' is here being used in a special technical sense. It does not mean what it means in other philosophical contexts. To say that the employer's (hiring policy enacting) utterance constitutes the harm of discrimination is *not* to say that the employer's utterance is contemporaneous with the discriminatory harms. The harm of discrimination is causally downstream from the utterance that enacts the discriminatory policy. It is *not* to say that the employer's utterance is sufficient for that harm either. Others need to follow the policy for the discriminatory harms to obtain. Constitution talk here, unlike elsewhere in philosophy, is not akin to an equals sign; it is instead a distinct norm-driven way of causing.

In order for an utterance to constitute harm then three conditions are required. The utterance enacts a norm; that norm is followed and harm results from following that norm.[42] Although, in what follows, the focus

[42] One might be tempted to say that certain norms are such that the mere enacting of them is harmful. Consider, for example, the employer's verbal enacting of the discriminatory hiring policy. Even if a discriminatory hiring practice does not result from the enacting of this policy (because, say, the business is shut down shortly thereafter), that policy in place might be harmful in a counterfactual way. Options are unjustly limited and this is so even if no particular red headed person is denied employment. Although I here concentrate on cases where actual harm ensues, I leave this possibility open.

is on the norm-enactment part of things, harm constitution requires that the norm is followed and that following it is harmful.

1.8 On social norms

We are here exploring ways in which speech constitutes harm by enacting norms that prescribe that harm. Although there are different sorts of norms, I am primarily interested in the enacting of *social* norms; these are the norms that guide our social practices. Although social norms guide our actions, we are typically barely conscious of them. An American may remain blissfully ignorant of the personal space norms that have been guiding her life in the United States until, that is, those norms are violated by a European friend when she is an adult. Social norms are not mere regularities. Being right-handed is the norm (in a purely descriptive sense) in my current logic class but this does *not* mean that the left-handed students really ought to be right handed. Social norms, by contrast, are prescriptive: they give rise to talk about what a person ought to do; they afford incentives and reasons for action; they are used to explain behavior, and they ground criticism of those who do not comply.

Whether or not certain social norms apply to someone is typically a function of that person's social role and position; the application of a norm to a person does not require that that person be consciously aware of that norm and it does not require that that person endorse that norm.[43] A woman who emphatically rejects the (patriarchal) norms of femininity, for example, will nevertheless be evaluated in terms of her response to those norms. Because she socially counts as a woman, the norms are relevant to her and this is so whether she agrees or not.

Bicchieri argues that social norms are "behavioral rules that are supported by a combination of empirical and normative expectations."[44] They are behaviors we expect others to follow (empirical expectation) and we believe that others believe that we ought to follow them too (normative expectations).[45] This means that we expect plenty of compliance and we

[43] See Witt 2011. See also Haslanger 2000 and 2012 and Sveinsdottir 2017 for social constructionist analyses of gender.

[44] See Bicchieri and Mercier (2014). This is a gloss on Bicchieri 2006.

[45] According to Bicchieri, social norms are *constituted by* the (empirical and normative) expectations of individual people and this opens up the possibility of changing them.

expect negative social consequences for failures to comply. The prescriptive force of these social norms is considerable. Individuals routinely go against self-interest in order to avoid the social censure of non-compliance and even practices that seem collectively irrational (or at least suboptimal) nevertheless persist because of the self-propelling nature of these norms.[46] Clearly, social norms are action-guiding.

Thus far, we have one example of speech constituting harm. When I enacted a discriminatory hiring policy and a discriminatory hiring practice ensues, my utterance constitutes the harm of discrimination. In this case, the enacted harmful norm is my company's hiring policy. This norm is both official and explicit. The focus in the remainder of this book, by contrast, is on the enacting of harmful social norms that are neither. When I enacted that policy, I also did so via an exercise of my authority over my company. My policy-enacting utterance was a standard exercitive. The focus in this book, by contrast, is with a different mechanism of norm-enactment.

1.9 Conclusion

In the next chapter, I argue that conversations are rife with norm-enacting utterances. I show that just about every time one makes a contribution to a conversation, one also thereby enacts permissibility facts (or norms) for that conversation. This phenomenon, which I call the conversational exercitive, illustrates another (non-authoritative) way that speech enacts norms and thus it bring us one step closer to seeing how our words might inadvertently enact harmful norms.

Altering our expectations in the right way will transform social norms. For a discussion about altering social norms, see Bicchieri and Mercier (2014).

[46] Lessig (1995) discusses dueling in the American South. Bicchieri and Mercier (2014) discuss female genital cutting.

2

Conversational Exercitives

2.1 Introduction

Recall that we are primarily interested in identifying previously overlooked ways in which speech constitutes harm. Speech constitutes harm by enacting norms that prescribe that harm. In this chapter, I explore the kinematics (i.e. the mechanics) of conversation and I argue that conversational contributions routinely enact norms and they do so in a previously overlooked manner. In subsequent chapters, we shall see how this conversational phenomenon generalizes and this will open up the possibility of speech enacting *harmful* norms in a relevantly similar and hidden manner. In the present chapter, however, I focus on the subtle mechanisms involved in conversational norm-enactment.

Conversation is a cooperative human endeavor. As such, it is a social practice governed by norms.[1] By exploring the kinematics of conversation and the norms governing its appropriate practice, we shall see that conversational contributions routinely enact changes to what is subsequently permissible in that very conversation. In other words, when one contributes to a conversation by adding to it, one thereby also enacts norms for that conversation; one enacts permissibility facts for the conversation to which one is contributing. Moreover, since conversational contributions enact permissibility facts, they are exercitive speech acts. Furthermore, since the permissibility facts in question concern the bounds of conversational permissibility, they are what I call conversational exercitives.

The chapter proceeds as follows. In Section 2.2, I argue for the phenomenon of conversational exercitives within the scorekeeping framework of conversational kinematics. Then, in Section 2.3, I argue

[1] Thus, some of these norms are social norms. See Chapter 1 section 1.8.

that the phenomenon generalizes in a certain important way and, in Section 2.4, I argue for conversational exercitives within the alternative common ground framework. Differences between these two frameworks are discussed in Section 2.5 and considerations in favor of the scorekeeping framework are offered. In Section 2.6, the multiple functions of speech are explored and, in Section 2.7, complexities regarding timing and accommodation are presented.

2.2 On conversational exercitives: a scorekeeping presentation

I turn now to the first task, that of presenting the phenomenon of conversational exercitives. Since I do so by drawing on Lewis' work on scorekeeping, I start with that.

2.2.1 Lewis on conversational score

In his "Scorekeeping in a Language Game", Lewis argues that there are several ways in which conversations are like baseball games.[2] One of the ways in which these two activities are similar is that they each have a score. The notion of baseball score that Lewis countenances is considerably more inclusive than the familiar one. The commonsense concept of a baseball score tracks only the number of runs, but Lewis's considerably more inclusive notion of score includes *all* facets of the game that are relevant to its assessment and proper play. It tracks, among other things, the inning, number of balls, strikes, outs, and errors as well as the number of runs. So, too, the score of a conversation keeps track of *everything* that is relevant to its proper development. (It is thus not about who "wins" the conversation.[3]) Rather, the conversational score tracks those things that matter with respect to what counts as appropriate for the ongoing conversation. This includes, among other things, the presuppositions, the appropriate standards of accuracy, and the relevant topics. Since the various components of conversational score affect such a wide variety of linguistic phenomena (which may not be familiar to some readers), it is worthwhile to consider some examples.

[2] See Lewis 1983.

[3] I thank Lynne Tirrell for suggesting that I make this explicit.

Definite descriptions are one such linguistic phenomenon; they are descriptions that purport to uniquely refer.[4] In other words, definite descriptions seem to refer to exactly one thing. Examples include 'the tallest student in my PHIL 207 class,' 'Helen McGowan Gardner's oldest son,' and 'my favorite color.' Each of these descriptive expressions are routinely used on particular occasions to uniquely refer; on each occasion, it seems that these expressions refer to one and only one thing. As is well known, many definite descriptions appear to succeed in uniquely referring even though these descriptions fail to uniquely describe their referent. The expression 'the desk,' for example, may pick out a particular desk even though there are many desks in the universe and there may even be several desks in the room in question. Salience appears to account for this.[5] On this account, a definite description refers to the most salient satisfier of the description.[6] Suppose, for example, that Bobby mentions that his dog has just been to the vet and I ask if the dog is healthy. Bobby's dog is certainly not the only dog in the universe and his dog may not even be the only dog present, but I have nevertheless managed to refer to his dog with this use of the expression 'the dog.' This is because Bobby's dog is the most salient dog in the context of this particular conversation. Salience is a component of the conversational score and this salience component of the conversational score helps to settle the appropriate use of definite descriptions in the conversation at hand by fixing the unique referent of such descriptions.

Consider now another linguistic phenomenon that draws our attention to a different component of the conversational score, the scope of quantifiers. When we use words like 'all,' 'some,' 'every,' or 'any,' we are making claims about groups of things. We might be saying that *all* of the things in the group have some property or that *some* of them do. The *scope* of these quantificational terms is a technical way of specifying the

[4] I leave it open whether this uniqueness requirement is semantic or pragmatic and whether it is necessary for reference. See Russell 1905; Szabo 2000; Roberts 2012.

[5] There are other ways to account for this. Perhaps 'the desk' is shorthand for a longer description that satisfies the uniqueness condition. Russell himself used this ellipsis strategy by taking proper names to be shorthand for definite descriptions. See Russell 1918/1956. Alternatively, one might argue that the objects under consideration are restricted in such a way that this uniqueness condition is met. For an especially accessible discussion of this uniqueness problem, see Lycan 2000. For further details see, for example, Neale 1990 and Stanley and Szabo 2000.

[6] Many theorists appeal to salience. See Lewis 1983 and Clark 1996.

group of objects in question. To see that the scope of such terms is a component of conversational score, consider the following. Suppose that Whitney, while talking to her son Jack about her shopping list, asks him whether there is any sour cherry juice. In this conversational context, the group of objects in question is the collection of things in their possession right now. Whitney is not asking whether there is any sour cherry juice anywhere in the universe and she is not asking whether there is any sour cherry juice at the store in Fairhaven (where she normally buys it). She is asking, of the things in their possession right now, is any of it sour cherry juice. As one can see then, the scope of quantificational terms is a component of conversational score.

Other components of conversational score include standards of accuracy, presupposition, and relevance. This list is not meant to be exhaustive. In fact, this notion of score is highly inclusive and includes, by definition, *whatever* is relevant to the assessment and proper development of the conversation. Thus, if some factor Y is shown to be relevant to the assessment and proper development of a conversation then (so long as Y is distinct from the other components of the score) Y is a component of the score.[7] Nothing else needs to be shown. The score just is the combination of that which matters for the purposes of conversation. This is an especially inclusive notion of score and not all ways of specifying the conversational score are as inclusive.[8]

This inclusive conception of score also tracks various meta-linguistic facts. The fact that a conversation is taking place and that all participants speak the same language are meta-linguistic facts that are also components of score. There are also other sorts of meta-linguistic facts tracked. Suppose, for example, that Greg asserts something that is then rejected by his interlocutor. Although the *content* of Greg's assertion does not become a background assumption shared in the conversation, the meta-linguistic fact that he asserted it is a component of the conversational score.[9]

[7] Technically, the distinctness qualification is unnecessary. A score with redundant components is perfectly adequate. Although I hope to avoid unnecessary (and ultimately irrelevant) complications regarding the distinctness of components, I am nevertheless inclined to exclude obviously equivalent components.

[8] Narrower conceptions of score include Thomason 1990; Lepore and Stone 2015; Camp 2018. There are many ways to specify the score—in terms of what it does and does not track, in terms of how it works, and in terms of what it is ontologically.

[9] Complexities regarding score change with blocked contributions are discussed in Section 2.7.

Furthermore, score change (sometimes called 'updating') is an ongoing and temporally complex process.[10] To see this, consider what happens with an accepted assertion. Suppose, for example, that Albert says, "I love Rolling Road" and his interlocutor gladly accepts his assertion. Even in this simple case, though, an ongoing series of score changes are enacted; the score must be updated multiple times and in multiple respects. Since the score tracks what is relevant for the proper development of the conversation, it essentially captures all contextual information required for the proper interpretation of Albert's conversational contribution. Since Albert uses the word 'I' (and the referent of 'I' depends on who is speaking), the score must already include the fact that Albert is speaking. Of course, the score could not reflect that fact *before* Albert started speaking. Moreover, Albert's accepted assertion adds the content of his assertion to the score and that can happen only *after* his assertion. As one can see, a single conversational contribution will involve several successive score changes.

2.2.2 Argument via conversational score

Lewis also stressed other similarities between baseball and conversation. In particular, each of these activities is governed by rules. (Lewis speaks of rules. I prefer the more general notion of norms. While discussing Lewis, though, I will stick with talk of rules.[11]) Just as it is impermissible for a runner to walk after only three balls are thrown to him, it is unacceptable for a participant in a conversation to cite what is known to be entirely irrelevant to the topic at hand. Although, as we shall see, the nature of these rules can differ considerably, both baseball and conversations are activities that are governed by rules (or norms). Furthermore, each activity is such that the permissibility of future behavior in that activity depends on the rules and what has already happened in the game or conversation. Whether or not it is appropriate for a runner to walk immediately after a ball is thrown to that runner depends on the rules of baseball and how many balls have already been thrown to that runner during the current at-bat. Since the number of balls that have

[10] These sorts of successive score (or common ground) changes are discussed in Stalnaker 1998 and von Fintel 2008.

[11] Rules, in Lewis's sense, need not be explicitly codified, consciously believed, or exception-less. For these reasons, I prefer the related notion of a norm.

been thrown to a runner during a single at-bat is a component of this more inclusive notion of the baseball score, we see that the permissibility of a runner walking to first base depends on the rules of baseball and what has happened thus far as captured by the score. Similarly, whether it is appropriate for a participant in a conversation to start talking about lemons depends on the rules of conversation and whether lemons are somehow relevant to the conversation. Since relevance is a component of conversational score, the conversational permissibility of talking about lemons depends on the rules and the score for that conversation. As one can see then, since the conversational score captures the relevant bits about what has happened thus far in the conversation, the permissibility of any particular conversational contribution depends on the score (and the rules).

Despite such similarities, there is an important difference between the rules governing baseball and those governing conversations. As Lewis stresses, the rules of baseball are rigid in a way that at least some of the rules of conversation are not. In baseball, if a runner walks after only three balls are thrown to him, the runner has violated the rules. That he walked under these circumstances does not make it correct for him to have done so and this is so even if no one takes notice and the runner nevertheless manages to get away with it. Some of the rules governing conversation are importantly different. Lewis calls them *rules of accommodation*. These rules adapt to the actual behavior of participants by changing the score so that what happens counts as conversationally appropriate. Rules of accommodation make the score automatically adjust (within certain limits of course) so that what actually transpires counts as fair play.

Standards of accuracy are another component of conversational score and this component sometimes adjusts to *accommodate* what is said.[12] Suppose, for example, that Donal says that Ireland is shaped like a sideways teddy bear and his interlocutors happily accept his claim. This shows that the standards of accuracy (for shapes of countries anyway) operative in the conversation at the time of Donal's utterance

[12] These standards are plural because they can vary between different sorts of objects. The appropriate standards for the boundaries of countries in a certain conversation might be quite different from the standards of accuracy in the same conversation for other sorts of objects or claims. I thank Rebecca Mason for this point.

are such as to render his utterance accurate enough. Suppose that Seamus subsequently points out that Italy isn't really shaped like a boot because it is squiggly on both sides and boots generally aren't. Seamus' denial that Italy is boot-shaped requires higher standards of accuracy (for country shapes) than were operative in the conversation at the time of Donal's utterance. So long as Donal accepts Seamus's claim as conversationally appropriate, the standards immediately and automatically adjust so that what Seamus said is appropriate.[13] Since standards of accuracy are a component of the score, this is a case where the score adjusts itself to accommodate what is said.

Of course, conversational contributions are constantly open to challenge: Donal need not accept Seamus' s utterance as apt. Suppose for example that Donal had said in response, "Whaddya mean it's not shaped like a boot? We're talking about landmasses here, Seamus! Get a grip. You are always such a pain—insisting on irrelevant detail!" Were Donal to say this in response to Seamus, then he would be rejecting Seamus's utterance on the grounds that it violates the standards of accuracy operative in the conversation at the time. In such a case, Donal would effectively prevent Seamus's utterance from having an ongoing effect on this standard of accuracy component of conversational score.[14]

Here is another example of a rule of accommodation in action. As we just saw, when Whitney asks her son Jack whether there is any sour cherry juice, she is asking a question about the things currently in their possession. Namely, is any of it sour cherry juice? This shows that, at the time of Whitney's utterance, the scope of the relevant quantifier ranges over the collection of things currently in their possession. Suppose that Jack were to then respond, "I think that the Old Company Store in Wareham has some." Jack is here indicating that Whitney and Jack don't have any sour cherry juice and they need to buy some more. But notice how Jack's utterance requires that the scope of the relevant quantifier be broadened. After all, Jack's utterance is conversationally

[13] Note that to accept an utterance as conversationally appropriate does not require believing that it is true or even probably true. It requires only that the utterance count as an apt contribution to the conversation.

[14] Technically, on my view anyway, Seamus's conversational contribution enacts changes to the standards of accuracy component of the conversational score and then Donal's utterance (that rejects Seamus's contribution) changes the score back in the relevant respects. See Section 2.7.

apt only if things in the Old Country Story are (now) within the scope of the relevant quantifier. As one can see then, so long as Whitney accepts Jack's conversational contribution as apt, this is also a case where the (quantifier scope component of the) score automatically adjusts to accommodate the appropriateness of what is said.

As I shall now point out, something very interesting follows from the flexible nature of these rules. Although Lewis did not point this out, the accommodating nature of these rules offers a way to illuminate another phenomenon: Any conversational contribution that triggers one of these rules thereby enacts permissibility facts for the conversation in question. Even though this is not immediately apparent, our conversational contributions routinely enact changes to the bounds of conversational permissibility.

Here is the argument in a nutshell: Since rules of accommodation make the score automatically adjust so that what actually happens counts as fair play, any conversational contribution that triggers a rule of accommodation thereby enacts a change to the score. Since what counts as fair play depends on the score, changing the score changes the bounds of conversational permissibility. Thus, any conversational contribution that triggers a rule of accommodation enacts changes to what is subsequently permissible in that conversation. For this reason, I shall henceforth refer to such conversational contributions as *conversational exercitives*. They are *exercitives* since they enact facts about what is permissible in some realm and they are *conversational* exercitives since the realm in question is a particular conversation.

2.2.3 Further examples of conversational exercitives

Since the phenomenon of conversational exercitives is so subtle and since my argument thus far is both general and abstract, some examples may help to illuminate the phenomenon. Before such examples are offered, however, a clarification concerning my methodology is warranted. In what follows, I briefly describe conversational contexts and I argue that certain utterances enact changes to the bounds of conversational permissibility on the grounds that the utterance in question renders other potential subsequent utterances conversationally impermissible. A problem may seem to arise from the fact that such conversational contexts are inevitably under-described. After all, there are always an infinite variety of factors that are (or may be) relevant to the proper specification of any such context. Because of this, there may well be ways of filling in unmentioned details that falsify particular claims I make about which utterances are subsequently conversationally impermissible. Even if it were always possible to do so, this does not establish that such utterances are not conversationally impermissible (at least sometimes or even most of the time). That there are some ways to fill in the details such that the utterance in question is permissible does not establish that there are not other ways to do so such that it is indeed impermissible. Since it is impossible to avoid under-describing conversational contexts, the best I can do is to specify those details most likely to be relevant. I now turn back to further examples of conversational exercitives.

Consider first changes regarding which possibilities are relevant to a conversation. Suppose, for example, that my adulterous friend Maureen and I are discussing what she should do about her husband's suspicions and we have been considering only those courses of action that would keep her adulterous activities secret. There are plenty of things she *could* do (e.g. kill or hypnotize her husband) that are, in this context, simply beside the point. They are not within the class of possibilities under conversational consideration. Suppose, however, that I were to then say something that required the scope of relevant possibilities to broaden. Suppose I said, "Why don't you just come clean and tell the truth for once!"[15] In such a case, my utterance requires that a previously irrelevant possibility (that Maureen tell the truth) be relevant. The score automatically adjusts, though, through a rule of accommodation, so that the possibility I mention is conversationally relevant. My utterance effectively broadens the scope of relevant possibilities. Moreover, by enacting a change to the score, my utterance enacts changes to what is subsequently permissible in the conversation. Unless things change again, Maureen is no longer conversationally permitted to ignore these options.[16] Since my

[15] This example is similar to one in Lewis 1983: 247.

[16] Of course, participants are free to try to block one another's moves. Maureen might ignore what I said and there may be contexts where her doing so counts as a conversational move and even one that changes the score right back to what it was. That said, conversationally broadening what is conversationally relevant seems easier than narrowing. In other words, for reasons that are not entirely understood, it is more difficult to say something that makes relevant options irrelevant than it is to make irrelevant options relevant.

utterance enacts changes to the bounds of conversational permissibility, my utterance is a conversational exercitive.

Here is another example illustrating the phenomenon of conversational exercitives. Conversational contributions that introduce presuppositions also enact facts about what is subsequently appropriate in the conversation at hand. Suppose that I have just finished jogging (without my dog) and I meet a friendly stranger who is walking her dog along the trails. While we are chatting about the weather, her dog starts chewing on my shoes and I say, "My dog Fido also loves chewing on shoes!" Notice that this utterance *introduces* a presupposition. At the time of my utterance, my being a dog owner is not already a component of the conversational score but my utterance requires for its conversational appropriateness that my being a dog owner is a component of the score. Suppose that my new friend does not question this presupposition (that I have a dog) and we go on to have a lengthy and informed discussion about the best vets in the area. In such a case, the proposition that I own a dog has become a part of the score; it would be conversationally inappropriate for my new dog-walking friend to then ask me if I have any pets. This query is conversationally weird because my being a dog owner has become a shared part of the conversation. To later question that presupposition is conversationally impermissible. Since my utterance enacts a change to the score (through a rule of accommodation, namely that for presupposition introduction), this conversational contribution thereby changes facts about what subsequently constitutes fair play in this conversation. Thus, although it may not be obvious, my utterance enacts changes to what is conversationally permissible and is therefore an exercitive speech act; it is a conversational exercitive.

In this case, my interlocutor did not verbally question my presupposition but that does not mean that she actually believed it. In fact, she could have thought that I was faking being a dog owner all along. Even if this is the case, however, my being a dog owner is nevertheless a component of the conversational score. By treating my presupposition-introducing contribution as apt and by continuing the conversation as if I am a dog owner, my interlocutor treats my being a dog owner as a background fact for the purposes of this conversation. As such, it is a component of the conversational score.

All of this is compatible with the plain fact that conversational contributions are always open to ongoing challenge. This means that it *is* possible to conversationally question presuppositions. After all, my dog-walking interlocutor might have immediately questioned my presupposition-introducing conversational contribution by responding, "Wait? What? You have a dog? But I've seen you at this park, running or walking, every day for two years and I've *never* seen you with a dog!" Were she to say this, she would prevent (or at least postpone) the presupposition that I am dog owner from being an ongoing component of the conversational score.[17]

So open to ongoing challenge are conversational contributions that it is even permissible to question a presupposition long after it has been introduced and even after it has been relied on repeatedly. To see this, suppose that, after having a lengthy and informed discussion of area vets, my dog-walking interlocutor says, "I know we've been talking about dogs all this time but it's really been bothering me and I didn't know how to bring it up but my friend Sean knows someone who doesn't have a dog but who likes to pretend to have one just to see if anyone says anything and... well... are you doing that right now?" Even conversationally entrenched presuppositions can be conversationally questioned in (highly unlikely but) conversationally appropriate ways.

But, as we just saw above, there are conversationally inappropriate ways to conversationally question entrenched presuppositions. It would not be conversationally apt for my interlocutor to simply ask me if I have any pets after we have been discussing my dog's experiences with area vets for the last twenty minutes. That the presupposition that I am a dog owner is a component of the conversational score thus affects what is conversationally permissible. Since my presupposition-introducing utterance enacts that score change, it therefore also enacts the conversational permissibility facts enacted by that score change. Thus, despite the ongoing challengability of conversational contributions, my utterance is nevertheless a conversational exercitive.[18]

[17] I say 'ongoing' since her objection changes aspects of the score back. For ease of presentation, I sometimes speak as if the hearer blocks the score change when really the hearer's rejection of the contribution changes the score back in at least some relevant respects. See Section 2.7.

[18] Witek denies that conversational contributions are exercitive. See Witek 2016. Witek here assumes that exercitive speech acts must involve an exercise of speaker authority. He is here relying on Austin's original characterization of exercitives as "involving the exercise of powers, rights, or influences"(Austin 1975: 151). I explicitly depart from Austin's characterization. For me, the core of exercitive speech is the enacting of permissibility facts; speaker authority is not required. For Austin, an exercitive was a *type* of speech act. For me,

2.3 One way the phenomenon generalizes

Thus far, I have argued that any conversational contribution that triggers a rule of accommodation thereby enacts a change to the conversational score, and thus enacts new permissibility facts for the conversation to which it contributes. Since many conversational contributions trigger such rules, many such contributions are conversationally exercitive. As we shall now see, though, the triggering of rules *of accommodation* is not actually necessary. Since the conversational permissibility facts are enacted by the *change to the score*, any conversational contribution that enacts such a change (whether it does so via a rule of accommodation or not) thereby enacts conversational permissibility facts. Since the score tracks that which is relevant to the proper development of a conversation, any contribution to a conversation will enact a change to the score. Since the score, in conjunction with the "rules" or norms of conversation, determines what is subsequently permissible in that particular conversation, conversational contributions routinely enact conversational permissibility facts.

To see this, consider the following. Suppose that Joanne asks me if Tom has called Mike and I say 'Yes.' (Suppose further that Joanne accepts my assertion.) My utterance (directly) enacts a change to the conversational score: the proposition that Tom called Mike is now a component of the score and we each accept that proposition for the purposes of the conversation. Now notice this: that the score has changed in this way is not due to a rule of accommodation. It is not as if what I said would have been inappropriate had it not been for a change in the score. It is just that what I said contributes to the conversation and thus changes what has happened in the conversation and, since the score keeps track of what has happened in the conversation, my utterance directly enacts a change to the score. All conversational contributions will directly enact changes to the score and thus thereby enact changes to what is subsequently permissible in the conversation at hand.

it is a ubiquitous aspect of virtually all speech. Despite an apparent disagreement, Witek concludes that "it is true that any move made in an illocutionary game that invokes a rule of accommodation changes the personal component of the illocutionary score relative to which it is evaluated and thereby brings about a change in the domain of permissibility facts"(Witek 2016: 20) and this is tantamount to acknowledging the phenomenon of conversational exercitives. The disagreement is thus merely terminological.

Here is another example of a conversational exercitive that does not work via a rule of accommodation. Conversationally changing salience facts changes the score and thereby enacts facts about what is subsequently permissible in the conversation at hand.[19] Suppose that, when discussing Bobby's dog, I say, "When I was child, we had a hyperactive Irish setter named Finbar who stole undergarments from neighborhood clotheslines and so we had to get rid of the dog." By introducing Finbar into the conversation, I thereby made Finbar the most salient dog (and that is why I managed to refer to Finbar with this use of the expression 'the dog'). Because of what I said, it would be inappropriate for Bobby to try to refer to his dog with the expression 'the dog' (until the salience facts change back again).[20] My utterance changed the salience facts that are a part of the conversational score and thereby changed the bounds of conversational permissibility. Thus, although it may not be obvious, my assertion about Finbar is also a conversational exercitive.[21]

2.4 Common ground

So far, I have argued for the phenomenon of conversational exercitives within the framework of conversational score but there is another important framework, the common ground framework.[22] In this section, I will present the common ground framework, mostly in connection to work on presupposition, and argue for the phenomenon of conversational exercitives within this framework.[23]

[19] One could treat salience changes as governed by a rule of accommodation for salience. I here treat changes to the salience component of the score as working without such an accommodation rule.

[20] Of course, if Bobby were to say something that *required* that his dog be the referent of the expression 'the dog,' then a rule of accommodation would likely kick in and adjust the salience component of the score so that his utterance is appropriate after all. If this sort of thing were to happen all of the time, then these acceptability facts would be unviolatable. For a discussion of this worry, see my 2004 and 2003.

[21] Because the update to the salience component of the score obtains prior to my use of the expression 'the dog' a rule of accommodation is not required. Updating occurs throughout an utterance. See Section 2.2.1.

[22] Arguably, the common ground literature arose from Lewis' (1969) notion of common knowledge. For an especially detailed and empirically informed discussion of common ground, see Clark 1996. Stalnaker (2002) credits Grice's William James Lectures (1989: 65, 274) with the introduction of the notion of common ground.

[23] I have in mind here Stalnaker's highly influential work on presupposition. See his 1973; 1974; and 1998.

Common ground tracks certain aspects of conversational context; it is the set of propositions that the participants in a conversation take for granted for the purposes of that conversation.[24] These propositions need not be believed; they may merely be accepted for the purposes of the conversation. Suppose, for instance, that I am talking to my uncle who believes that his beloved son Chris is a talented singer and he says something that presupposes this. Although I do not believe that Chris is talented, I let it go and just accept it for the purposes of the conversation.[25] Acceptance falls short of belief.[26]

The common ground changes as the conversation develops. It is usually understood to be a set of possible worlds; those worlds in which the propositions in question are true.[27] As a specification of the conversational context, the common ground functions in much the same way as the conversational score. To see this, we will now consider the accommodation of presupposition within the common ground framework.

2.4.1 Presupposition

Very roughly, a presupposition of an utterance is information that is taken for granted rather than expressed.[28] 'My husband enjoys beer' presupposes that I have a husband. 'The cat sat on the mat' presupposes that there is a (salient and hence identifiable) cat and that there is a (salient and hence identifiable) mat.

There are two types of presuppositions commonly discussed in the literature. The first type is semantic; it concerns the meaning of words and the truth-value of utterances. On the standard way of defining semantic presupposition, an utterance U semantically presupposes P if

[24] Some components of the common ground will be broad cultural beliefs (e.g. Boston is the capital of Massachusetts) and others will be more specific to the conversation at a time (e.g. Uncle Charlie is speaking now). These sets of propositions can be structured; there may be multiple common grounds, and the common ground framework can be extended to account for different kinds of conversation. See Green 2017b.

[25] There are lots of reasons why one might do this. It's polite. Chris's vocal talent may be a low stakes topic in the conversation. Conversations go more smoothly when interlocutors accommodate one another's contributions.

[26] See Stalnaker 1974: 202.

[27] Ontological commitment to possible worlds can be avoided in a variety of ways.

[28] For a discussion of the related but distinct notion of not-at-issue content and its role in propaganda, see Stanley 2015.

and only if P must be true in order for U to be either true or false.[29] Consider the utterance, "It was Peter who took the apple." This utterance presupposes that someone took the apple and it seems that this presupposition must be true in order for the original utterance to be either true or false. If it is true that it was Peter who took the apple then someone took the apple. If it is false that it was Peter who took the apple, then it is still true that someone took the apple; it just wasn't Peter who took it. And, if it is false that someone took the apple, then it seems that my utterance ("It was Peter who took the apple") is neither true nor false.[30]

The other type of presupposition is pragmatic; it concerns the assumptions made by participants (i.e. speakers and hearers). An utterance U pragmatically presupposes P if and only if the speaker assumes that P is taken for granted (and thus in the common ground) between participants in the conversation at hand. When I told Sally that it was Peter who took the apple, I made several pragmatic assumptions. I assumed that Sally speaks English, that someone took the apple, and that Sally cares about who took the apple. These things are taken for granted in this conversational context and thus they are already a part of the common ground. As such, they are pragmatically presupposed by my utterance.

Notice that semantic presuppositions are also (typically) pragmatically presupposed. When I said, "It was Peter who took the apple," I assumed that someone took the apple and I assumed that Sally assumed that someone took the apple. In other words, I assumed that the proposition that someone took the apple was already a part of the common ground.[31] As one can see then, semantic presuppositions are (typically) pragmatically presupposed. For this reason, it makes sense to focus here on pragmatic presupposition.[32]

[29] This notion has its roots in Frege and Strawson. For a classic presentation of this characterization of semantic presupposition, see van Fraassen 1968. This negation test is just one of many. Semantic presuppositions tend to project across different sorts of embeddings, not just negation. Other embeddings include: possibility ('It is possible that it was Peter who took the shoes,' belief operators ('Sally believes that it was Peter who took the apple'), questions ('Was it Peter who took the apple?') and probability adverbs ('Probably, it was Peter who took the apple'). This projectability varies and this variation requires theoretical explanation. The status of semantic presupposition is contested. See note 32.

[30] Another option is to attribute a third truth-value to sentences with false presuppositions.

[31] I also assumed that there is a salient (and hence identifiable) apple and I assumed that Sally would be able to figure out which apple that is.

[32] There are other reasons to focus on it. For starters, it is unclear that there is even such a thing as semantic presupposition. See, for example, Lycan 1986: 73–108.

There are two different sorts of cases of conversational contributions involving pragmatic presuppositions. With the first sort of case, the presupposition in question is already a part of the common ground. With the second sort of case, it is not. Let's consider an example of the first sort of case. Suppose that Mike and I both know that someone took the apple that I placed on the kitchen table earlier that day and we are discussing who most likely took it. When I say, "It was Peter who took the apple," I operate on the assumption that someone took the apple and I assume that Mike operates on that assumption too. The proposition that someone took the apple is already a part of the common ground. My utterance does not *add* this proposition to the common ground. It's already there.

The second sort of case is more interesting for our purposes. Let's consider an example. Suppose that Mike and I are talking about what a despicable person Peter is and suppose further that, although there has been mention of a missing apple, there has been no mention of anyone actually taking it. When I say, "It was Peter who took the apple," my utterance requires that the proposition that someone took the apple be a part of the common ground but that proposition is not a part of the common ground just prior to my utterance. In such a case (and so long as my interlocutor accepts what I say), the common ground adjusts to accommodate what I say.[33] My utterance *introduces* the presupposition that someone took the apple; the common ground *accommodates* that presupposition.[34] In possible worlds talk this means that all worlds in which no one took the apple are thereby excluded from the common ground; the common ground henceforth only includes worlds in which someone took the apple.

[33] According to Stalnaker (1998), there is no need to posit special rules of accommodation to account for this. Operating on the assumption that I am a cooperative and competent conversational participant, my interlocutor can work out that my utterance presupposes that someone took the apple and my interlocutor can work out that I would only presuppose this if it were appropriate for me to do so. Because of this, my interlocutor will accept this proposition in light of my utterance and these inferences and this proposition will thus become a part of the common ground.

[34] The term 'accommodation' comes from Lewis and is still used in the literature. There is considerable discussion about the scope of what is accommodated, the principles guiding accommodation and whether it concerns local (as opposed to global) contexts. For a summary of these issues, see von Fintel 2008; Beaver and Geurts 2011.

Notice that, in this case, my utterance is a conversational exercitive. By changing the common ground, my utterance thereby changed what is subsequently permissible in the conversation at hand. Once the proposition that someone took the apple becomes a shared part of the conversation, it would be conversationally impermissible to then simply and directly question that proposition. Suppose, for example, that this presupposition becomes entrenched in our conversation: Mike and I go on to discuss (at some length and detail) the apple that was taken and the times and ways that it might have been taken. If Mike were to then say, "Hey, did someone take the apple?" his utterance would be conversationally out of bounds; it would violate the norms operative in this particular conversation. Thus, although my utterance ('It was Peter who took the apple') does not seem to be enacting normative facts for the conversation, it is. My utterance is a conversational exercitive.[35]

Conversational contributions that introduce presuppositions alter the common ground and are thus conversational exercitives. If the phenomenon were limited to such presupposition-introducing utterances, then conversational exercitives would not be that widespread in the common ground framework. As it happens, though, plenty of other sorts of contributions also alter the common ground. A consideration of assertion, for instance, shows that the phenomenon of covert exercitives is routine in the common ground framework. When I said, "It was Peter who took the apple," in addition to presupposing that someone took the apple, I also *asserted* that Peter took the apple. So long as my interlocutor accepts my assertion, it is also added to the common ground.[36] It adds the proposition that Peter took the apple to the common ground. (All worlds in which Peter did not take the apple are thereby excluded and only worlds in which Peter took the apple remain.) Moreover, this change to the common ground enacts changes to what is subsequently permissible in the conversation at hand. Once the proposition that Peter took the apple becomes a part of the common ground, the conversationally

[35] Again, although conversational contributions are subject to ongoing challenge, there are norms guiding the appropriate way to do so. See Section 2.3.

[36] It does so, that is, so long as my interlocutors accept my assertion. Stalnaker treats assertion as a sort of proposal to change the common ground. Since common ground is what is shared amongst participants, assertions become a part of the common ground only if they are accepted. See Stalnaker 1998 and 1999. This complexity will be discussed in Section 2.7.

permissible ways to then question that proposition (or anything required by it) are limited. It would be conversationally impermissible, for example, to then ask if Peter has ever taken anything. Such a query is conversationally impermissible in a conversational context where Peter's having taken the apple is a part of the common ground. Thus, although it may not be obvious, my utterance ('It was Peter who took the apple') enacts changes to what is conversationally permissible. My utterance is a conversational exercitive.

We have now seen the phenomenon of conversational exercitives within the common ground framework. In what follows, I explore some differences between the two frameworks and then explain why I prefer the scorekeeping framework.

2.5 Why I prefer score

As one can see, both the conversational score and the common ground track relevant facts about conversational context. Both the score and the common ground change as the conversation develops and each framework exhibits the phenomenon of conversational exercitives. Despite these similarities, however, there are important differences between these two frameworks.

First, the common ground tracks only psychological facts.[37] It tracks those belief-like states of acceptance shared by participants. The score, by contrast, captures all sorts of facts—both psychological and non-psychological—relevant to the conversation. Second, the common ground tracks only what is *shared* by *all* participants. The score, by contrast, tracks *everything* relevant. To be shared is to be recognized by all participants and for each participant to realize that every other participant recognizes it. Not everything relevant to a conversation is shared in this way. Thus, the score captures more and, for this reason, I prefer the score framework.

Although these two frameworks are often treated as competitors, they are better seen as complementary or overlapping.[38] After all, they each

[37] The common ground tracks (only) psychological facts but it need not be *composed* of such facts. Changes to common ground can thus be (directly) enacted even if the facts tracked by it are caused to obtain. In this regard, common ground is much like score. I thank Matt Moss for this clarification.

[38] Langton sees them as complementary. See Langton 2011: 87. She helped me to see that they are not competing.

track important aspects of conversational kinematics. The score tracks those facts relevant to the proper development of the conversation whereas the common ground tracks (certain aspects of) participants' awareness of and attitudes towards the propositions relevant to the conversation. I see them as overlapping; on my inclusive Lewisian conception of conversational score, it captures everything the common ground does and then some.[39]

2.6 Multiple functioning

We are now in a position to see that conversational contributions do many things at once. In addition to whatever speech act a conversational contribution may be on the surface (e.g. an assertion, a question, or a command), since it also enacts a change to the conversational score, it is also simultaneously a conversational exercitive that enacts permissibility facts for the conversation. Although this may seem surprising or counterintuitive, it is commonplace in the philosophy of language that any single utterance performs a multiplicity of functions. Conversational exercitives are just another such function.

It is well known, for example, that utterances express content in a wide variety of ways simultaneously. They state, presuppose, and implicate (both conversationally and conventionally).[40] Even at the illocutionary level of what our words *do*, a simultaneous multiplicity of function is widely accepted. On the standard account of indirect speech acts, for instance, single utterances have multiple illocutionary forces.[41] Saying, for example, "Can you pass the salt?" during a meal is, on this account, both literally a question about the addressee's physical abilities and an indirect request that the addressee pass the salt.[42] If what I have argued here is correct, then the (simultaneous and often unintended) enacting of

[39] Again, there are different ways to define score and thus different ways to distinguish score from common ground. For a different difference, see Camp 2018.

[40] For an account of implicature (both conversational and conventional) see Grice 1989: 26–31.

[41] See Searle 1979a and Lycan 1986: 157–86.

[42] This standard account is not without its critics. Bertolet (1994), for example, denies indirect force altogether. For a response, see McGowan et al. 2009.

conversational permissibility facts is yet another thing our utterances do along with everything else.[43]

Regarding multiplicity of function, it is also worth mentioning that a single utterance can be both a standard exercitive and a conversational exercitive. Suppose, for instance, that while discussing Bobby's dog, my bubble gum chewing three-year-old son walks into the room and blows a bubble clear out of his mouth and into the hair of Bobby's frail elderly mother. Suppose that, in response, I set a new rule for my son by saying: "You are no longer permitted to chew bubble gum in public." Since this utterance enacts a permissibility fact for my son via my authority over him, it is a standard exercitive. Since it also renders gum chewing a relevant topic in the current conversation, though, it also enacts a change to the relevance component of score and thereby enacts changes to the bounds of conversational permissibility. As one can see, this standard exercitive is also a conversational exercitive.

Finally, the phenomenon of conversational exercitives is perfectly compatible with the fact that other things besides conversational contributions can enact changes to the conversational score and thereby enact changes to the bounds of conversational permissibility. Suppose, for example, that while discussing Bobby's dog, my neighbor's dog, Sage, runs into the room and starts chewing on Bobby's leg.[44] Since all conversational participants witness Sage's misbehavior, Sage is thereby rendered the most salient dog at this point in the conversation. Sage's behavior (and our all noticing it) enacts a change to the score and, as a result, it would be conversationally improper for any conversational participant to try to refer to any other dog with the expression 'the dog' (until, of course, the salience facts change again). That Sage's behavior changes the bounds of conversational permissibility, though, in no way undermines the fact that conversational contributions do so too. After all, what can be done through conversational means can also often be done non-conversationally.[45]

[43] Again, exercitives are not a type of speech act; they are a ubiquitous aspect of language use. See note 18.

[44] Lewis makes a similar point in his 1983: 240–3.

[45] Suppose, for example, that I want to communicate my desire that Deirdre share her chocolate with me. I can do so verbally (by requesting that she do so) or I can do so non-verbally (by gazing longingly at her box of chocolates as I lick my lips). This example is based on examples from Rod Bertolet but is used here to make a different point. See Bertolet 1994.

2.7 Timing, blocking, and accommodation

Although I sometimes speak as if the score change is enacted only once the conversational contribution is accepted by one's interlocutors, this is not technically accurate. It is a convenient shorthand for typical cases, but the full story is more complex. Strictly speaking, the score change is immediately and directly enacted. Just as my skipping to work directly enacts the truth that I skipped to work, my asserting that Peter took the apple directly enacts the conversational truth that I asserted that Peter took the apple. If my assertion is then rejected by the interlocutor ("No, he didn't, I did!"), then my interlocutor's utterance will enact score changes of its own. In particular, the proposition that Peter took the apple will be removed from the set of claims treated as background in the context of this conversation and the claim that my interlocutor took the apple will be added. As one can see, questioned or rejected contributions do not enact *ongoing* score changes, but they do enact temporary score changes.[46] On my view, they enact changes immediately even if those changes are soon reversed. So although it sometimes makes sense to talk as if the score change is blocked by one's interlocutor's rejection of one's conversational contribution, this is really shorthand for the more complicated truth that the score change enacted by one's utterance is soon undone by that subsequent rejection.

Things work differently in the common ground framework. Blocked utterances are not shared and thus never enter the common ground. Thus, when my interlocutor rejected my assertion that Peter stole the apple, she effectively prevented that claim from entering the common ground. This result may seem intuitive but it comes at a cost. In particular, the common ground theorist must accept quite a lot of temporal indeterminacy. Consider an utterance that introduces a presupposition. That presupposition becomes a part of the common ground only once it is shared but since there is no temporal fact of the matter regarding when a participant accepts a presupposition, there is no temporal fact of the matter regarding when that presupposition is shared.[47] As a result, there

[46] Even this is a simplification since any move enacts multiple score changes and *some* of the score changes (i.e. the fact that the speaker spoke) are enduring.

[47] This temporal indeterminacy is not discussed in the common ground literature but has been confirmed in private correspondence with Robert Stalnaker, Steven Yablo, and Kai von Fintel.

is no fact of the matter regarding when that presupposition enters the common ground. So, too, with assertions. Such temporal indeterminacy provides yet another reason to prefer the conversational score framework.

In recent work, Langton, who works in the scorekeeping framework, offers an account of blocked utterances that is importantly different from mine. According to Langton, presupposition accommodation by interlocutors is a necessary felicity condition for certain types of (what she calls back door) speech acts. So, on her account, when that sort of speech act is not accommodated, the attempted speech act retroactively misfires.[48]

Suppose, for example, that I tell Rae that even Van could pass the test. On the surface, my utterance is an assertion but, because my utterance also presupposes that Van is not very bright, there is an additional back door speech act of verdictively ranking Van as of inferior intelligence. This verdictive relies, according to Langton, on my interlocutor accommodating this presupposition. If Rae rejects it, then my back door verdictive speech act fails (even if my utterance succeeds in other illocutionary ways). Moreover, the verdictive fails because of what my interlocutor failed to do *afterwards*. Langton here stresses the important role of interlocutors thereby highlighting ways that we can undermine the harmful speech of others. This is all to the good but my account does the same without the temporal indeterminacy of accommodation and without the (mysterious and counter-intuitive) retroactive result.

Blocking conversational moves is a process that is both complex and multi-faceted. It is not as if objecting to a certain conversational move thereby undoes all of the score changes directly enacted by that conversational move. One cannot change the fact that the contribution was made. That contribution might introduce topics and alter salience facts and these score changes will not be undone by subsequent moves objecting to it. Clearly, some score changes will remain intact; others will go back to what they were before the objectionable move was made and still others change yet again. What matters for our purposes is how

[48] See her 2018. On her account, *all* speech acts are accommodation dependent and thus have this retroactive feature. Langton here operates with a broader conception of accommodation; she includes uptake and score change as instances of accommodation. Back door speech acts can also be performed via implicatures. For other discussions of objecting/blocking, see Haslanger 2010; Ayala and Vasilyeva 2016; Johnson 2018; Horisk manuscript; and McGowan 2018a.

effective and/or easy it is to reverse the score changes that result in harm and the answer to this important question remains to be seen.

2.8 Conclusion

In this chapter, I have shown that conversational contributions routinely enact facts about what is subsequently permissible in the conversation. Such conversational exercitives involve an important but overlooked mechanism of verbal norm enactment. Since conversational exercitives enact permissibility facts, they do what standard exercitive speech acts do but they work differently. In Chapter 3, similarities and differences between standard exercitives and conversational exercitives are explored.

3

On Differences Between Standard and Conversational Exercitives

3.1 Introduction

As we saw in the previous chapter, conversational contributions routinely enact changes to what is conversationally permissible. By enacting changes to the conversational score, such utterances thereby change what is subsequently permissible in that very conversation. In this way, conversational contributions are like standard exercitives; they enact facts about what is permissible in some realm. Despite this important similarity, however, there are also several important dissimilarities between standard exercitives and conversational exercitives. Moreover, these differences will be important in later chapters when evaluating hypotheses about allegedly harmful speech.

Before we begin, though, a clarification is warranted. When I speak of conversational exercitives, I refer to *that aspect* of a conversational contribution that enacts permissibility facts for the conversation in question. As we saw in the last chapter, such conversational contributions will do many other things besides enacting such permissibility facts. (Asserting p will assert p as well as enact conversational permissibility facts in virtue of the score change involved in asserting p.[1]) The conversational contribution is the total speech act in context and the conversational exercitive is but one aspect of what that utterance does in context. The same is true of standard exercitives. An utterance that enacts permissibility facts via the exercise of speaker authority is likely to do several other things

[1] It will likely presuppose and implicate as well. See Chapter 1.

as well. If the utterance is a conversational contribution, then it will also enact changes to conversational permissibility. The utterance may also be the answer to a request or an insult and so forth. Thus, when I speak of standard exercitives, I refer to that aspect of the utterance in question that enacts permissibility facts in this way.[2]

Let us now turn to the task of exploring the differences between standard exercitives and conversational exercitives. One important difference concerns their respective mechanisms of production. As we have seen, standard exercitives enact permissibility facts via an exercise of speaker authority. Conversational exercitives, by contrast, do so via the norm-governed nature of conversation. By saying something that enacts a score change, such utterances thereby enact, via the norms governing conversation, a change to what is subsequently permissible in that very conversation. As one can see, these two sorts of exercitives do what they do through very different means. We shall explore this difference in a bit more detail in the present chapter by investigating the respective role of (linguistic) intentions in the functioning of these two types of exercitives.

Here is another difference: It is already evident that conversational exercitives are much more common than standard exercitives are. In fact, since every conversational contribution enacts a score change, every conversational contribution enacts changes to conversational permissibility and is thus a conversational exercitive. Plainly, the same cannot be said for standard exercitives. They require an exercise of speaker authority and are comparatively less common.

As we shall see in the following sections, though, there are further important differences between these two sorts of permissibility-fact-enacting utterances. In particular, they have different success conditions and they enact very different sorts of permissibility facts. Before we can explore these differences, however, it is first necessary to present some further details about the nature of communicative intentions.

[2] Thus, when we say that conversational contributions *are* conversational exercitives, we are using the 'is' of predication, as opposed to the 'is' of identity. Being a conversational exercitive is one of the properties of that conversational contribution; it is not equal to and thus exhaustive of it.

3.2 On gradations of communicative and informative intentions

As discussed in Chapter 1, we are here working within a broadly Gricean framework wherein language use is a tool for communicating and communication is essentially a matter of recognizing the speaker's communicative intention. Certain complexities about communicative intentions are relevant when considering the differences between standard and conversational exercitives. For this reason, the relevant complexities are presented here.

Recall that communicative intentions are higher-order intentions. When I communicate some content, I intend to communicate that content (this is the informative intention) and I intend for the addressee to recognize my intention to communicate that content (this is the communicative intention). Since my communicative intention is an intention about my informative intention (namely that it be recognized), my communicative intention is a higher-order intention. An example may help. Suppose I tell Celia that Nora loves second grade and Celia realizes that I am telling her that Nora loves second grade. In this case, Celia realizes this via her recognition of my intention to tell her this. Notice that just hearing the sounds of what I say and recognizing the linguistic meaning of those sounds would not be enough. The very same sounds with the very same meaning would have been produced/expressed had I been reading aloud from a book. No, this is an example of communication because Celia recognizes that I intend to tell her that Nora loves second grade (that is, Celia recognizes my informative intention) and she also recognizes that I intend for her to recognize that intention (that is, she recognizes my communicative intention).

This higher-order (communicative) intention and its recognition are crucial. After all, I might intend to cause a belief in someone but not intend for that intention to be recognized. Suppose, for example, that I want Celia to believe that I am rich; I might put on airs to cause her to believe that I am well-to-do but since I do not want her to recognize this intention (to cause her to believe that I am rich), this is not a case of communication even if I am successful and Celia comes to believe that I am rich. Although I intend for Celia to make this inference (that I am rich), since I do not intend for her to recognize that intention, this is not a case of communication. Communication happens via the recognition of an intention that the speaker intends to be recognized.

In this fairly simple case (of telling Celia that Nora loves second grade), I am quite aware of this communicative–informative intention pair and they are also fairly explicit in my mind. Not all informative intentions are so straightforward. Suppose, for example, that Celia also takes me to be telling her that I am comparing our daughters; that I am keeping track of how our daughters are doing in relation to one another and I really want my daughter to do better than her daughter. Although I might not have been so aware of this when I said what I said, it may well be that I was in fact communicating this. If I were to ask myself if that was one of the things I wanted to get across in saying what I said, and if I were to be completely honest with myself, I might come to realize that, yes, that is part of what I intended to communicate. Notice, however, that this part of my communicated meaning is significantly less conscious and less explicit (than the claim that Nora loves second grade). How conscious speakers are of an informative intention (or how conscious they are of the entire content of that intention) and how explicit those intentions are to speakers appear to be a matter of degree. The same is true for the hearers. How conscious hearers are of their recognition of an intention and how explicit hearers' understanding of the (entire) content of that intention appear also to be a matter of degree.

Relevance theorists (who also work, as I do, within a broadly Gricean linguistic framework) have a way of capturing this gradation in terms of 'manifestness.' As Robyn Carston puts it: "A communicative intention is a higher-order intention to make it mutually manifest to audience and communicator that the communicator has a particular informative intention" and manifestness is a matter of degree.[3] It is, as she says, "the degree to which an individual is capable of mentally representing an assumption and holding it as true or probably true at a given moment."[4] The proposition that Nora loves second grade is made more mutually manifest by my utterance than the proposition that I am comparing our daughters. Manifestness can also differ between participants. One can certainly imagine contexts in which my utterance renders the proposition that I am comparing our daughters much more manifest to Celia

[3] See Carston 2002: 376. [4] See Carston 2002: 378.

than to me. That informative and communicative intentions admit of such degrees will be important in what follows.

3.3 On the role of intentions

In short, the relevant intentions associated with standard exercitives tend to be at the high end of the manifestness spectrum while those associated with conversational exercitives tend to be at the (very) low end.

3.3.1 Speaker intentions

Let's start with standard exercitives and let's look at a paradigmatic case. Suppose that during a department meeting (the purpose of which is to discuss, design, and enact new policies regarding the Philosophy Department's Honors Program) the chair enacts a new policy by saying, "OK from now on then, only students who have completed both history requirements will be eligible."

In this case, the speaker is well aware of her (illocutionary) intention to enact a policy (that is, to enact a permissibility fact for the department's honors program). She is also well aware of her intention to enact that particular policy. In other words, the content of that policy is quite explicit in her mind. Moreover, this content is also tied quite closely to the linguistic meaning of the words she actually utters.

Contrast this with a paradigmatic example of a conversational exercitive. Suppose, for instance, that Bobby and I are talking about how much work his house needs and I say, "Well our house isn't even structurally sound so we sure have our work cut out for us!" By bringing up my house, I thereby enact a change to the salience component of the score and this score change in turn enacts conversational permissibility facts. In particular, it makes it the case that my house is the proper referent (in this conversation and until the salience facts change again) of expressions like 'the house.'

Consider the extent to which the speaker intends to be enacting this conversational permissibility fact. One might be tempted to say (as I have elsewhere) that the speaker simply does not intend to do so.[5] After all, my primary aim is to assert a claim about my structurally unsound house

[5] See my 2003 and 2004.

and not to enact a change to the bounds of conversational permissibility. It may seem that enacting permissibility facts is the furthest thing from my mind. To think so, however, would be hasty. After all, we have just seen how complex and how graded these intentions are. Since I intend to be talking about my house and since I am aware of the permissibility consequences of so doing at least in so far as I would recognize violations of these conversational permissibility facts, it seems that I do intend—in some less conscious and less explicit way—to bring about these permissibility changes. I am aware of contributing to an activity that is governed by norms and I am aware that I am changing the conversation in a way that changes what ought to happen subsequently. So although the intention to enact a conversational permissibility fact may not be foremost in my mind and although the precise content of that fact might not be explicitly understood by me when I speak, there is nevertheless a sense in which I do have the relevant speaker intentions. With conversational exercitives, these intentions are considerably less conscious and less explicit; it seems that they are fairly far down on the scale of manifestness.

Although this discussion may seem to stretch the concept of intentionality to an extreme, it is important to note that not everything our utterances do will turn out to be intentional (even with this graded notion of intentionality). To see this, consider an example. Suppose that when I spoke to Bobby about his house, I was the first person in that conversation to utter the word 'structurally.' The truth that I was the first person in that conversation to utter the word 'structurally' is (directly) enacted by my utterance; this is something that my utterance does along with everything else that it does (e.g. assert that our house is structurally unsound; enact changes to the salience component of the conversational score and so forth). Even though my utterance (directly) enacts this truth (that I am the first person in this conversation to utter the word 'structurally') and even though my utterance is an intentional action, there is no sense in which I intended to enact this truth. Doing so is just no part of what I set out to do. This is so even if I am later made aware of my utterance enacting this fact. "'Hey do you realize that you are the first person in this conversation to say 'structurally'?" That I realize I have done so does not mean that I *intended* to do so.

Under different circumstances, though, my enacting of this fact would be intentional. Suppose, for example, that we were playing some sort of word game in which who says a word first matters for the purposes of the game. If this were the case, then my enacting of this fact would be intentional. It might be intentional in this watered down (low on the manifest scale) sense or it might be highly intentional in the way that my telling Celia that Nora loves second grade is. If being the first to say 'structurally' matters a lot then it is likely to be highly intentional; if it matters but only little and tangentially, then it is likely to be intentional in the attenuated sense in which most conversational exercitives are.

Of course, we have thus far only considered paradigmatic examples. No doubt there are non-paradigmatic cases of standard exercitive speech acts in which the relevant speaker intentions are significantly less conscious and less explicit than they are in the above example. Speakers may be extremely distracted for instance. There are also (non-standard) cases of conversational exercitives where the relevant speaker intentions are much more conscious and explicit. One could even imagine a case where one of the speaker's main aims is to enact a certain conversational permissibility fact. Suppose that I intentionally exploit the phenomenon of conversational exercitives in order to steer a conversation as I wish. I may, for example, be chatting with self-absorbed Kate and so I intentionally keep bringing up other topics in order to avoid listening to her drone on about herself (or in order to enjoy watching her struggle to bring the topic back to herself). In this case, I am well aware of the conversational permissibility-fact-enacting consequences of my contributions. In fact, one of my aims in speaking is to bring about such consequences. Thus, I am well aware of my intention to enact conversational permissibility facts and I am also well aware of my intention to enact the particular permissibility facts that I do enact.

In sum and in general, the speaker intentions associated with standard exercitives are more conscious and more explicit than those associated with conversational exercitives. With conversational exercitives, it seems that the enacting of conversational permissibility facts is more like a pragmatic side effect of making a contribution to the norm-governed activity of conversation than it is one of the speaker's intended actions. With standard exercitives, by contrast, the enacting of permissibility facts is in fact the very point of speaking.

3.3.2 Hearer recognition

A consideration of the hearer's recognition of the speaker's (various) intentions illuminates yet another difference between these two types of exercitives. Consider the above paradigmatic example of a standard exercitive. Consider the department chair who enacts a new permissibility fact for the honors program by saying, "OK from now on then, only students who have completed both history requirements will be eligible." As we just saw, in this case, the speaker is well aware of her intention to enact a permissibility fact and she is also well aware of her intention to enact this particular permissibility fact. Moreover, the hearers recognize both of these intentions. The other faculty present at the meeting recognize both that the chair is enacting new departmental policy and that she is enacting this particular policy. Thus, the chair's illocutionary intention (to enact policy) and her locutionary intention (regarding the content of the policy) are made mutually manifest. In other words, the speaker is well aware of these things and her speaking makes the other participants well aware of them as well.

Contrast that with a paradigmatic example of a conversational exercitive. Recall my saying "Well our house isn't even structurally sound so we sure have our work cut out for us!" to Bobby during our conversation about how much work his house needs. This utterance is a conversational exercitive; it enacts a change to the salience component of the conversational score and thus enacts changes to the bounds of conversational permissibility. I argued above that there is an attenuated sense in which I intended to enact the relevant conversational permissibility fact. I am aware of contributing to an activity that I know to be norm-governed; I am aware of steering the conversation towards my own house and I would recognize any violations of the permissibility facts enacted. In a similar fashion, there is an attenuated sense in which hearers recognize the speaker's (attenuated) intentions. The hearers too recognize that this utterance is a contribution to a norm-governed activity; it steers the conversation towards a consideration of my house and the hearers would also recognize violations of the conversational permissibility facts enacted. Of course, the hearer's recognition of these things is significantly less conscious and considerably less explicit than the hearer's recognition of the various speaker intentions with standard exercitives. Even so, there is nevertheless an attenuated sense in which hearer's *do* recognize the relevant speaker intentions.

Again we have thus far only considered paradigm cases of the two types of exercitives. There will be non-paradigmatic cases of standard exercitives where the relevant speaker intentions are significantly less manifest to the (or a) hearer for one reason or another. Perhaps, the hearer is distracted and would only be fully conscious of the speaker's intentions if someone asked her the right questions. Typically, with standard exercitives, the hearers are well aware of what the speaker is intending to do but in some cases a hearer may be significantly less so. It is also possible for a certain hearer to be keenly aware of the typically attenuated intentions relevant to a conversational exercitive. Perhaps a student of linguistics, who has been thinking a lot about conversational kinematics, is especially aware, on some occasion, of the sense in which a speaker intends to be enacting conversational permissibility facts when adding to a conversation. Although possible, it is certainly not typical.

3.3.3 *Comparative reliance on intention and intention recognition*

We have thus far considered the typicality of the presence of certain sorts of speaker intentions and the typicality of the recognition of those (speaker) intentions with the two sorts of exercitives. Now, we shall consider the comparative importance of both the presence of these speaker intentions and their recognition between the two sorts of exercitives. The speaker's intention to enact a permissibility fact, the speaker's intention to enact that particular permissibility fact and the hearer's recognition of both of these intentions matters a lot more with standard exercitives than with conversational exercitives.

To see this, we shall consider cases where each of these conditions fails. Consider first a case of a standard exercitive in which the speaker does not intend (in even an attenuated sense) for her utterance to have exercitive force. Suppose, for instance, that Cindy is the C.F.O. and during a corporate meeting the purpose of which is to enact new money-saving policies, she says, "From now on, we cannot allow overtime to be approved by middle management." Suppose that rather than intending to enact a new overtime policy, Cindy merely intends to be expressing her personal opinion about, and her frustration with, the current budget crisis. Suppose further that even if she were questioned afterwards about her aims in speaking, she would honestly—and on reflection—deny that enacting such a policy was any one of those aims.

In such a case then, there is not even an attenuated sense in which Cindy intends to enact an overtime policy.

In a case such as this, her speech act, if it manages to be a standard exercitive at all, is far from ideal. In fact, many would regard Cindy's failure to intend to enact overtime policy as a fatal defect of the standard exercitive speech act. On this view, which is a widespread view in the philosophy of language and speech act theory, Cindy's failure to intend to enact such a policy prevents her utterance from doing so.[6] Suppose, however, that one does not treat speaker illocutionary intention as necessary for illocution in this way. Even if other conditions are met and in virtue of these conditions being met the utterance manages to enact the overtime policy in question, the fact that Cindy did not intend to do so is nevertheless at least a non-ideal aspect of this standard exercitive. It's non-ideal because the speaker is supposed to be intending to enact the policy; it's non-ideal because a condition that is supposed to be satisfied is not.

Suppose now that Cindy does intend to enact an overtime policy but her intention to do so is not foremost in her mind. Suppose that she becomes aware of this intention only after she is asked clarificatory questions about her aims in speaking and only after she reflects long and hard about things. There is room for people to disagree about whether or not Cindy's utterance manages to have standard exercitive force in such a case. One might regard the low manifest level of her intention to enact the overtime policy as a fatal defect of her speech act. Even if one were to regard the utterance as successfully enacting such a policy in this case (say because other conditions are satisfied), Cindy's standard exercitive speech act is nevertheless non-ideal. It's non-ideal

[6] It is a widespread assumption that the speaker's intention to ¥ is a necessary condition for the speaker to perform the illocutionary act of ¥ing. The possibility of (what is sometimes called illocutionary implication) may afford an exception. It might be possible for someone to intend to enact a verbal contract (and not intend to promise) but by enacting that contract that person thereby automatically also promises. Suppose, for example, that verbal contracts are just like promises except that they enact much stronger obligations. For an exploration of these sorts of possibilities, see Searle and Vanderveken 1985. Kukla and Lance (2013) argue that it is a mistake to assume (as Searle does) that the normative facts enacted by various sorts of speech acts differ only with respect to strength. According to Kukla and Lance, each type of speech act enacts its own peculiar sort of normative fact. Kukla and Lance downplay the role of intentions in language use (and work outside the broadly Gricean framework in which I operate here). For another influential example, see Brandom 1994.

because she is supposed to be highly aware of her intention to enact the policy in question; it is non-ideal because an important success condition is not fulfilled.

Consider, by contrast, conversational exercitives and the speaker's intention to enact a conversational permissibility fact. As we have already seen, speakers typically are not highly conscious of their intentions to enact conversational permissibility facts. It is only in a highly attenuated sense that conversational contributors intend to do so at all. Moreover, that this is the case in no way undermines the exercitive force of conversational contributions. While the speaker's intention to enact a permissibility fact ought to be highly manifest to the speaker with a *standard* exercitive, this is simply *not* the case with conversational exercitives. Being highly aware of one's intention to do so is just not part of how they work. As a result, a failure to be highly aware of one's intention to do so does not render the conversational exercitive non-ideal in any manner.

What about the full out failure to intend to enact a conversational permissibility fact? What if the speaker fails to intend to enact a conversational permissibility fact in any sense whatsoever. It's not clear what this would actually look like. To see this, suppose that a conversational contributor fails to recognize the permissibility consequences of her contribution even after those consequences are patiently pointed out to her and suppose further that she insists sincerely and on reflection that she did not intend to enact any them. Even in a case like this, though, it seems that there is nevertheless a sense in which she intends to enact conversational permissibility facts since she realizes at some level or other that conversations are norm-governed activities and she also intended with her contribution to add to the conversation. So even if she had not consciously connected the dots and realized that making such a contribution will enact changes to conversational permissibility, she still in some sense intends—perhaps in a more attenuated sense than usual—to enact conversational permissibility facts. What would we say, though, about a contributor who did not even realize these things? Consider, that is, a speaker who is not aware of adding to the conversation or who fails to realize that conversations are activities governed by norms. Perhaps such a speaker is not competent to contribute to a conversation at all and her utterance fails to be a genuine contribution. Or maybe her contributions are genuine contributions but they are non-ideal in some sense in virtue of her failure to realize these things. Either way, it seems that conversational exercitives do depend on speaker intention in this highly attenuated sense. As we saw above, though, unlike standard exercitives, they do not depend on that intention being highly manifest to the speaker.

In addition to the intention to enact permissibility facts, speakers also have (locutionary) intentions regarding the content of the permissibility fact being enacted. With standard exercitives, the intention to enact a permissibility fact with a particular content is also an important condition. Moreover, that intention ought to be highly manifest to the speaker. When that condition fails or when the intention is not highly manifest to the speaker, the standard exercitive is (at least) non-ideal. With conversational exercitives, by contrast, there is no expectation that the speaker be highly conscious of the content of the conversational permissibility fact being enacted. If, however, there is not even an attenuated sense in which the speaker intends to enact a conversational permissibility fact with that content, the conversational exercitive is (at least) non-ideal.

Hearer recognition is the flip side of speaker intention. With standard exercitives, participants ought to be highly aware of the relevant speaker intentions; the recognition of these intentions is an important part of how standard exercitive speech acts work. With conversational exercitives, by contrast, this is not the case. In what follows, I consider a series of cases in order to demonstrate this.

First, let us consider the speaker's illocutionary intention to enact a permissibility fact. Suppose, for example, that my children think I am only kidding when I say that they will have to go to bed early unless they finish the rubbery scallops that I have prepared for their dinner. Their failure to recognize my illocutionary intention to enact a new rule renders my standard exercitive speech act non-ideal. It is controversial whether uptake (the hearer's recognition of the speaker's illocutionary intention) is necessary for illocution. Austin took it to be.[7] Either way, we can safely conclude that uptake is an important success condition of standard exercitives.

The hearer's recognition of the speaker's locutionary intention is also important with standard exercitives. Suppose, for instance, that my

[7] See Austin 1975: 116–17.

children misunderstand what I said and think that I intend to be declaring a new rule such that they must go to bed *oily* unless they finish their dinner. In this case, they recognize my illocutionary intention (to enact a new rule), but they misunderstand the content of that rule. Such a misunderstanding also renders my standard exercitive non-ideal.[8]

Although the relevant speaker intentions ought to be highly manifest (and correctly identified) by hearers with standard exercitive speech acts, this is simply not the case with conversational exercitives. Conversational exercitives are perfectly successful and even ideal in cases where the hearers are not well aware of the speaker's attenuated intention to enact a conversational permissibility fact, the speaker's attenuated intention to enact that particular conversational permissibility fact, the fact that a conversational permissibility fact is being enacted or the fact that that particular conversational permissibility fact is being enacted. It is simply not the case that the relevant speaker intentions (or the relevant facts about which conversational permissibility facts are being enacted) ought to be highly manifest to hearers with conversational exercitives.

That said, there is certainly an attenuated sense in which hearers do and ought to recognize all of these things. Competent participants in some sense recognize these (attenuated) speaker intentions as well as the permissibility consequences of conversational contributions in virtue of several factors. First, participants recognize the permissibility consequences of conversational contributions at least in so far as they manage to operate within the bounds of conversational permissibility. Second, participants are and ought to be aware of the norm-governed nature of conversation even if this awareness is not foremost in their minds. Third and finally, participants realize that the utterance in question is a contribution to, and they even realize that it is an intentional contribution to, the conversation in question. Hearer recognition in this attenuated sense

[8] Since I leave open the possibility that a speech act can have a particular illocutionary force and/or a particular locutionary content without the speaker intending that her utterance have that force and/or that content, there are two more ways in which hearer recognition may fail and standard exercitives are sensitive to both of these failures. A standard exercitive is defective if the hearer fails to recognize the actual illocutionary force of the utterance (whether intended by the speaker or not) and/or the actual locutionary content of the utterance (whether intended by the speaker or not). According to a prevalent account of illocution, though, unintended illocutionary force is impossible. For a discussion of this, see Chapter 4 section 4.3.

is important for the success and proper functioning of conversational exercitives.

In sum, standard exercitives work by making certain speaker intentions mutually manifest. The speaker is well aware of her intention to enact a permissibility fact and to enact a particular permissibility fact and her speech act aims at rendering these very intentions manifest to the hearer as well. In short, standard exercitive speech acts work at the level of the consciously communicated intention to do so. Conversational exercitives, by contrast, do not work by making the intention to enact a conversational permissibility fact mutually manifest. Nor do they work by making the intention to enact a particular conversational permissibility fact mutually manifest. The relevant intentions with conversational exercitives are typically not very manifest to *any* of the participants and this is as it should be. In Section 3.5, we shall investigate the success conditions of conversational exercitives, but in the meantime, it is clear what they do *not* depend on.

3.4 On the role of speaker authority

Another important difference between these two types of exercitives concerns the role of speaker authority.

3.4.1 Standard exercitives

As we saw in Chapter 1, standard exercitives are authoritative speech acts. In order to enact permissibility facts in some particular domain (via a standard exercitive), a speaker must have, and be exercising, the authority to do so. I am unable to enact new speed limits in Massachusetts, for example, exactly because I do not have the requisite authority to do so. Only certain state officials can do so and when and how they can do so are officially specified.

With standard exercitive speech acts, it is important not just that the speaker has the required authority to enact the permissibility fact in question but that the speaker is also exercising that authority on that occasion. Even though I am in a position to order my son to clean his room, for example, I may nevertheless merely suggest that he do so when he asks me what to do on some rainy day. Although I have the authority to order him, I am not exercising that authority on that occasion.

With standard exercitives, though, the speaker has and is exercising the authority to enact the permissibility fact in question.

The hearer's recognition of the speaker's authority and the hearer's recognition that the speaker is exercising that authority on that particular occasion are also important conditions of standard exercitives. If a speaker has the authority but the addressee falsely believes that the speaker does not have it, then the standard exercitive speech act will be (at least) non-ideal. Suppose, for example, that the on-site health inspector verbally enacts a cease and desist order for the delinquent cupcake factory but the manager of that factory falsely believes that only the health inspector's boss has the authority to do this. In this case, the health inspector's standard exercitive speech act is non-ideal exactly because the manager addressed by the speech act fails to recognize that the health inspector does in fact have the requisite authority to successfully perform this speech act. The hearer's recognition that the speaker is exercising that authority on that occasion is also an important condition for standard exercitives. Suppose, for example, that during a frustrating department meeting, I throw up my hands and say, "Well, I've had it. Meeting over." Suppose that my colleague Helena, who recognizes that, in my capacity as department chair, I have the authority to terminate department meetings, falsely believes that I am kidding around in order to lighten the mood. In this case, Helena recognizes that I have the authority to terminate the meeting, but she does not recognize that I am here exercising that authority. My standard exercitive speech act is non-ideal exactly because Helena (and perhaps others as well) fails to recognize this fact.

3.4.2 *Authority, expertise, and standing*

This notion of authority is rich and complex. While it is true that standard exercitives sometimes depend on a highly official sort of authority, as it does in enacting law, naming ships, and marrying people (some of Austin's favorite examples), the authority in question need not be so very official. Parents, for example, have a less official sort of authority over their children. Parents can verbally enact rules for their children that other people cannot. Of course, parenthood is somewhat official; it is legally sanctioned in a variety of ways but other sorts of authority do not seem to be official at all. Consider, for example, the mean girl in middle school who announces that Maddy is no longer cool.

It seems that she has the authority to oust Maddy even though her authority is not officially sanctioned in any way. Among her peers, though, she counts as having that authority and this seems to be sufficient for her to actually have it.

It seems that, even in the adult arena, counting as having authority is sometimes constitutive of having it. Suppose, for example, that there is a traffic accident and motorists are at a loss with respect to what the subsequent traffic pattern ought to be. Suppose that one of these motorists takes it upon herself to start directing traffic. Maybe the other motorists will ignore her and continue to scratch their heads in bewilderment but maybe they won't. Since this is a (classic) coordination problem and since everyone is better off if there is an agreed upon strategy for dealing with it, it makes practical sense to follow her direction and, in fact in real life, people often do. Moreover, once people start following her instructions, she counts as the director of traffic and thereby has the authority to direct it. Once this process is under way, she can order cars to stop, reverse, and change directions. Normally, only a police officer or other designated official has the authority to do this. Maitra calls this phenomenon licensing. Authority is licensed when it is conferred upon those who act as if they already have it.[9] Licensing shows that authority can be fairly unofficial and it is partially constituted by the recognition or treatment of others.

Authority is a kind of comparative power. On this view, to have authority in some context is to be able to do things that other people cannot do and it is to be able to do these things because one socially counts as having the power to do them. In other words, one is able to do these things because one has conferred upon her by others a certain status.[10] One might count as having this power because one has been officially declared the person with such power or one might count as having the power because one has been licensed as having it on some particular occasion.

It is important to distinguish authority from expertise. *Being* an authority is different from *having* it. Being an authority on some subject

[9] Maitra 2012.

[10] Since authority must involve the imposition of, what Searle (1995) calls, a status function, it is socially constructed. Searle (1995) affords a helpful discussion of the ontology of social construction.

matter is to have a lot of knowledge about it. Having authority, by contrast, is to have powers conferred upon one that enables one to do things that others cannot do.

Of course, authority and expertise are related. Sometimes expertise grounds authority. Certain experts about antique furniture, for example, are empowered to appraise the value of antiques for the purposes of an insurance claim. In this case, the antiques expert has been officially designated by the insurance company as someone who is able to do this. No doubt, the insurance company designated this person to do this because of his expertise. This is a case where the authority is officially conferred in virtue of expertise but the conferral need not be so official. Those recognized to have the relevant expertise, for example, may be more likely to have (a much more informal sort of) authority licensed to them.

In sum, although expertise and authority are related, they are nevertheless distinct. Authority involves a status conferred by others that constitutes a power to do things others cannot. Expertise, by contrast, is a kind of knowledge.[11]

3.4.3 *Conversational exercitives*

Consider now the role of speaker authority with conversational exercitives. Does the successful enacting of conversational permissibility facts require that the speaker has and is exercising authority over the relevant domain? Recall that, with standard exercitives, the authority required of the speaker is limited to the domain over which the enacted permissibility fact presides. Since conversational exercitives enact permissibility facts in the very conversation to which they are a contribution, the speaker authority condition would require that conversational participants have and are exercising authority over that very conversation. In light of this, one might be tempted to say that conversational exercitives are also authoritative speech acts. After all, there is a sense—perhaps a very thin sense—in which a contributor to a conversation is an authority over that conversation and is exercising that authority when he or she contributes to it. Since authority is a *comparative* kind of social power, though, and since just about everyone is able to contribute to

[11] Tirrell treats expertise as a type of authority. See Tirrell's "Authority and Gender: Flipping the F-Switch," an unpublished manuscript.

conversations, we run the risk of stretching this notion of authority too far. My concern is that, by treating even conversational participation as an exercise of authority, we are at risk of ignoring the very sorts of power dynamics crucially at play in our broader investigation.

That said, it is clear that a speaker must have a certain kind of *standing* in order to successfully contribute to a conversation.[12] Eligibility for participation in conversation is governed by a complex set of social norms. Suppose that I approach two women chatting at the Beverly Yacht Club in Marion and they flat out refuse to acknowledge that I have spoken to them. Their reaction to my attempted contribution makes it clear that, as far as these snotty Marion ladies are concerned, I am not welcome to join their conversation; I lack the requisite (in this case, social) standing. Other sorts of cases of this are less hierarchical. Suppose, for instance, that my good friends Greg and Claudia are talking and I walk over and say hello. Suppose that they accept my greeting but nevertheless exclude me from the ongoing conversation because they are having a pressing discussion about town politics and I don't live in their town; I know nothing about it; I could not care less and they know it. In this case and despite our friendship and mutual regard, I nevertheless lack standing to join their conversation.

This (conversational) standing can also be licensed. One can come to have it as a result of acting as if one already has it. Suppose that when I walked over to the Beverly Yacht Club ladies and chimed into their conversation, they each assumed that I belonged there and so they accept my conversational contribution and chat with me for a good long while. In this case, I acted as if I had the standing to be in their conversation and they treated me as if I had that standing and their treating me this way is sufficient for me to have that standing (at least on this occasion).[13] Standing can be licensed.

The difference between authority and standing may be a mere matter of degree. After all, they are each constituted by a status conferred by others. Although one might stress the similarities, I prefer to mark the

[12] I distinguish standing from authority; others treat it as a type of authority. See, for example, Herbert and Kukla 2016, a fascinating discussion of what they call "peripheral speech".

[13] One might think that I merely "passed" as having that standing. Similar issues arise for social constructionist accounts of race. See, for example, Mallon 2004.

differences. On my view, standing is just too wide spread to count as a form of authority. To appreciate my concern, consider the speech act of assertion. Even though we are all in a position to assert things, one must be (minimally) eligible to assert particular things. Here is an example. Since I am not there and the house is no longer even in the family, I have no idea whether there is a lamp on right now in the living room at 113 Osborne Avenue in Catonsville, Maryland. Since I do not have the evidence and since everyone knows that I do not have the evidence, I lack the standing to make an assertion (one way or the other). Although assertions require standing in this sense and although standing is like authority in some respects, I think it would be a mistake to treat assertion as an authoritative speech act. If assertions are authoritative speech acts, then all speech acts are. After all, every speech act requires that the speaker be socially positioned such that the making of that speech act makes minimal sense. Just as to stress all syllabus is to stress none, to say that all speech acts are authoritative speech acts is to lose sight of the important role that power plays in only some types of speech acts. Thus, although conversational exercitives require that the speaker has the standing to make the conversational contribution in question, on my view, it would be a mistake to treat conversational exercitives as authoritative speech acts.

Although conversational exercitives are not authoritative speech acts, speaker authority nevertheless has an undeniably important role to play with them. After all, speaker authority affects who says what (and when) in any given conversation and this in turn, affects which particular conversational permissibility facts a particular contributor enacts with her contributions. Suppose, for instance, that Deirdre is talking to her boss and her boss is the only person who can declare a leave day for the company. Suppose further that, while talking to Deirdre, the boss announces that she is declaring a leave day for the following Monday. The boss's utterance is a standard exercitive. As such, it enacts a leave day for the company and it does so via an exercise of the boss's authority. In addition to this, however, as a conversational contribution, the boss's utterance also enacts several permissibility facts for the conversation. In particular, it makes leave days a relevant topic of the conversation and it introduces (into the common ground of that conversation) the fact that next Monday will be a leave day for the company. Because only the boss could enact the leave day, only the boss could make this particular conversational contribution and thus only the boss could change the conversational score in just these ways.[14] As one can see then, since speaker authority affects who can say what (and when), speaker authority can affect which particular conversational permissibility facts a speaker can enact (and the conversational circumstances under which she can enact them).

Note that plenty of other things do this too. Politeness, for example, affects what people say (and the circumstances under which they say it) and this, in turn, affects which particular conversational permissibility facts are enacted (when and by whom). Suppose, for example, that I am talking to Shirley who has a huge and highly visible blemish on her nose. Thinking that it would be impolite to say anything about her festering carbuncle, I pretend that I do not notice it. Once she mentions the infection in her nose sore, however, it is socially acceptable for me to discuss it with her. As one can see, although I *could* have asked her about her blemish (and thereby changed the score by introducing a new topic), politeness considerations tell strongly against *my* doing so. Shirley, however, is under no such constraint. As one can see, politeness considerations, just like speaker authority, also affect the enacting of conversational permissibility facts by affecting which conversational contributions are made when and by whom.[15]

Expertise also plays an important role with conversational exercitives. First, expertise contributes to standing. One ought to be an authority on the relevant topic in order to make certain sorts of claims about it. If I lack expertise about the real estate market in Florida, then I really have no standing to claim that it is the third most volatile real estate market in the United States. Expertise also affects credibility, which in turn affects participants' beliefs and those beliefs are captured by the score (and, when these beliefs are shared, they are also captured by the common ground). Because Maeve is an expert on traditional Irish dance, her claim that Liam Harney is the best living male step dancer is accepted (even believed) by all conversational participants but it wasn't when Lori said

[14] Of course, once the boss has enacted the leave day, others can bring up the topic and introduce this fact into the conversation.

[15] One might think that the *conversational* permissibility of discussing the subject is one thing while the *social* acceptability of doing so is quite another. Although tempting, this assessment treats conversational norms as entirely distinct from broader social norms and, since conversation is a social practice, this is a mistake. The norms governing conversation need not be peculiar to conversation; they might include more general norms of cooperation.

it. Although Maeve and Lori asserted the very same claim in the very same conversation, Maeve's enacted different changes to the score (and common ground) because her assertion was believed. Thus, although conversational exercitives are not authoritative speech acts, they are nevertheless affected by both authority and expertise.

In sum, conversational exercitives do not work the way that standard exercitives do. While standard exercitives rely on making certain linguistic intentions (highly) mutually manifest between speaker and hearers, conversational exercitives do not. While standard exercitives are authoritative speech acts, conversational exercitives are not. Although both of these sorts of exercitives enact permissibility facts, they each do so via quite different mechanisms. Standard exercitives are a verbal exercise of power that communicate the speaker's intention to exercise that power in a certain way but conversational exercitives are generated by the norm-governed nature of conversation. Since the mechanisms of production are different, it really should be no surprise that the success conditions are also different.

That the success conditions for the two types of exercitives are different will be important in later chapters when judging the plausibility of various hypotheses regarding how speech functions. Suppose, for example, that a certain racist comment is alleged to constitute an act of oppression in virtue of enacting oppressive permissibility facts. If the utterance in question enacts these oppressive permissibility facts via an exercise of speaker authority, then it ought to satisfy the various success conditions of standard exercitives. If it fails to do so, then this tells against the hypothesis that it is oppressive. If, by contrast, the racist utterance enacts the oppressive permissibility facts in some other way (say, as a conversational exercitive or via some related mechanism) then the hypothesis ought to be tested against *different* conditions of success. In this way, we see that the differences in success conditions can be put to use in assessing specific hypotheses regarding how speech does what it does.

3.5 Conditions of success for conversational exercitives

Thus far, I have argued that conversational exercitives do not share the same success conditions as standard exercitives. Although we have seen what the success conditions of conversational exercitives are *not*, one might well wonder what they are. I now turn to this important task.

3.5.1 Being a conversational exercitive

The success conditions for conversational exercitives are really quite minimal. Before investigating the success conditions, a distinction is warranted. On the one hand, there is the question of what is required for an utterance to enact conversational permissibility facts at all. On the other hand, is the question of what is required to enact a certain set of conversational permissibility facts. I shall focus first on the former issue regarding what is required for an utterance to be a conversational exercitive. As we shall see, it requires only that the utterance enact a change to a conversational score.[16] It does not require that the utterance is or is regarded as a conversational contribution and it does not require that the utterance in question succeed as the particular conversational contribution the speaker intended it to be. We shall proceed by considering a series of cases where various recognition conditions fail to see whether that failure prevents the utterance in question from enacting conversational permissibility facts at all.

Consider first a case where the addressee fails to recognize the content of the utterance. Suppose, for example, that my mother wants to get my husband interested in set dancing again and, as she pulls a videotape out of her bag, she cheerfully says to him, "I hope this will get you interested in sets again." Suppose further that my beloved and hearing-impaired husband, Mike, mishears her and mistakenly thinks that she says 'I hope this will get you interested in sex again'. In this case, the addressee (Mike) misunderstands the content that the speaker (my mother) intends to get across so he fails to recognize the speaker's informational (locutionary) intention. Although this failure renders my mother's assertion far from ideal, it does not prevent her utterance from being a conversational exercitive.

Despite the comic miscommunication, my mother's utterance nevertheless enacts conversational permissibility facts. In cases of miscommunication, though, the difference between common ground and conversational score is especially relevant. Let's start with the common ground. Recall that the common ground is by definition shared. Although Mike misunderstands what my mother says, her contribution nevertheless results in an addition to the common ground. After all, since my mother is understood

[16] This condition coincides with the technical definition of a move, introduced in Chapter 4 section 4.2.1.

as making a conversational contribution, the fact that she has done so is added to the common ground. (This fact is also a component of the conversational score.) Moreover, that my mother just added to the conversation has permissibility consequences for the conversation: it is now Mike's turn to speak. Since this fact is also a part of the common ground both Mike and my mother recognize this fact and thus abide by the subsequent conversational permissibility fact.

Since the miscommunication has not yet been detected, though, it is not a part of the common ground. Recall though that the score need not be shared; it captures all facts relevant to the proper development and assessment of the conversation. As such, it tracks participants' beliefs that are not shared. In particular, it captures facts about what my mother actually said and what Mike mistakenly believes her to have said. These score changes enact (quite different) conversational permissibility facts for Mike and my mother. Given what he took her to have said, Mike is now warranted in being taken aback, confused, and perhaps even fearful of both the content of the videotape and my dear mother. An indignant "Excuse me?" is conversationally appropriate after my mother's utterance but it would not have been appropriate before her utterance. Given what she takes herself to have communicated, by contrast, my mother is warranted in expecting Mike to smile politely and thank her for the videotape. The clash between their expectations will likely cause them to soon discover the miscommunication and this mutual realization will effect changes to both the score and the common ground.

At this point, one might be concerned about an alleged difference between the norms of the conversation and what the participants take those norms to be (given what they each believe about the conversation). In cases of miscommunication, one might wonder who is right about what the norms actually are? Is it my mother? Is it Mike? Or is it that there are different norms for different participants so that they are each correct? I am agnostic on this matter. One important point is that since the common ground tracks only what is shared and the score tracks participant beliefs that are not shared, the score is able to capture facts relevant to the proper development of the conversation that the common ground simply cannot.[17] Furthermore, even in cases of miscommunication, the miscommunication itself enacts conversational permissibility

[17] This is an additional reason to prefer the score framework. See Chapter 2 section 2.5.

facts. Thus although my mother did not manage to make the conversational contribution she intended to make, her utterance nevertheless enacts permissibility facts for the conversation and is therefore a conversational exercitive.

Consider now a different case involving a different sort of miscommunication: uptake failure. This involves the addressee's failure to recognize the speaker's illocutionary intention. The addressee is wrong about what sort of speech act the speaker intends to be performing. Suppose, for example, that Mike and I are discussing what to do next weekend and he says, "I wouldn't mind going to a movie" with the intention of proposing that we go to see a movie (because going to see a movie is what he wants most to do). Suppose that, instead of recognizing his intention to propose that we see a movie, I think that he is merely going on record as saying that he would be willing to see a movie if (and perhaps only if) going to see a movie is something that I am especially interested in doing. In this case, although I recognize the content of what he says, I nevertheless fail to recognize what sort of speech act Mike intends to be performing in saying what he says. He intends to be proposing that we go to see a movie but I take him to be doing something else. Although my failure to recognize his illocutionary intention renders his speech act non-ideal, it does not prevent his utterance from being a conversational exercitive.

For starters, Mike still counts as making a conversational contribution and, as we have just seen, this alone is sufficient for his utterance to enact a conversational permissibility fact: he spoke, so it is now my turn. Furthermore, he goes on record as being willing, under some circumstances, to see a movie and this becomes part of both the common ground and a component of the score. Our seeing a movie next weekend is now under discussion and movies are now a relevant topic of conversation. As one can see, despite the communicative failure, Mike's utterance nevertheless alters the conversational score and thereby enacts permissibility facts for the conversation. It is therefore a conversational exercitive.

I have thus far argued that even when there are different sorts of miscommunication during a conversation, even when important success conditions of certain attempted speech acts are unmet, an utterance nevertheless enacts a change to the score and thus enacts conversational permissibility facts and is therefore a conversational exercitive. In light of this, one might well wonder what sorts of failures prevent an utterance from being a conversational exercitive. What if the utterance is completely drowned out? What if the addressee falsely believes that the utterance is not even an act of speech? What happens when the addressee falsely believes that the utterance is not intended as a conversational contribution? In short, just how minimal are the success conditions of conversational exercitives?

To begin to answer this question, consider the following. Suppose that when I mention my most recent disagreement with my neighbor, a truck drives by and completely drowns out what I say so that, although my interlocutor realizes that I spoke and although she realizes that I am intending, by so doing, to contribute to our conversation, she does not hear a single word that I utter. Even in this case, my utterance is a conversational exercitive. Since my interlocutor recognizes my intention to contribute to the conversation, the meta-linguistic fact that I spoke but was not understood becomes a part of the score. (Since these facts are a shared part of the conversation, they are also a part of the common ground.) Moreover, this score change clearly affects what is subsequently appropriate in the conversation at hand. Proceeding in recognition of my attempted contribution and allowing, perhaps even inviting, me to repeat myself are made appropriate by this recognition. As one can see then, even this (massively unsuccessful) utterance nevertheless enacts changes to the bounds of conversational permissibility; it is thus a conversational exercitive.

What about other recognition failures? Suppose now that my interlocutor sees that I am speaking, but, although she does not hear the content of what I say, she falsely believes that I am talking to someone else on my cell phone so she fails to recognize that my utterance is intended as a contribution to our conversation. Despite this recognition failure, my utterance is still governed by the norms of this conversation and it is taken by my interlocutor as a violation of those norms. After all, talking on one's cell phone while in the middle of a conversation is in violation of the (politeness) norms of conversation. Although this is not what I have actually done, it is what I am taken by my interlocutor as having done. As a result, this utterance counts as an inappropriate move according to my interlocutor (and the norms governing conversation). Moreover, this utterance alters the conversational score by introducing the meta-linguistic fact that I spoke and that I was taken to do so "out of bounds" as it were.

Moreover, this score change enacts conversational permissibility facts. For one thing, it is conversationally appropriate for my interlocutor to react as if I have just done something rude and/or perplexing but such behavior would not have been appropriate before my utterance. As one can see then, even in a case where one's interlocutor fails to recognize one's intention to contribute to the conversation, one's utterance may nevertheless enact a change to the score and thus enacts a change to the bounds of conversational permissibility.[18]

Consider one final case. Suppose that I am sitting in my office alone and I say something to the computer screen. In this case, my utterance is not a contribution to a conversation; it is not taken by anyone to be a contribution to a conversation and, although it enacts the fact that I said what I said, since that fact is not relevant (to the proper development and assessment of any conversation) it does not enact a change to the score of any conversation. As a result, this utterance is not a conversational exercitive.

As one can see, the success conditions for conversation exercitives are extremely minimal. In order for an utterance to enact conversational permissibility facts requires only that the utterance in question enact a change to a conversational score and this requires only that it be relevant to the proper development and assessment of that conversation. It does not require that the conversational contribution succeed as the speech act intended by the speaker and it does not require that the hearer recognize that the utterance is intended as a conversational contribution.

Given the minimal nature of the success condition for an utterance to be a conversational exercitive, it is clear that conversational exercitives are simply ubiquitous. Since the vast majority of utterances are in fact relevant to some conversation or other, the vast majority of utterances enact score changes and are thus conversational exercitives.

That they are ubiquitous, however, does not make them trivial. After all, it is important to know both that and how we make changes to the normative facts around us. Furthermore, other phenomena (e.g. conversational implicatures) are no less important for being widespread. Finally, the second half of the book demonstrates the social, moral, and even legal importance of the phenomenon.

[18] Not every utterance that directly enacts a conversational score change is a conversational move. See Chapter 4 section 4.2.1.

3.5.2 Being a particular conversational exercitive

A different question concerns what is required for a conversational contribution to enact the particular conversational permissibility facts that it does enact. In short, it depends on three things: the conversational score at the time of utterance, the conversational contribution made, and the norms governing the conversation in question. This may sound simple enough, but it is anything but simple. A wide variety of factors affect which particular conversational contribution is made and, as a result, these factors in turn affect which particular conversational permissibility facts are enacted at any given point in a conversation.

Once again, it is best to proceed with an example. Suppose that Susan and I are discussing the best way to repair my wooden boat. I cannot afford to have Beetle Inc. do it properly and the temporary repairs we have been using have now given way. In this conversational context I say, "Well, I'm afraid to tell you that it is time for a fiberglass cap on the bow." Let us assume that this conversational contribution is understood perfectly. In other words, let us assume that the various success conditions for this somewhat complex assertion are met. This assertion is somewhat complex because it is also an indirect speech act. It is directly an assertion about what I am afraid to tell Susan but it is also an indirect assertion that it is time for a fiberglass cap on the bow. Suppose then that Susan hears what I say and realizes that I am contributing to the conversation by so doing. Suppose that the various speaker intention conditions are met. Suppose, that is, that I intended to get across both claims and I also intended to assert two claims. Suppose also that the various hearer recognition conditions are met: Susan recognizes all of these intentions (and meta-intentions) and she does so via her recognition of the conventional meaning of what I say along with background information about the politeness of indirection, her love of wooden boats and consequent distaste for fiberglass, her astute ability to reason and so on.

This conversational contribution is a conversational exercitive and it enacts a variety of conversational permissibility facts. Here are just some of them. It makes it Susan's turn to talk. It commits me to the two claims asserted and this affects what is conversationally permissible for each of us. I ought to be able to back up my claims and Susan is entitled to ask me to. It would be conversationally out of bounds for me to deny these commitments (or anything implied by them). My assertions also entitle

Susan to epistemically rely on my claims and it requires her to respond in some way or other. In particular, by asserting these claims, my utterance essentially proposes the addition of these claims to the common ground.[19] As such, it makes it incumbent on Susan to either accept or reject them. Moreover, by treating Susan in a polite manner (via indirection), this utterance affects the permissible ways for Susan to respond and it makes it more incumbent on her to be polite to me. Furthermore, it introduces the possibility of repairing the boat with a fiberglass cap and it introduces fiberglass as a topic of conversation. As one can see then, there are a rather wide variety of conversational permissibility facts (dependently) enacted by the score changes (directly) enacted by this particular conversational contribution in this particular context.

Before proceeding, though, a clarification is warranted. We have already distinguished between the conversational contribution (which is the total speech act in context) and the conversational exercitive (which is that aspect of the conversational contribution that is the enacting of conversational permissibility facts). Because any one conversational contribution typically enacts several different conversational permissibility facts, this (conversationally exercitive) aspect of the conversational contribution is itself multiplicitous. In what follows, though, we shall focus on the enacting of just one such conversational permissibility fact.

To that end, let us focus, in particular, on the enacting of the permissibility fact that Susan must now engage with the claim that it is time for a fiberglass cap on the bow. Engaging with this claim might involve accepting it, rejecting it, or considering its merits. As we saw earlier in this chapter (Section 3.1), the enacting of this conversational permissibility fact does *not* depend on speaker intention in the ways that standard exercitives do. That neither my intention to enact a conversational permissibility fact nor my intention to enact this particular conversational permissibility fact is highly manifest to myself in no way undermines the exercitive force of my contribution. Such failures, by contrast, would render a standard exercitive non-ideal if not a complete failure. It also does *not* depend on hearer recognition in the ways that standard

[19] This is how Stalnaker (1978) treats assertion (as a proposed addition to the common ground). There are plenty of other accounts. See, for example, Bach and Harnish 1979; Brandom 1994; and Williamson 1996.

exercitives do. That neither my attenuated intention to enact a conversational permissibility fact nor my attenuated intention to enact that particular permissibility fact is highly manifest to Susan in no way undermines the exercitive force of my conversational exercitive. These recognition failures would, by contrast, render a standard exercitive (at least) non-ideal if not entirely unsuccessful.

That said, the enacting of this particular permissibility fact is sensitive to speaker intention and hearer recognition *in other ways*. In short, it depends on the success of the assertion (that it is time for a fiberglass cap on the bow) and this, in turn, depends on the successful communication of the intention to assert this. Suppose that when I said, 'Well, I'm afraid to tell you that it is time for a fiberglass cap on the bow,' I did not assert that it is time for a fiberglass cap on the bow. Suppose, that is, that I only intended to tell Susan that I was afraid to tell her this and something about the way that I said it enabled Susan to realize that I was not also intending to assert it.[20] In this case, my utterance does not assert the claim (that it is time for a fiberglass cap on the bow) and thus my utterance does not make it incumbent on Susan to engage with this claim. Since this assertion relies on the communication of linguistic intentions, the enacting of this particular conversational permissibility fact thus depends on the speaker's intention to assert it and the hearer's recognition of this intention.

That this is so should not be at all surprising. After all, the differences between the cases change what the conversational contribution is. In the original example, the utterance was a successfully communicated indirect assertion but, in the second case, it was not an indirect assertion at all. Although the same words are uttered at the same point in the same conversation, they are nevertheless distinct conversational moves.[21] Moreover, these differences are captured by the score and thus affect which particular conversational permissibility facts are enacted.

[20] A more complex case would involve my intending to indirectly assert (that it is time for a fiberglass cap on the bow) but Susan fails to recognize this. Another tricky case involves my not intending to assert this but Susan falsely believing that I do. In each of these cases, the utterance is a different conversational contribution and the score would capture the differences between them with subtle subsequent corresponding differences to conversational permissibility.

[21] Technically, due to constant updating, there will be differences in the score by the time Susan realizes (that I did not intend to indirectly assert that it is time for a fiberglass cap on the bow) and these differences enable her to realize this.

Finally, as we saw in Section 3.1, although the intention to enact conversational permissibility facts and the intention to enact a particular conversational permissibility fact are typically at the very low end of the manifestness spectrum, they can, in some cases, be highly manifest. Moreover, when they are highly manifest to speakers, and especially when those intentions are made manifest to one's interlocutors, this changes the conversational contribution and thus affects which particular conversational permissibility facts are enacted by the utterance in question. This is yet another way in which the enacting of particular conversational permissibility facts is sensitive to speaker intention and hearer recognition.

In sum, we have seen that it does not take much for an utterance to be a conversational exercitive. It does not take much, that is, for an utterance to enact conversational permissibility facts of some sort or other. Indeed, it seems to be a nearly universal feature of language use. In order for an utterance to enact a conversational permissibility fact requires only that the utterance in question be relevant to some conversation or other. By being relevant to some conversation, the utterance in question thus enacts a score change for that conversation and thus, in virtue of the norms governing conversation, enacts permissibility facts for that conversation.[22] As we have seen, this minimal standard is met even when the utterance is not heard at all and even when it is not taken to be an intended conversational contribution.

The enacting of particular conversational permissibility facts, by contrast, requires much more. As we have seen, this is sensitive to a wide variety of factors. That this is so, though, makes perfect sense. After all, what the conversational contribution is depends on all these factors too. Moreover, since the particular conversational permissibility facts enacted by a conversational contribution depends on the score, the norms governing the conversation, and the conversational contribution itself, any change that makes an utterance a different conversational contribution would also be a change to which particular permissibility facts are enacted by that conversational contribution.

[22] There are norms that govern all conversations (Gricean norms, norms of politeness, norms of cooperation and social interaction) and there are the conversation-specific permissibility facts (also norms) enacted by conversational contributions. The different sorts of norms at play are further discussed in Chapter 4 section 4.1.2.

3.6 The permissibility facts enacted

There is another important difference between standard exercitives and conversational exercitives and it concerns differences between the permissibility facts enacted by them. First, standard exercitives can enact all manner of permissibility facts. By uttering a standard exercitive, one can enact law, restaurant policy, or a new bedtime for one's children. Conversational exercitives, by contrast, can only enact permissibility facts for *conversations*. Moreover, conversational exercitives can only enact permissibility facts for the *particular* conversation for which they enact a score change.[23] In this way, we see that the permissibility facts enacted by conversational exercitives are, and must be, highly localized while those enacted by standard exercitives need not be and typically are not.

Second, the permissibility facts enacted by conversational exercitives are often temporary since the bounds of conversational permissibility are constantly shifting as the conversation progresses. When I mention my house in a conversation, for example, I thereby make my house the most salient house in the context of this particular conversation and this, in turn, changes the appropriate use of the expression 'the house' in this conversation. This particular conversational permissibility fact, however, will change as soon as any other house is made more salient than mine in the context of this conversation. If the conversation is about the comparative value of houses, this is likely to happen many times over. Thus, although my utterance enacts a permissibility fact for the conversation, that particular permissibility fact is unlikely to preside over the conversation for very long.

The permissibility facts enacted by standard exercitives, by contrast, are not like this. When the C.E.O. enacts a new policy or when I set a new bedtime for my children, the permissibility facts enacted are not of this fleeting variety. Although such permissibility facts can certainly be

[23] The individuation of conversations is an interesting and complex issue. Conversations can be intermittent and extended across time especially in cases of ongoing relationships. Suppose that Greg and I have a conversation about Bill's drinking when I see Greg at the band concert and then, four months later, when I see him at Dennis' mother's funeral, I pick up where we left off by saying "Any good news for me about our favorite imbiber?" In responding to me, Greg will rely on our previous conversation. It is unclear, in this case, whether our exchange at Dennis' mother's funeral counts as a continuation of the earlier conversation or if it is a new but related conversation.

replaced or changed, it is not inevitable that, in the natural course of things, they very soon will be.

3.7 Conclusion

In sum, since conversational exercitives enact permissibility facts, they do what standard exercitives do. As we have seen, however, the similarities pretty much end there. Conversational exercitives enact permissibility facts via an entirely different mechanism from that of standard exercitives; they are more plentiful, their success conditions are importantly different, and the permissibility facts enacted are different in nature.

The most important difference between these two sorts of utterances, however, is still to be made explicit. In the following chapter, I shall argue that the enacting of conversational permissibility facts by conversational exercitives is not a communicative phenomenon at all. Moreover, there are several important ways in which the phenomenon of conversational exercitives generalizes.

4

The General Phenomenon

Covert Exercitives

Conversational contributions routinely dependently enact permissibility facts for the very conversation to which they contribute and they do so by directly enacting changes to the conversational score. I shall argue, in the present chapter, that the phenomenon generalizes. Our utterances sometimes constitute contributions to activities other than (but usually in addition to) conversation. When they do and when those other activities are norm-governed in the appropriate way, the utterance in question (also) dependently enacts permissibility facts for that other norm-governed activity. Conversational exercitives are but a special case of a more general phenomenon.

The chapter proceeds as follows. In Section 4.1, I clarify the nature of norm-governed activities and distinguish between the different sorts of norms involved. Then, in Section 4.2, I argue for the general claim that contributions to norm-governed activities dependently enact permissibility facts for those activities. Finally, in Section 4.3, I argue that the act of dependently enacting permissibility facts via contributions to norm-governed activities is not an illocutionary act. It is, rather, (what I am calling) a parallel act.

4.1 On norms

Since the mechanism of norm enactment identified in the previous chapter relies on the norm-governed nature of conversation and since I here aim to argue that that phenomenon generalizes, clarity regarding the nature of the norms and what makes an activity or practice norm-governed are required.

4.1.1 *On being norm-governed*

An activity counts as norm-governed just in case some actions count as inappropriate with respect to that activity. This is sufficient to show that the activity in question is governed by prescriptive norms. If at least some actions would count as out of bounds or otherwise inappropriate with respect to that activity, then that activity is norm-governed in the relevant sense. Clearly, this condition is easily and widely met. Conversations, dancing with a partner, informal social interactions, playing improvisational jazz, chess, checkers, and baseball are all norm-governed in this sense.

The norms in question need not be explicit, formal, exception-less, or even consciously recognized.[1] To see this, consider social norms. They apply to a person primarily in virtue of that person's role in a social practice. A woman's appearance and behavior, for example, are evaluable under the norms of femininity even if those norms are not explicitly stated, even if they are not formally sanctioned, even if they admit of exceptions, and even if a woman is barely conscious of those norms. Such norms nevertheless guide action and have prescriptive force.

The prescriptive force of social norms and their interaction with one another can be quite complex and nuanced. As a feminist, for example, I reject many of the norms of femininity. Although I consciously reject the norms of femininity, however, I am nevertheless judged in terms of them and I am sometimes socially sanctioned for my failure to abide by them. Because I am "responsive to and evaluated under"[2] these femininity norms, they have prescriptive force for me even though I do and should reject them.[3] Social norms do not need to be endorsed to be prescriptive. It requires only that we expect others to abide by them; we expect others to expect us to abide by them, and we expect negative consequences for those who not abide by them.[4]

4.1.2 *Different sorts of norms*

As one can see, it doesn't take much for an activity to be norm-governed. So long as some actions would count as somehow inappropriate with

[1] They also do not need to be peculiar to that norm-governed activity. The norms of cooperation, for example, will govern a wide variety of practices, all of which count as norm-governed. I thank Mark Richard for raising this issue.

[2] Witt 2011. [3] Witt 2011.

[4] This is how Bicchieri (2006) defines social norms.

respect to a certain activity, then that activity is norm-governed in the relevant sense. That said, there are different sorts of norms governing these activities and they ought to be distinguished.

As Lewis himself stresses, there is an important difference between the rigid rules of baseball and the rules of accommodation operative in conversational contexts.[5] If a batter returns to the dugout after receiving only two strikes, the batter's action violates the rules of baseball and this is so even if no one notices and his action is treated as correct. With the rules of accommodation operative in conversations, by contrast, the rules adjust (within certain limits, of course) so that what actually happens counts as fair play. If I say something that requires higher standards of accuracy to be operative in the conversation in order for what I say to be appropriate, then the rules of accommodation make the score adjust so that what I say counts as correct.

Although there is this important difference between different sorts of rules and hence different sorts of norms, it is also true, and worth pointing out, that both sorts are operative in conversation and both sorts are operative in baseball. First, conversations are also governed by the rigid sort of rules. When I say, "Joe ain't no good at making mescaline salad," my utterance violates several rules (of grammar, word choice, and pronunciation) and, in some contexts anyway, this is so even if my interlocutor does not notice.[6] As one can see, even the cooperative activity of conversation is governed by some of the more rigid rules of language use. Second, norms of accommodation are operative in baseball too. After all, what counts as a strike is in part constituted by the judgment calls of individual umpires.[7] Thus, there are occasions where a pitch is high (and thus would not count as a strike) but is called as such. In at least some cases, the strike zone is automatically adjusted so that the umpire's call counts as correct. As one can see, there are accommodating norms operative in baseball as well.

In addition to this distinction between rigid and accommodating norms, there is also an important difference between norms (whether

[5] See Lewis 1983. As indicated earlier, Lewis speaks of 'rules' although I prefer the more general notion of norm.

[6] Once a "mistake" is regarded as acceptable by a large enough percentage of language users, it might cease to be a mistake. Even these "rigid" rules can evolve with use.

[7] For a discussion of the constructive (fact-enacting) aspect of verdictive speech acts, see my 2005 and Langton 2009.

rigid or accommodating) that govern *all* instances of the (sort of) activity in question and those norms (whether rigid or accommodating) that govern only a particular instance of that (sort of) activity. Consider first the general or global norms. I call them *g-norms*.[8] G-norms govern all instances of the norm-governed activity in question and they are not enacted by the performing of any particular such activity. The g-norms governing conversations, for example, include the (relatively rigid) rules of grammar and (the accommodating norm of) Grice's cooperative principle.[9] Note that these conversational g-norms apply to all conversations and they are not enacted by any particular conversation.[10]

Some of these g-norms are very general and others are more localized. The norms of cooperation that Grice stresses, for example, are very general norms of conversation. One ought to speak in a manner that enables one's interlocutor to understand what you mean by what you say. This is a very general norm of conversation. Of course, the appropriate to way to do this can vary from one context to another. In other words, there are more localized g-norms of manner operative in specific contexts. Using technical philosophical language while conversing with a supermarket teller is likely to violate local g-norms of manner of expression while failing to use that technical language would be a violation at an APA session on indexicals. G-norms can be more or less localized.

Other norms, by contrast, are quite specific and they are enacted by the performing of the very token-instance of the norm-governed activity over which they preside. I call such (token-activity-specific) norms *s-norms*.[11] Consider another example from a conversation. Suppose that my Uncle Jack and I are talking about his house when I say, 'Oh yeah, well, when we bought our house, we thought about how difficult it would be to maintain it but we decided that we loved the house so much that we just had to buy it!' When I said this, I changed the salience facts for the conversation (making my house the most salient house) and this in turn changes what is subsequently permissible in that conversation.

[8] See my 2009b. [9] See Grice 1989: 26–31.

[10] Again, to say that these norms are conversational does not require that they be peculiar to conversation. These "conversational" norms may just be more general norms of cooperation.

[11] See my 2009b. The distinction between g-norms and s-norms may not be a sharp one and there is likely to be a complex feedback system between the two sorts of norms. Such details are not pursued here.

My utterance constitutes a move in the conversation that makes it conversationally impermissible (for the time being) to try to refer to any other house with the expression 'the house.' My utterance enacts a new *s-norm* for the conversation.

Several things are worth noticing about these s-norms. First, they are of limited duration. The s-norm I enact, for example, will be altered as soon as another house is made more conversationally salient. Second, s-norms are of limited scope. Unlike the rules of grammar (which are g-norms), this norm applies only to this particular conversation. Third, s-norms are enacted by the performing of the particular token instance of the conversation in which such norms preside. When I made a move in the conversation, I thereby enacted a new s-norm *for that particular conversation*. Fourth, the permissibility facts enacted by conversational exercitives just are s-norms. Participating in a conversation will involve the perpetual creating and altering of s-norms, the constant creating and destroying of fleeting activity-specific conversational permissibility facts.

4.2 How this generalizes

The phenomenon of conversational exerctives generalizes. Many activities (not just conversations) are such that contributions to them thereby change what is subsequently appropriate in them. I shall now argue that any move in a norm-governed activity thereby enacts permissibility facts (s-norms) for that activity.

In order to argue for this general claim (i.e. that any contribution to a norm-governed activity thereby enacts s-norms in that activity), it is first necessary to be clearer on what is required for an action to count as a contribution to, or a move in, such an activity.

4.2.1 On being a move

An action is a *move* in an activity just in case it is a contribution to that activity and is thus governed by the g-norms of that activity. Conversational participants make conversational moves whenever they say things that contribute to the conversation. Since these utterances are contributions to the conversation, they are governed by the various g-norms of conversation. Similarly, swinging the bat while at-bat is a move in baseball and dipping one's partner is a move in ballroom dance. Each of these actions is governed by the g-norms of these activities.

Clearly, one must be positioned in order to make a move in such an activity. That is, one must be a participant or player in that activity; one must have the requisite "standing" (Section 3.4.2). Even if I were one of the best batters in the universe, I cannot just jump down from the stands and bat at a Red Sox game. If I did, my action would not be a contribution to the game. (It would be grounds for having me arrested.) Since I am not one of the players, I simply cannot contribute to the game. Making moves requires that one be a player.

Being a player will also involve at least some degree of awareness that one's action contributes to the norm-governed activity in question. Suppose that I say something to Peter not realizing that Joe thinks I am interjecting in his conversation with Lucy. In this case, my utterance is a move in the conversation with Peter but it is not a move in the conversation between Joe and Lucy (even though Joe mistakes it as one). It is not a move in that conversation because I am not a player in that conversation; I am utterly unaware of making a contribution to that conversation; I have no intention (not even an attenuated one) to contribute to that conversation and my utterance is not governed by the g-norms of that conversation.

Although my utterance is not a move in the conversation between Joe and Lucy, it nevertheless enacts score changes in it. Because Joe takes it as a contribution, my action is relevant to the proper development and assessment of his conversation with Lucy. As a result, it is tracked by the score of that conversation. Thus, my utterance is a move in the conversation with Peter but a mere event that enacts a score change in the conversation between Joe and Lucy. Not all actions that enact score changes in an activity are moves in the activity.

The standing required to be a player can be (and often is) licensed. I may not be a part of a particular conversation, but when I interject my two cents and the others welcome me into the conversation, I thereby become a participant. By treating me as having the standing to contribute to that conversation, I come to have it. Players can also refuse to license standing to another. Suppose that I join in (on my flute) with some session players and they stop playing and stare me down. In this case, my contribution is not accepted and I do not become a player. Licensing is at the discretion of the participants.

Notice that it is possible to make a move in a norm-governed activity while being pretty oblivious to what move you're actually making. To see this, suppose that I grow hungry while driving along I 95 South so I pull off the highway and stop at a Burger King restaurant in Providence, Rhode Island but I do not realize that this part of Providence has very few (or no) white people. When I walk into the restaurant, I expect there to be other people present so I know that I am entering a social situation. I also know that social interactions are norm-governed and that there are complex social g-norms governing the appropriate behavior and treatment of people in various roles and social positions. I know, for example, that there are certain ways to interact with the teller and other ways to interact with the other people in line and yet other ways to interact with other people in the bathroom. In short, I am aware that my action of entering the restaurant is, and I intend for it to be, a move in a complex combination of norm-governed activities of social interaction. Although I have made such an intentional move, I am utterly unaware (at first anyway) of precisely what move I have made.

As it turned out, my move was in stark violation of local g-norms. I did not realize (when I first entered the restaurant anyway) that my action was in violation of race-based and class-based social g-norms governing who should be where. I noticed everyone noticing me and wondered why. When the kitchen staff alerted one another to stare out at me, I realized—in a flash—that I was the only white person in the restaurant and, given the reaction of others, I inferred that it was highly unusual for white people (or for white people who look like me) to enter that restaurant. Thus, although I made an intentional contribution to what I knew was a norm-governed activity, I did not realize that I was, and I did not intend to make, the particular move that I socially counted as making. Ignorance of local g-norms is one way that this can happen.

As this example shows, an action that violates the g-norms of a norm-governed activity is nevertheless a contribution to, and thus a move in, that activity. Being *governed* by the g-norms does not require *abiding* by them.[12] A baseball player who shoves a runner off of a base in order to tag that runner has made a move in the baseball game even though that action is prohibited by the g-rules and norms governing the baseball game. As a violation of the rules and g-norms, this action is clearly governed by them. As such, it counts as a move in this technical sense.

[12] Robert Mark Simpson (2013) assumes that a move in my sense requires *abiding* by the norms. I realize that I was insufficiently explicit on this point in my 2009b (to which he is responding).

Finally, although this technical sense of move is quite inclusive, plenty of actions performed by participants in norm-governed activities will nevertheless fail to count as moves in this sense. Suppose, for example, that a baseball player were to scratch his nose while waiting in the outfield. This action is not governed by the g-norms of baseball. As a result, this action is not a move in the baseball game and this is so even though it is performed by a participant of the game; it is an intentional action and, it is performed while that participant is playing the game. Since it is not governed by the rules and g-norms of baseball, it is not a move in this technical sense.

4.2.2 Moves enact s-norms

We are now in a position to see that any move in a norm-governed activity thereby dependently enacts s-norms (permissibility facts) for that activity. Notice first that moves directly enact score changes. Since a move is an action governed by the g-norms of the activity in question, moves are relevant to the proper development and assessment of that activity. Since the score, by definition, tracks all such relevant facts, the score tracks all moves. Consequently, any move directly enacts components of score.

Since what is permissible at any point in a norm-governed activity depends on what has happened so far in that activity (along with the g-norms) and since what has happened so far is captured by the score, directly enacting a change to the score thereby dependently enacts s-norms (permissibility facts) for the activity in question. Therefore, any move in a norm-governed activity (dependently) enacts s-norms for that activity.

Examples abound. When my opponent moves her checker, for example, her doing so makes it permissible for me to subsequently move mine. As soon as Pat mentions a certain in-joke, he thereby makes it permissible for others to mimic Charles singing show tunes at last year's picnic. When an Irish session player starts a tune at a certain pace, it thereby makes it impermissible for other players to play at a different pace or to play other tunes.[13] As one can see, our actions are

[13] The norms are different in other musical traditions (e.g. improvisational jazz).

often contributions to norm-governed activities and when they are they enact changes to what is subsequently permissible in those activities.

Recall that although all moves (directly) enact score changes, not everything that (directly) enacts a score change is a move. Suppose, for example, that while I am talking to Bob about his sailboat, we both witness our friend Mike falling off of his boat. In this case, Mike falling off of his boat (directy) enacts a change to the conversational score (and, since we both notice it and notice each other noticing it, it also changes the common ground). Moreover, this score change has permissibility consequences: now that Mike's boat is the most salient boat in the context of this conversation, it is now conversationally permissible for me to refer to Mike's boat with the expression 'the boat' whereas it would have been conversationally inappropriate to do so before that score change. Although Mike's fall enacts a score change, it is not a move in the conversation. Mike's fall is not governed by the g-norms of our conversation; it is not a contribution to that conversation; it is merely an event that is relevant to the conversation. Being relevant to a norm-governed activity falls short of being a contribution to it.

4.2.3 Covert exercitives

Thus far, we have focused on the s-norm-enacting property of moves in norm-governed activities but we have not focused specifically on cases where the move in question is speech. Clearly, speech is sometimes a move in a norm-governed activity other than conversation. When it is, it (dependently) enacts s-norms for the activity and is thus exercitive. Since the exercitive feature of the utterance in question is somewhat hidden, I call these utterances *covert exercitives*. (Again, my use of 'covert' departs from the technical usage in linguistics. See Section 3.4.) Covert exercitives dependently enact s-norms in the norm-governed activity in which they are a move.

Conversational exercitives just are (a type of) covert exercitive. Since conversations are norm-governed activities and since conversational contributions are moves in the norm-governed activity of conversation, conversational contributions are covert exercitives; they enact s-norms for the very conversation in which they are a move.

Suppose that while discussing high school memories with my friend Greg I say, "Paul is doing well. He recently landed his dream job and got married. I am so happy for him! He's really gotten it all together."

My utterance is a move in the conversation; it thereby dependently enacts s-norms for the conversation and is thus a conversational exercitive. In addition to this, however, my utterance is also a move in the norm-governed activity of social interaction. Suppose that Paul had treated me terribly in high school and everybody (Greg included) knows it. By expressing happiness for Paul's successes, I treat him well and I do so even though I am warranted in resenting him. This magnanimous action sets the tone for my interaction with Greg and thereby has normative consequences. It encourages taking the high road and it discourages pettiness. By making the particular move I made, I thereby affect what sorts of moves ought to be made going forward. My action makes it less permissible for Greg to be uncharitable and petty (towards Paul or anyone else).

Moreover, as we shall see in subsequent chapters, our words are often unwitting contributions to various norm-governed activities in our social world. As a result, we are often unknowingly enacting s-norms for those activities too. Bringing this to light, along with its social, political, moral, metaphysical, and even legal importance, is the focus of the second half of this book.

4.3 On illocution and parallel acts

In Chapter 3, important differences between standard exercitives, on the one hand, and conversational exercitives (a type of covert exercitive), on the other, were explored. There, we saw that although both sorts of utterances enact permissibility facts (which are s-norms), they do so via distinct mechanisms and they each have quite different conditions of success. I shall now argue that there is an additional important difference between them.

The enacting of permissibility facts via a standard exercitive is an illocutionary act, but the enacting of permissibility facts via a covert exercitive is not. Since the enacting of permissibility facts via a standard exercitive works via making the speaker's linguistic intentions mutually manifest to participants (that is, it works via the hearer's recognition of the speaker's conscious and fairly explicit intention to do so *and to do so via* the speaker's meta-intention that the addressee recognize that intention), it is a communicative phenomenon. Since the enacting of permissibility facts (s-norms) via a covert exercitive does not work this way, it is not a communicative phenomenon. It is not an illocutionary phenomenon either.

4.3.1 Illocution revisited

The illocutionary force of an utterance is the act constituted by the utterance in virtue of the utterance functioning as speech. This speech-functioning qualification matters. To see this again, consider the following example. Suppose that I say to my parish priest, "I promise to go to Mass each week, Father Mullaney." This utterance constitutes many different actions but only some of these actions are illocutionary.

My utterance constitutes the act of making sounds and moving my tongue, but such purely physical acts are not illocutionary acts.[14] This is because these acts do not depend on the speech functioning as such. Such purely physical acts do not depend on the recognition of the speaker's communicative intention via the hearer's recognition of the conventional meaning of what is actually said.

My utterance also directly enacts the fact that I spoke. Although my utterance directly enacts this fact, this enacting action is not an illocutionary act either. It too fails to depend on the recognition of either the meaning of what is said or the speaker's communicative intention. Not all enacting actions performed by speech are illocutionary.

My utterance is also the act of promising. My utterance undertakes an obligation on my part to go to mass each week and by saying what I say I thereby obligate myself to Father Mullaney to do so. (Note that this is so whether or not I also intend to keep the promise; insincere promises are still promises.) Now, this act of promising *does* depend on the speech functioning as speech. First, it depends on various minimal recognition conditions. It depends on Father Mullaney hearing what I say, recognizing it as speech, and recognizing the conventional meaning of the words I utter. Second, and more to the point, my utterance constitutes a promise exactly because Father Mullaney recognizes my intention to promise (to go to mass each week); he recognizes my intention that he recognize that intention *and* he does this via his recognition of the conventional meaning of what I actually say. In other words, my promise

[14] Just as the physical act of speaking (i.e. producing sounds) is not an illocutionary act, neither the physical act of writing (i.e. placing ink on paper) nor the physical act of typing (i.e. pressing buttons on a keyboard) are illocutionary acts either.

is successful exactly because my utterance succeeds as speech. My utterance manages to enact this obligation in virtue of linguistically communicating my intention to undertake that very obligation. Because of this, my promise is an illocutionary act.

What about the s-norm enacting action of covert exercitives? Are they illocutionary acts? I shall now argue that they are not. When an utterance dependently enacts permissibility facts (s-norms) by triggering the g-norms of norm-governed activities, the act of dependently enacting those s-norms is *not* an illocutionary act.

4.3.2 Not an illocution

Focus first on conversational exercitives. The enacting of conversational permissibility facts (s-norms) via a conversational exercitive is not an illocutionary act. The mere fact that something *depends on* an illocutionary act (e.g. a conversational contribution) is insufficient to show that it *is* one. Conversational contributions enact conversational s-norms without the speaker having a highly manifest intention to do so (Section 3.3). There is typically only an extremely attenuated sense in which speakers intend to be enacting the conversational s-norms that the speaker's contributions enact. Since speakers are aware that conversations are guided by g-norms at least to the extent that speakers tend to work within the bounds of conversational permissibility, there is a thin sense in which speakers intend to be bringing about the conversational permissibility changes that the contributions dependently enact. We have also seen that hearers are not highly aware of the speaker's (highly attenuated) intention to enact conversational s-norms. There is a thin sense, though, in which hearers are aware of the s-norms enacted. Hearers tend to operate within the parameters set by the enacted conversational s-norms; they know that conversations are g-norm-governed and that the speaker knows this; they also know that the speaker just contributed to what the speaker knows is a norm-governed practice. So there is a thin sense in which the speaker's (highly attenuated) intention to enact conversational s-norms is recognized.

The mark of the illocutionary, however, is at the intentional *meta-level.* When I assert that P, I not only intend to commit to the truth of P, I also intend that my interlocutor recognize my intention to commit to the truth of P. Moreover, my success in asserting P depends on both the presence and the recognition of that meta-intention. As we have repeatedly seen, though, the enacting of conversational s-norms does not work this way. First, it is far from clear that conversational participants have the requisite meta-level intentions (whether attenuated or not) regarding their (highly attenuated) intention to enact conversational s-norms. Moreover and even more to the point, even if conversational contributors do have a (highly attenuated) intention that interlocutors recognize their (highly attenuated) intention to enact conversational s-norms, we have seen repeatedly that the enacting of those s-norms does *not* depend on the recognition of *that* meta-intention. It depends instead on the norm-governed nature of conversational practice.

Thus, although the enacting of conversational s-norms piggybacks on something that is clearly and highly communicative (the conversational contribution in question), the act of enacting conversational s-norms is not. The act of enacting conversational s-norms via a conversational exercitive is therefore not an illocutionary act. The same reasoning applies to the s-norm enacting action of covert exercitives. Since the norm-enacting action does not depend on the communication of the (meta-)intention to enact those s-norms, the act of enacting them is not an illocutionary one.

4.3.3 *Parallel acts*

Although the covert enacting of s-norms is not an illocutionary act, it is nevertheless connected closely with speech. When a conversational contribution directly enacts a (conversational) score change, *parallel* to these directly enacted score changes, are dependently enacted permissibility facts (or s-norms). Similarly, when an utterance constitutes a move in any norm governed activity, that covertly exercitive utterance directly enacts score changes for that token instance of that norm-governed activity and, *parallel* to those direct score component enactments, are dependently enacted s-norms for the token instance of that norm-governed activity.[15] For this reason, I call them parallel acts.

To emphasize the difference between parallel acts and illocutionary acts, consider the following (highly abstract) example. Suppose that

[15] Just in case my terminology is confusing, the following may help. Any action (whether it is speech or not) that constitutes a move in a norm-governed activity thereby performs the parallel act of enacting s-norms for that activity. When the action in question is speech, that utterance is a covert exercitive that performs the parallel act of enacting s-norms.

when I get home from work, my husband, who is struggling with skepticism, asks me to state a simple accessible truth and, being a wonderful and always obliging wife, I respond, "2 + 3 = 5." Unknown to either one of us, however, our two children are playing a silly word game whereby our son Shea is the winner if Mommy says the word 'equals' and our daughter Nora is the winner if Mommy says the word 'grue'. By saying what I say then, I thereby make Shea the winner.

My act of uttering '2 + 3 = 5' is describable in many different ways. Moreover, whether an act is intentional (and how intentional it is) can depend on how that act is described. To use a familiar example from Davidson, a single act of flipping a light switch can also be described as turning on the light, illuminating the room, and alerting the burglar one did not know was there. The very same act is both intentional on some descriptions and unintentional on others.[16]

When I uttered '2 + 3 = 5' I asserted that 2 + 3 equals 5 and, under this description, what I did is an intentional act. In asserting this, I intend to commit to the truth of the claim that 2 + 3 equals 5. I intend that my husband recognize that intention via his recognition of the meaning of what I say. My assertion is an illocutionary act.

The very same action (of uttering '2 + 3 = 5') also makes Shea the winner of this silly word game. Although my utterance does this, I do not intentionally do it. Since my action directly enacts a change to the score of their word game, my action dependently enacts permissibility facts (s-norms) for their game. However, since I am utterly unaware of this game and my affect on it and I am not a player in the game, my action is not a *move* in the game; it is merely an event that directly enacts a score change. Because my action is relevant to the proper development and assessment of that word game, it is tracked by the score and thus directly enacts a score change. In this case, making Shea the winner is neither an intentional nor a communicative act; it is instead a *parallel* act. Parallel acts are acts dependently enacted by directly enacted score changes. In this case and context then, performing the illocutionary and communicative act of asserting that 2 + 3 = 5 also constitutes the parallel act of making Shea the winner.

[16] See Davidson 1963. Although it is standard to treat this as one action with multiple descriptions, there is considerable controversy regarding the ontology of action. See Wilson and Shpall 2012.

Notice that my assertion that 2 + 3 = 5 is also a contribution to my conversation with Mike. As such, it directly enacts changes to the conversational score and thereby dependently enacts s-norms for this conversation. The enacting of those s-norms is also a parallel act. Plainly, a single act can directly enact score changes in different norm-governed activities simultaneously. My act of assertion is a move in the conversation and a mere score-enacting event in the silly word game. A single act can also simultaneously be a *move* in two (or even more) different norm-governed activities. Saying something in a conversation is simultaneously a move in that conversation and a move in the norm-governed activity of social interaction.

Verbally complimenting John on his work, for example, dependently enacts s-norms in our conversation but it also dependently enacts s-norms in our interaction. It affects our relationship, not just our conversation. We can also be fairly oblivious to the contributions that our words are making in these other (i.e. non-conversational) norm-governed activities. A patient turns to the male nurse and addresses him as the doctor.[17] As a social move, this signals, among other things, the social expectation that men should not be nurses. Although unintentional, it's a slight. During a wellness seminar, a Human Resources employee encourages all employees to take the stairs. By assuming that everyone is able to take the stairs, this employee reinforces ableist assumptions. At a dinner celebrating the life of the famous philosopher David Lewis, a senior male philosopher turns to me and says, "It must be so strange for you to be here with all of these philosophers" thereby signaling his assumption that I am not one.[18]

In all of these cases, the speaker's utterance constitutes multiple parallel acts. As a move in a conversation, the utterance directly enacts changes to the conversational score and thus dependently enacts s-norms for that conversation and thus constitutes the parallel act of

[17] For a fascinating discussion of how acts of address highlight certain social roles and norms thereby coordinating behavior, see Brooks's *The Law of Address*, an unpublished manuscript.

[18] This is a fictionalized real example. In the real example, the senior male philosopher in question intended to insult me. When I responded, "Why do you assume that I am not a philosopher?" he said (feigning surprise and apology) "Oh, I am so sorry. Did this little lady take an undergraduate course with David?". When I said that David supervised my dissertation in metaphysics, he smirked, turned away, and then ignored me for the rest of the dinner.

dependently enacting these conversational s-norms. In addition to being a move in a conversation, though, all of these utterances are also moves in the norm-governed activity of social interaction. Consequently, these utterances directly enact score changes in the relevant token instance of the practice and thus dependently enact s-norms in them too. Moreover, the act of dependently enacting these s-norms is a parallel act. Clearly, we are perpetually performing parallel acts and sometimes we are oblivious to the normative consequences of our words.

4.3.4 On collateral acts

In their *Linguistic Communication and Speech Acts*, Bach and Harnish identify a phenomenon they call a collateral act and they contrast collateral acts with illocutionary acts.[19] In what follows, I explain what collateral acts are; I offer examples of a few different sorts and I then argue that they are distinct from parallel acts.

Bach and Harnish accept the standard conception of illocution so that performing the illocutionary act of x-ing requires intending to x. In fact, for Bach and Harnish, who are primarily interested in the purely communicative aspect of illocutionary acts, the mark of the illocutionary is that the recognition of this intention is both necessary and sufficient for x-ing.[20] Collateral acts, by contrast, are actions constituted by speech that are collateral to, but distinct from, the purely communicative acts of illocution.[21] Examples will help to illustrate the phenomenon.

Suppose that I am lying when I tell Dave that I am not dating anyone else. When I say what I say, I intend to deceive Dave but my success in deceiving him will depend in part on Dave *not* recognizing my intention to deceive him. Suppose now that I am successful in deceiving Dave. The act of deceiving him is (what Bach and Harnish call) a *covert* collateral

[19] See Bach and Harnish 1979.

[20] Bach and Harnish (1979: 4) operate with a narrow conception of illocution according to which hearer uptake (the hearer's recognition of the speaker's illocutionary intention) *is* the illocutionary effect. Further effects are analyzed separately.

[21] Again, Bach and Harnish's (1979) conception of illocution is quite narrow; it includes only what one might call purely communicative acts. Consider, for example, the act of telling someone that p. This act will succeed only if the addressee recognizes the speaker's intention to tell her that p *and* it will succeed just in case the hearer recognizes that intention (as a result of recognizing the conventional meaning of what she actually says). Telling is a purely communicative act. (Conventional acts, by contrast, depend on convention and not on the communication of intention.)

act. (Again, my use of 'covert' is different from theirs.[22]) It is covert in *their* technical sense since my success in deceiving Dave depends in part on my intention (to deceive him) *not* being recognized by him; it depends on that intention not being mutually manifest. Moreover, it is a collateral act since it is not illocutionary; the recognition of the intention to deceive is not sufficient for its success. (Quite the contrary; it would prevent it from succeeding.) Thus, when I assert that I am not dating anyone else, I am also performing the collateral act of deceiving Dave.

Now consider another sort of example. Suppose that I like to impersonate the famous philosopher David Lewis and I mimic his mannerisms when I say, "Just as non-alcoholic beer isn't beer, non-mereological composition isn't composition." When I say this, I intend to be mimicking David. Since my success depends in part on others recognizing this intention, the act of mimicking is an *overt* one. Since communicating my intention to mimic is not sufficient (I would also need to succeed, at least to some extent, in behaving like David), the act of mimicking is not an illocutionary act. Rather, it is a collateral act constituted by saying what I say in the manner that I say it.

The third sort of collateral act succeeds independently of the recognition of the relevant intention. Suppose, for example, that Joanne and I are making small talk as we wait for the other guests to arrive. Wanting to avoid the social awkwardness that would be involved with silence, I politely ask about her family and her various social engagements. Since I will succeed in making small talk whether or not Joanne recognizes my intention to avoid social awkwardness, the collateral act of making small talk is neither covert (that is, dependent on the failure to recognize that intention) nor overt (that is, dependent on the recognition of that intention). Moreover, making small talk is not an illocutionary act since it is not constituted by the communication of the intention to make small talk. Rather, making small talk is a collateral act one performs when conversing for purely social purposes.

[22] Note that the Bach and Harnish (1979) notion of covertness qualifies intentions. An intention is covert so long as the person with the intention does not want that intention recognized; that intention is not made "mutually manifest"; it is not communicated. My use of 'covert' qualifies an act constituted by speech; that act is covert if it is enacted via the norms of a norm-governed activity (and not by the communication of a (meta-)intention to do so.

As one can see, collateral acts are actions performed by speech that are distinct from illocutionary acts. Since parallel acts are also acts performed by speech that are distinct from illocutionary acts, they are like collateral acts. Although there are these similarities, there are also important differences. To start with, collateral acts are highly intentional acts and parallel acts are not. Note that, in each of the three sorts of cases, the speaker is highly aware of a fairly explicit intention to perform the collateral act in question. (What marks the difference between the three sorts of collateral acts just discussed is the role that the *recognition of* that intention plays.) As we have seen, with parallel acts, by contrast, no such intention need be present and, even when it is, it is highly attenuated.

Another difference between collateral acts and parallel acts is the mechanism of production. Parallel acts are constituted by directly enacting score changes in norm-governed activities and collateral acts are not. An utterance constitutes a parallel act in virtue of being a move in (or an event that enacts a score change in) a norm-governed activity. This is not the case with collateral acts; they are highly intentional acts performed via illocutionary acts. Thus, although both collateral and parallel acts are acts performed by speech that are distinct from illocutionary acts, they are nevertheless importantly distinct phenomena.

4.4 Conclusion

The phenomenon of conversational exercitives generalizes. Any utterance that constitutes a move in a norm-governed activity (or that enacts a score change in such an activity) thereby enacts permissibility facts (s-norms) for that activity and is therefore a covert exercitive. Conversational exercitives are but a special case of covert exercitives; conversations are only one sort of norm-governed activity in which speech can enact score changes. The enacting of s-norms is not accomplished via the communication of any sort of intention (whether manifest or meta) to enact those norms; it is accomplished in virtue of the utterance being a move in, and thus directly enacting a score change to, the norm-governed activity in question. The enacting of s-norms is therefore a parallel act.

5

Speech and Oppression

5.1 Introduction

Thus far, we have focused on the phenomenon of covert exercitives. We have seen that when speech constitutes a move in a norm-governed activity, the utterance in question enacts permissibility facts (s-norms) for that norm-governed activity. We have also seen that this way of enacting permissibility facts is distinct from the more familiar way of doing so. With a standard exercitive, permissibility facts are enacted via an exercise of speaker authority. The mechanism of production, the felicity conditions, the degree of awareness of participants, and even the nature of the permissibility facts enacted are all quite different with covert exercitives.

Having explored and analyzed the phenomenon in some detail, it is time to apply it. The phenomenon of covert exercitives is not just a quirky fact about speech that is of interest to linguists, philosophers of language, and others who study language-use. Rather, this phenomenon illuminates a previously overlooked way that *ordinary* speech, in *ordinary* social situations, constitutes harm by enacting harmful s-norms.

In the next few chapters, the focus is on the enacting of *harmful* s-norms. (Covert ways that speech can enact positive normative changes will briefly be explored in the Conclusion.) In the current chapter, however, we focus on a particular type of harm and a particular type of speech: oppression and sexist remarks. I here explore how an offhand sexist comment can *be* an act of oppression. If a sexist remark enacts a permissibility fact (or s-norm) that oppresses, then the remark that enacts that oppressive permissibility fact constitutes, and does not merely cause, an act of oppression. We will here explore *two different* ways that speech can do this.

The chapter proceeds as follows. In Section 5.2, the nature of oppression is explored and, in Section 5.3, two mechanisms of oppressive speech are presented. The first involves a standard exercitive and the second involves a covert exercitive. In Section 5.4, various objections are discussed and assessed. Doing so further clarifies the framework here endorsed.

5.2 On oppression

Since the aim of this chapter is to explore ways in which speech may be an act of oppression, I shall begin with a presentation of the basic nature of oppression. In short, to be oppressed is to be systematically and unjustly disadvantaged in virtue of one's membership in at least one socially marked group.[1] As Frye stresses in her classic work on the subject, the systematic nature of oppression involves overlapping and unavoidable forces and barriers that are enforced via a complex web of social norms and penalties.[2] As a sign of the interlocking and "cage-like" quality of these norms and penalties, oppressed persons often face double binds.[3] Consider, for example, the working mother who is accused of neglecting her children and the stay at home mom who is regarded as a traitor to feminism. The female attorney who is either branded abrasive for being assertive or is overlooked because of her lack of assertiveness also faces a double bind, involving interlocking, competing, and unavoidably punishing social expectations. Oppressed persons must negotiate these complex and interwoven social norms that—working together—tend to systematically disadvantage them as a group. As Young argues, these disadvantages include marginalization, exploitation, powerlessness, cultural imperialism, and violence.[4]

On this sort of account, oppression is a complex human activity that ranks people according to their membership in these groups and this ranking involves some people being systematically and unjustly disadvantaged

[1] One might wonder about the difference between oppression and discrimination. Although this will be explicitly discussed in Chapter 7, here is a short answer. Oppression requires an antecedent and unjust social structure but discrimination does not. 'Discrimination' also has several senses, only some of them are morally loaded, and technical legal notions of discrimination vary across time and jurisdiction.

[2] Frye 1983a.

[3] Marilyn Frye (1983a: 4–5) likens oppressive forces to the patterns of wires in a birdcage. See also her (1983b: 17–40).

[4] Young 1992.

in virtue of their group memberships. Oppression involves "a network of forces and barriers which are systematically related and which conspire to the immobilization, reduction, and molding of"[5] oppressed persons; it "is a complex coordinated system of social interaction, which ranks people and imposes norms, with associated expectations and informal penalties, for how people are to be treated in view of their ranking".[6]

Certain points are worth highlighting about this picture of oppression. First, oppression involves genuine disadvantage. To be disadvantaged is to be made objectively worse off (relative to others) and this means that one is harmed.

It is worth pointing out that *feeling* hurt is neither necessary nor sufficient for being harmed. I was hurt when Mike forgot my birthday but I was not harmed. The person of color may not have felt hurt when denied service at the restaurant in the segregated south but she was nevertheless harmed. Second, as stressed above, oppression is a *structural* phenomenon. Limitations, suffering, or even harms that come about in random or haphazard ways, are not instances of oppression. To see this, consider Bob who had a stroke while sailing his boat around Nantucket. He was unable to call 911 because he had no cell phone reception and his marine radio happened to have been stolen the night before. Bob was certainly harmed by the resulting delay in medical attention but he is not oppressed. The absence of cell reception and the theft were random events and not the result of systematic social forces that collectively and in concert bind and limit his life options, as they do oppressed persons. Third, the harm in question must be tied to one's *membership* in at least one socially marked group. If I am mistreated because I have bushy eyebrows, for example, I may be harmed by the mistreatment and I might even suffer as a result of it but I am not thereby oppressed. This is because people with bushy eyebrows are not socially marked for mistreatment in our society. If, by contrast, I am mistreated because I am a woman, then the mistreatment in question may be an instance of oppression. As one can see then, oppression requires that the disadvantage (or harm) come about in virtue of one's membership in a social group that is (already) systematically socially disadvantaged. This is what it means for oppression to be structural.

[5] Frye 1983a: 7. [6] Simpson 2013: 562.

It is systematic in these ways. Unfortunately, in our society, many different groups are oppressed (e.g. non-whites, women, non-heterosexuals, non-cis-gendered people, the obese). These axes of oppression intersect in complex and deeply harmful ways. Focusing on one axis at a time can render invisible the compounded harms and erasure of those who are multiply-oppressed.[7] The social forces limiting an individual's options, experiences, and choices will be affected by that person's social identity along each of these axes. Although what is said here does generalize, my main focus is on race and gender. Finally, a group may be socially oppressed (e.g. the obese) even though the group in question is not recognized by the law as a protected group. (The legal status of body size is beginning to change, however, at least in some U.S. states.[8])

In seeking to further understand the nature of oppression, it is worth pointing out that not all cases of oppression involve an oppressor. Suppose, for example, that a certain employer requires his employees to have a valid driver's license in order to be eligible for employment. Although actually being able to drive is not a part of the job, this employer believes that having a valid driver's license is a good measure of responsible citizenship and he wants to hire only responsible citizens. Suppose further that, although unknown to the employer, non-whites in this community typically do not have valid driver's licenses and this is a direct result of racism in society.

There is some controversy regarding the nature of racism, where it resides, and what makes a society and its institutions and practices racist. Most agree that a differential harm condition is required. That is, racist institutions and practices systematically disadvantage, and thus harm, non-whites (relative to whites). Some argue, however, that a further moral attitude condition is also required. One might think, that is, that there must also be ill-will towards non-whites either in the present execution of these institutions and practices or somewhere

[7] This passing comment hardly does justice to the phenomenon of intersectionality. For classic work on this, see Crenshaw 1989; 1991; 2012.

[8] In California, for example, body size can qualify as a disability and thus as grounds for a discrimination claim. See *Cassista v. Community Foods, Inc.* See also, *Cook v. State of Rhode Island.* What constitutes a disability varies from state to state. How this affects body size as grounds for a discrimination case is discussed briefly in Chapter 7 (note 26). I thank Ann Garry for bringing this to my attention.

in the history of them. Garcia argues that actual ill-will towards non-whites is not necessary, however, just a failure to have the *right* sort of moral attitude.[9]

Bringing this back to our example, suppose that non-whites tend to be without valid driver's licenses because there is a racist plot down at the Department of Motor Vehicles. In this case, there is ill-will towards non-whites in the present. Supposing that our employer is unaware of this plot, his policy is racially oppressive in virtue of the non-accidental nature of the correlation between being non-white and not having a valid driver's license. After all, this correlation obtains as a direct result of conscious racism.[10] By excluding people without valid driver's licenses, this policy systematically disadvantages non-whites and it does so in a social context where non-whites are systematically disadvantaged. It is therefore a racially oppressive policy.

Suppose that there is currently no such ill-will towards non-whites in this society. Maybe non-whites tend to be without valid driver's licenses because non-whites tend to be unable to afford vehicles and maybe this is because of ill-will towards non-whites that has long since been eradicated. Even in a case like this, the employer's policy is racially oppressive. It systematically and unjustly disadvantages non-whites in virtue of a non-accidental correlation between being without a valid driver's license and being non-white and this correlation obtains because of racism.[11] Thus, by enacting that policy in this social context, the employer oppresses non-whites.

Despite enacting a racially oppressive policy, the employer in this case is nevertheless not an oppressor. This is (roughly) because the oppression resides in the antecedent and unjust distribution of social power and not in the individual actions of the employer.[12] After all, there is nothing intrinsically unjust about the employer's policy. The policy in question is problematic only because of the non-accidental correlation brought about by antecedent racial injustice. If, by contrast, a speaker intends

[9] See Garcia 1996, 5–45. [10] See Haslanger 2004.

[11] Failing to recognize and/or failing to take action regarding the financial consequences of historic racism is a failure to have the right sort of moral attitude towards non-whites and thus may constitute ill-will of the sort identified by Garcia (1996).

[12] For a discussion of this, see Haslanger 2004: 102. This case would count as (what Haslanger calls) non agent-based.

to enact permissibility facts that are themselves unjust (whether or not the speaker also realizes that the permissibility facts in question are unjust) and if those permissibility facts are also oppressive (that is, if they unjustly disadvantage those who are already systematically and unjustly socially disadvantaged in virtue of their membership in a social group), then I shall say that the speaker is an oppressor.[13] Since the employer's policy is not itself unjust, the employer does not satisfy the above conditions for being an oppressor. Moreover, this is so even though the employer's utterance constitutes an act of oppression. As one can see then, verbal acts of oppression do not require that the speaker be an oppressor.

It is also worth stressing that even in the more familiar cases of oppression that do involve an oppressor, an unjust social arrangement is nevertheless required.[14] This is because oppression must be systematic in the ways discussed above. Suppose, for example, that an employer were to refuse to promote non-white employees but that she does so in a world that is racially just. In such a case, her actions are akin to an employer discriminating against people with bushy eyebrows. Since people with bushy eyebrows are not systematically disadvantaged in our society, this (peculiar) form of discrimination is not an instance of oppression.[15] Similarly, in a racially just world, the employer's actions would be wrong but they would not be acts of *oppression*.[16] In order for her actions to be acts of oppression, non-white people must be systematically and unfairly disadvantaged in this society and they must be so disadvantaged in virtue of being non-white. In our society, this is (unfortunately) the case and so the employer's actions would be acts of (racial) oppression.

[13] This is where I draw the line between oppressing while being an oppressor and oppressing without being an oppressor. There may well be other defensible ways to do so. For others on this point, see, Haslanger 2004. If, by contrast, the employer was aware of the oppressive nature of his policy and he intended it, then he would be an oppressor.

[14] I thank Lynne Tirrell for a helpful discussion of this point.

[15] For a discussion of different senses of 'discrimination' (e.g. neutral, moral, philosophical, and legal), see Section 7.3.

[16] Similarly, suppose that a husband routinely abuses his wife but that he does so in a gender-just society. In such a case, his actions constitute abuse but they are not acts of gender oppression per se. In order for his abuse to oppressive, it must occur in a broader context where women are systematically disadvantaged in virtue of being women.

5.3 Two mechanisms of oppressive speech

Speech oppresses when it enacts (and does not merely cause) permissibility facts that oppress.[17] Thus, for speech to actually be an act of oppression, it must *enact* oppressive permissibility facts. Permissibility facts are oppressive if they unjustly disadvantage a person in virtue of that person's membership in a socially marked group and the group in question is systematically and unfairly disadvantaged in the relevant social context in virtue of that membership.

Since oppressive speech enacts oppressive permissibility facts, oppressive speech must (somehow) enact permissibility facts. We have already seen that there are two ways for speech to enact such facts: standard exercitives and covert exercitives. Standard exercitive speech acts enact permissibility facts via an exercise of speaker authority; covert exercitives do so by triggering the norms of norm-governed activities. These two sorts of utterances afford two different mechanisms of oppressive speech.[18]

5.3.1 *Mechanism one: authoritative speech*

As we have just seen, oppressive speech is speech that enacts permissibility facts that are oppressive and standard exercitives are one way for speech to enact permissibility facts. Since, as I shall argue, standard exercitives can enact *oppressive* permissibility facts, standard exercitives afford our first mechanism of oppressive speech.[19]

Let us begin with an example. Suppose that the proprietor of a certain restaurant makes the following declaration, 'From now on, non-whites are prohibited service and any employee of mine who serves a non-white customer will be fired!' This utterance enacts a new policy for his restaurant and thereby enacts permissibility facts for his establishment. It makes it impermissible for his employees to serve any non-white

[17] Again, for the permissibility facts to oppress, they must be followed and they must be such that following them oppresses (Chapter 1 section 1.7).

[18] I call them 'mechanisms' (and not 'models') because the difference between them concerns the mechanism of enacting the (oppressive) permissibility fact; they do not offer different models or accounts of what makes speech oppressive. In fact, these mechanisms can co-obtain. I thank Catherine Wearing for suggesting that calling them models might be misleading.

[19] This first mechanism has its roots in Austin and is inspired by work by MacKinnon and Langton in arguing that speech (in particular pornography) can subordinate. See Austin 1975; MacKinnon 1987; 1993; and Langton 1993.

person; it makes it against restaurant policy for non-white people to patronize the restaurant.[20] Furthermore, since his utterance enacts this policy (and thus these permissibility facts) via his authority over his restaurant, his utterance is a standard exercitive.

As we have seen, standard exercitives are authoritative speech acts. The speaker *must* have authority over the realm in which the enacted permissibility facts preside. It is only the proprietor, for example, who is able to enact policy for his restaurant. Had either a patron or an employee, for example, uttered the very same words on the very same occasion with all the same intentions, the utterance would not have enacted this new restaurant policy.[21] Thus, in order for an utterance to be oppressive in *this* way, the speaker must have (and be exercising) the requisite authority.

Notice that, in this case, the proprietor's standard exercitive is an act of oppression.[22] This is because the policy enacted by the utterance (that is, that non-whites are not permitted to patronize this restaurant) is oppressive. It unfairly disadvantages non-white persons; it does so in virtue of their non-whiteness and non-white persons are already systematically and unfairly disadvantaged in this social context in virtue of their non-whiteness. As we have seen, when speech acts enact permissibility facts of this sort, the speech in question is oppressive.

Notice also that, in this case, the proprietor is an oppressor. Since he intends to enact a permissibility fact (i.e. that non-whites are prohibited service) that is unjust (whether he realizes that it is unjust or not) and since that permissibility fact is in fact oppressive (whether he realizes that it is or not), the proprietor satisfies the conditions stated above for being an oppressor. Furthermore, this result seems correct. After all, by exercising his authority over his establishment, the proprietor intentionally enacts a policy that is, in fact, unjust to non-whites and that also, in fact,

[20] It may enact other permissibility facts as well. It may, for example, also make it inappropriate for any non-white person to try to patronize his establishment.

[21] If a customer or employee posts a sign stating this policy and the proprietor is aware that it has been posted but does not remove it, the law will regard the sign as authorized by the proprietor. I thank Frederick Schauer for this point.

[22] Harm is constituted when a harmful norm is enacted and it is followed (Chapter 1 section 1.7). One could argue, however, that the enacting of the norm alone (independent of the subsequent behavior prescribed by it) is harmful in virtue of unjustly limiting possibilities (even if those possibilities are never sought or attempted.)

oppresses them. So, even if the proprietor is unaware that this is what he is doing, he is nevertheless an oppressor by so doing.

This example also highlights the fact that there are non-legal non-moral permissibility facts. Although the proprietor is making it impermissible for his employees to serve non-white customers, he is not making it either illegal or immoral for them to do so. (In fact, it is both illegal and immoral for them to abide by this policy!) Rather, the proprietor is enacting a policy for his establishment; he is making it impermissible *according to the policies of that establishment* for his employees to serve non-white customers. Clearly, there are different sorts of permissibility facts and some are neither legal nor moral.

In sum, the proprietor's utterance affords our first mechanism of oppressive speech. As a standard exercitive, it is an authoritative speech act that verbally enacts permissibility facts via the speaker's exercising of his or her authority over the realm in question. Such utterances are oppressive when all or some of the enacted permissibility facts are oppressive. Oppressive speech acts of this sort are actually quite familiar. If a company executive were to say, 'I hereby declare that, from now on, female workers cannot receive over-time pay even if they work over-time,' such an utterance would be an act of gender oppression. Similarly, the 'No Irish Need Apply' signs of the 1920s are also acts of (racial) oppression. Although it may be difficult for some today to conceptualize the Irish as a racialized and oppressed group, what matters is the social context of the time.[23] All of these speech acts are standard exercitives that enact oppressive permissibility facts.

5.3.2 Mechanism two: covert exercitives

As we have seen, some speech enacts permissibility facts, not in virtue of an exercise of the speaker's authority and the communication of the speaker's intention to enact those permissibility facts, but in virtue of an utterance being a move in a norm-governed activity. When an utterance constitutes a move in a norm-governed activity, that utterance thereby enacts permissibility facts (s-norms) for that activity. Since the enacted permissibility facts (s-norms) can satisfy the conditions of being oppressive,

[23] At the time in the United States, the Irish were systematically disadvantaged as a (racialized) group. For a discussion of this history, see Ignatiev 1995 and Jacobson 1998.

it is thus possible for covert exercitives to oppress. As a result, covert exercitives afford a second mechanism of oppressive speech.

Oppressive covert exercitives might seem like a mere and remote possibility, but—as we shall see—they are not. Notice first that all social practices are norm-governed so whenever speech contributes to a social practice, the utterance in question is covertly exercitive. This is sufficient to show that such utterances enact s-norms in those social practices. Since not all s-norms are oppressive, however, we need reason to believe that some of these s-norms are actually oppressive.

Since various social groups are, as a matter of fact, oppressed, there are at least some oppressive g-norms governing our social practices. As a structural phenomenon (Section 5.2), oppression itself is a complex collection of human practices that unjustly ranks people according to their membership in social groups. This ranking involves treating persons in some social categories differently than (and some worse than) persons in other social categories. Such ranking practices are norm-governed; abiding by these norms oppresses so there are oppressive g-norms operative in many of our social practices.

That speech routinely contributes to social practices with oppressive g-norms is still insufficient to show that such utterances are oppressive covert exercitives. This is because individual moves can contribute to a norm-governed practice without interacting with the oppressive g-norms governing that practice. Not every move interacts with every g-norm. Moreover, moves can violate g-norms. Recall that being a move requires only that the action in question be a *contribution to* a norm-governed activity; this is sufficient for the action to be *governed by* (some of) the g-norms of that activity. Furthermore, being *governed by* (some of) the g-norms does not require *abiding by* those g-norms. A bowler who walks down the alley and kicks all the pins down performs an action prohibited by certain rules (or g-norms) of bowling but, since this action is a violation of those rules (g-norms), it is clearly governed by them. As such, it is a move in our technical sense.[24]

[24] See Chapter 4 section 4.2.1 for further details. Robert Mark Simpson (2013) assumes that a move in my sense requires *abiding by* the norms. On my view, moves are made by *participants* in rule-governed activities. Brown (2015: 88–9) mysteriously assumes that being a participant requires previously establishing one's credentials in that particular instantiation of that norm-governed system in that microenvironment. Being a participant requires only being socially situated to contribute.

To support the claim that some utterances enact oppressive s-norms, we need to identify utterances that are moves in norm-governed activities that also *abide by* the oppressive g-norms governing those activities. Unfortunately, such utterances are all too familiar and common. After all, how we speak to or even about someone is one way to differentially treat people according to that person's group membership. Since racist and sexist utterances mistreat oppressed persons in virtue of group membership, these speech moves abide by the oppressive g-norms operative. Moreover, this gives us positive reason to believe that the s-norms enacted by such speech moves are themselves oppressive.[25] Sexist remarks are oppressive covert exercitives.[26] Racist jokes and comments are too. Thus far, I have argued rather abstractly for the *prevalence of* oppressive covert exercitives. I shall now focus on a particular example.[27]

Suppose that Steve and John are co-workers at a workplace in the contemporary United States. Further suppose that there are very few female employees at this workplace and the following exchange takes place in the employee lounge:

JOHN: So, Steve, how did it go last night?
STEVE: I banged the bitch.
JOHN: [smiling] She got a sister?

Consider Steve's utterance. Although this might not be immediately apparent, Steve's utterance is simultaneously a move in at least two different norm-governed activities. First, Steve's utterance is a contribution to a conversation and is thus a conversational exercitive; it enacts s-norms (i.e. conversational permissibility facts) for that conversation. Among other things, Steve's utterance enacts changes to the salience facts of this particular conversation thus rendering a particular woman (i.e. the woman with whom he had a date the previous evening) the most

[25] Anti-racist and anti-sexist utterances, by contrast, violate the oppressive g-norms in operation. As contributions to (and moves in) the oppressive social practice in question, these actions also directly enact changes to what has happened in the practice and thus to the score. Such anti-racist and anti-sexist remarks would abide by more egalitarian g-norms.

[26] For a discussion of the difference between sexism and misogyny and an account of the latter, see Manne 2018.

[27] This example has been modified from a similar one used in my 2009b. I altered the example to avoid the possible implication that sexism is confined to the working class. See fn. 23 of 2009b: 399 and fn. 5 of Simpson 2013: 562.

salient woman in the context of this particular conversation. As a result, she is the proper referent of pronouns like 'her' and 'she' until, of course, the salience facts change again. Arguably, Steve's utterance also makes it conversationally appropriate, in this particular conversational context, to use degrading terms for women.[28]

That it is *conversationally* permissible to degrade women, though, falls (far) short of showing that it is otherwise appropriate to do so. Conversational permissibility is one thing. Broader social permissibility is another.[29] How do we go from changing the conversational score (so that conversationally degrading women in this particular conversation here and now is locally appropriate) to changing the normative facts *outside of* speech and conversation (so that it is somehow "permissible" to treat women as inferior at this time and in this particular employee lounge)?

That Steve's utterance is also a contribution to broader (extra-conversational) social practices is sufficient to establish that his utterance also enacts s-norms in these broader social practices. Moreover, since Steve's utterance is a verbal means of mistreating women, it is a verbal move that abides by oppressive g-norms. As a result, it is a covert exercitive likely to enact similarly oppressive s-norms.[30]

What might those oppressive s-norms be exactly? Since the s-norms depend on the (score and the) g-norms, identifying which particular s-norms are enacted by any particular move will require first identifying all the relevant g-norms but here we face an epistemic challenge. Unlike institutionalized games with their explicit rules and unlike conversations with their well-studied norms, the g-norms of our social practices are significantly less well understood. Additional empirical work is required.

[28] How long the enacted s-norms persist will depend on John's accepting Steve's utterance as (conversationally) appropriate. For a discussion of blocking, see Chapter 2 section 2.7.

[29] Of course, conversational permissibility is a type of social permissibility since conversations are social activities. We are here concerned with how enacting changes to conversational norms can also enact changes to non-conversational (social) norms.

[30] One might doubt that Steve's remark oppresses women if no women are present to hear it. Strictly speaking, it is not necessary that a member of the oppressed group be present in order for an utterance to oppress. So long as the enacted permissibility fact (s-norm) disadvantages members of the relevant group in virtue of membership in that group, the utterance in question is oppressive. The hanging of a 'Whites Only' sign, for instance, will oppress non-whites even if no non-white person is present when the oppressive restaurant policy is enacted. One may also modify the example so that a woman is present when Steve speaks.

Although we may not have complete knowledge of the g-norms governing our social practices, we do have important knowledge about how the oppressive g-norms operate. We know that such norms will, in general, advantage men over women; they will rank men above women and they will prioritize men's interests over women's interests thereby disadvantaging women relative to men. Moreover, such norms do so on the basis of (mere) group membership. Thus, although the g-norms of gender oppression are not as well understood as games and conversations, we can nevertheless make an educated guess regarding what the enacted s-norms are in Steve's case.

Here's a hypothesis: Steve's utterance makes it permissible, in this immediate environment and at this time (here and now), to degrade women. By so doing, his utterance makes women count as second-class citizens (locally and for the time being). Notice that if Steve's utterance enacts these s-norms and they are followed, then it is an act of gender oppression. It systematically and unfairly disadvantages women because they are women and it does so in a social context (i.e. the contemporary United States) where women are already systematically and unjustly disadvantaged in virtue of being women. Thus, *if* I am right about the enacted s-norms, then Steve's covert exercitive is an act of (gender) oppression.

How might enacting this s-norm harm actual women in that workplace? What tangible effect might result from the covertly exercitive functioning of Steve's remark? What behavioral changes would count as following the oppressive s-norm enacted? Actions potentially rendered appropriate by the s-norm enacted by Steve's utterance might include visually lingering on a woman's legs, expecting women to make themselves as attractive as possible, assuming that female employees ought to be more polite, undervaluing women's professional contributions, and/or expecting the women in the workplace to wipe the counters and clean out the communal refrigerator. By altering the normative landscape of the workplace in these ways, Steve's utterance enacts norms that prescribe behaviors that oppress women. As such, his remark constitutes an act of oppression.

Finally, if Steve's utterance enacts the hypothesized s-norms, then it is akin in its functioning to a sign reading: 'It is hereby permissible, in this local environment and at this time, to treat women as second class citizens.' Such a sign hanging in an employee lounge would not and should not be tolerated. It enacts a policy that systematically and unjustly disadvantages women because they are women and it does so in a social context where women are structurally disadvantaged relative to men. In short, it is an act of gender oppression.[31]

5.4 Potential objections

To some readers, this hypothesis may seem nothing short of preposterous. In this section, I consider several objections of varying quality and argue that, on reflection (and when properly understood), the hypothesis is both theoretically sound and plausible.

5.4.1 Individuals cannot enact structures

One might think that the hypothesis that Steve's utterance oppresses women is confused at best. After all, oppression requires a systematic social structure and there is just no way that Steve, a regular guy with no particular social standing, could possibly bring such a social structure about. As a result, it simply cannot be the case that Steve's utterance actually *oppresses* anyone.[32]

This objection is confused. Oppressive utterances need not enact oppressive social *structures*. Rather, they enact a certain sort of s-norm *in a social context where* such oppressive structures already obtain. To see this, suppose that a racist employer were to verbally enact a company policy such that non-white employees cannot be promoted. This (standard exercitive) utterance is oppressive; it enacts a permissibility fact that disadvantages non-white employees in virtue of their non-whiteness *and* it does so in a social context where non-white persons are already systematically and unjustly disadvantaged in virtue of their non-whiteness. As one can see, this utterance does not enact the oppressive social structure. It enacts a (certain sort of) permissibility fact in a *social context with* such a structure.

Thus, the hypothesis that Steve's utterance oppresses (women) does not require the implausible claim that Steve single-handedly enacts an

[31] It would also be an actionable act of gender discrimination. Potential legal applications of the phenomenon of covert exercitives are explored in Chapter 7.

[32] This objection has been raised repeatedly in conversation and in unpublished manuscripts.

entire complex social system of oppression with this one sexist remark. To think so is to be confused about the nature of both oppression and oppressive speech.

A consideration of this objection, though, does more than merely dispel a confusion; it helps to highlight just where the power to oppress resides with a covert exercitive. The power is in the oppressive social structure; it is in the norm-governed social practices and not in the individual participants. On this view, individuals say things that (whether they consciously realize it or not) count as moves in broader practices and, by so doing, these individuals thereby enact new norms (s-norms) for those practices. With standard exercitives, the power lies with the speaker who intentionally exercises that power. With covert exercitives, by contrast, individual speakers are often unwitting channels through which social structures operate. Robert Mark Simpson puts the point nicely:

> [W]hat Steve's remark does is bring the latent force of that gender system to bear in the local context. The oppressive power of Steve's comment is derived from something for which he is not responsible—the underlying system of social organization—but the activation of that oppressive power in the local context is something for which Steve is causally responsible and (defeasibly) morally responsible. McGowan's contention, in summary, is that Steve's speech functions as a conduit through which the underlying structural oppression of women gains purchase on particular individuals, both men and women, at a particular time and place.[33]

5.4.2 Enact versus inform

One might object that Steve's utterance does not *enact* these oppressive permissibility facts; it merely enables the hearer to infer that such permissibility facts *already* obtain. After all, it is only because women are already locally subordinated that Steve feels comfortable talking this way in the first place.

In response, recall, first, that we have already established that Steve's utterance enacts permissibility facts (s-norms). Exactly because it is a move in norm-governed activities, it is a covert exercitive that enacts permissibility facts (s-norms) in those activities. What remains open is which particular permissibility facts (s-norms) are enacted by his utterance.[34]

[33] Simpson 2013: 563.

[34] Furthermore, the distinction between enacting a fact and informing people about an antecedent fact is not sharp when the fact in question is socially constructed and

Moreover, the fact that women are already oppressed in society at large does not *undermine* the claim that Steve's utterance enacts an oppressive s-norm. As we have seen, acts of oppression actually *require* the antecedent existence of an oppressive social structure. Since this point bears repeating, consider the following example. Suppose that John hangs a 'Whites Only' sign in his burger joint in Mississippi in 1954. At that time and place, non-whites were certainly oppressed. Furthermore, the fact that non-whites were already oppressed helps to explain both John's inclination to hang such a sign and his ability to get away with it. That this is so, however, in no way undermines the fact that John enacts an oppressive restaurant policy by hanging the sign. Doing so is an act of oppression and this is so (not despite the antecedent existence of the oppressive structure but) *because of* the antecedent existence of the oppressive structure. Similarly, even if women are antecedently oppressed and even if this explains why Steve said what he said and how he manages to get away with it, this in no way undermines the claim that his utterance enacts an oppressive s-norm.

Keep in mind that Steve could have said something else and, if he had, he would have thereby made a different collection of moves and thus enacted different score changes to the various norm-governed activities at play. Suppose, for instance, that he had said: "We had a great time. She's smart, funny, and really accomplished!" Had he said this, different changes to the conversational score would have been enacted and more to the point different non-conversational s-norms would have been enacted. Since his utterance does not abide by and thus perpetuate oppressive g-norms, it is unlikely to enact oppressive s-norms.

The Steve case highlights the role that individual actions play in broader social structures. Whether we realize it or not and whether we intend to do it or not, our individual actions contribute to these broader social structures. We actually add to them by enacting s-norms that partially constitute such structures. Our actions, albeit often unwittingly, bring these structures to bear in the micro-context of our actions. Many theorists interested in oppression stress that it is a structural and macroscopic phenomenon. It is and it is important to realize that it is. That said, it is also true that such macro-structures are partially enacted by

permissibility facts are socially constructed. For a discussion of the role of collective recognition in constituting (i.e. enacting) social constructions, see Searle 1995.

individual actions in micro-contexts. Oppressive structures have their effect and gain purchase at the micro-level of individual action and interaction.

Finally, suppose that the oppressive s-norm allegedly enacted by Steve's utterance was already operative in the conversation (and that employee lounge) before Steve's utterance. (Suppose, for example, that a similarly sexist comment had been made earlier in that particular conversation.) In such a case, it may seem that Steve's utterance cannot enact that s-norm exactly because that s-norm is already operative and thus had already been enacted. To conclude this, though, is to overlook something important about the ontological status of permissibility facts, in particular, and of social constructions, in general.

Because social constructions ontologically depend on (a complex form of) collective recognition, all social constructions (not just permissibility facts) need to be re-enacted in order to obtain. If, for example, we all ceased to regard a certain permissibility fact as obtaining, it would cease to obtain. If no one regarded a certain currency as valuable, then it would cease to function as currency. The collective recognition of that fact (at time t) makes it the case that it obtains (at time t). Thus, whatever constitutes the collective recognition of a permissibility fact at a time enacts the permissibility fact at that time. Arguably, Steve's utterance does just that (even in a case where the s-norm in question is already operative). Since his utterance is part of what makes it the case that the permissibility fact in question is regarded as obtaining at that time, his utterance enacts that fact at that time.[35]

That said, there is nevertheless an important difference between cases where Steve's utterance is the first to enact oppressive s-norms in that social and conversational context and cases in which it is not. Because of the nature of covert exercitives, all of these cases are cases of enacting harmful s-norms but the former cases are indeed more potent. The difference here is akin to the important difference between utterances that introduce a presupposition (to the score or common ground) and those that merely rely on existing presuppositions. The emerging picture is this: The (oppressive) g-norms are operative in the broader society, but

[35] This way of thinking about social construction is influenced by Searle 1995. This perpetual re-enactment of social constructions may well be what Butler means by reiteration. See Butler 1997).

they gain purchase in micro-contexts of personal interaction when individual actions/utterances enact (oppressive) s-norms via those (oppressive) g-norms. The first time this happens in a particular micro-context can be especially powerful.

To see this, consider the following example. The Capital Slam poetry contest at the Mercury Lounge in Ottawa, Canada is organized by a man named Rusty Priske, who describes the following events on his blog.[36] According to Rusty, the CapSlam community is an open and constructive one but on March 16, 2014, a poet named Omar took the stage and in Rusty's own words:

> It was a very angry poem. That's okay. I have a number of very angry poems myself. But then it turned.
>
> He started ranting about the evils of women. I caught some stuff about porn and he seemed to be blaming women for his problems in life. Then (with what I could call hatred in his voice) said "feminists" with venom... then he caught himself and said "fucking feminists" with a real sneer.[37]

Rusty goes on to describe the effect Omar's poem had on him and the audience. Rusty himself struggled to keep his cool; he was fuming with anger and utterly unable to concentrate on his own poem. His mind was fully engaged with trying to work out how he ought to react. He says:

> Listening to hate speech on our stage, which I hold as close to sacred as I get, had me seeing red.[38]

It is clear from Rusty's description that this sort of misogynist speech was downright alien to the micro-culture of CapSlam. In light of this, one might wonder how and why Omar's venomous poem had such an effect. After all, Omar is entirely alone in his sentiments, at least in this context. Omar's poem had such a powerful effect, I contend, because it enacted harmful s-norms for the first time in this micro-context. Although the oppressive g-norms were already and unfortunately part of our broader culture, those norms did not come to bear on CapSlam until Omar brought them there via his poem. Were CapSlam a different sort of

[36] https://rustythepoet.wordpress.com/2014/03/16/my-night-at-the-slam-reacting-to-oppressive-speech/ accessed on February 25, 2015, reprinted with permission.

[37] https://rustythepoet.wordpress.com/2014/03/16/my-night-at-the-slam-reacting-to-oppressive-speech/ accessed on February 25, 2015, reprinted with permission.

[38] https://rustythepoet.wordpress.com/2014/03/16/my-night-at-the-slam-reacting-to-oppressive-speech/ accessed on February 25, 2015, reprinted with permission.

community where misogynistic poetry was less rare or even common, Omar's poem would still enact oppressive s-norms but it wouldn't be the first or only time such s-norms are operative in that context. On my view, the power to oppress in this case is not in Omar, the speaker, but in the social structure brought to bear via Omar's words.[39] So it is with Steve. How powerful the enacting of oppressive s-norms is depends on the context in which such s-norms are enacted and the history of such norms in that context.

5.4.3 *Too easy to reverse*

One might worry that covert exercitives cannot possibly afford a useful mechanism of oppressive speech exactly because the enacted permissibility facts (s-norms) are too fleeting and too easy to reverse to manage to oppress in any substantive sense. Consider again Steve's utterance. The hypothesis that his utterance is oppressive appears to be undermined by the realization that one could immediately object to what he said and thereby, it seems, undo or (even block) the allegedly oppressive s-norm enacted by his utterance. If the enacted s-norms are so easy to undo, then they hardly seem *oppressive* per se.

First, it may be that Steve's utterance *seems* easy to reverse because conversational moves *seem* easy to reverse. Recall that Steve's utterance is simultaneously a move in the norm-governed activity of conversation and a move in the norm-governed activity of gender oppression. As a conversational move that enacts s-norms for the conversation, Steve's utterance may well *seem* easy to reverse. After all, in order to reverse (or even block) the objectionable s-norm (i.e. that it is subsequently appropriate, in this particular conversation, to use degrading terms for women) it seems that one would just need to object to what Steve said (on grounds, say, that it is sexist). Of course, in actual practice, speaking back in this way may prove to be quite difficult. As the growing literature on silencing shows, there are a variety of ways in which harmful speech can disable (or altogether prevent) the speech of those targeted.[40] Moreover, the empirical evidence suggests that those targeted by harmful

[39] Omar's poem places a burden on the audience and the CapSlam community. Unless the oppressive s-norms are to be allowed to reign, they must somehow be reversed.

[40] The literature on silencing is vast. See, for example, Langton 1993; MacKinnon 1993; Anderson 1995; Hornsby 1995; McGowan 2003; West 2003; Maitra 2009; and Dotson 2011.

speech rarely actually speak back.[41] As a result, certain conversational s-norms may not be so easy to reverse in practice.

Moreover, that Steve's utterance is (or seems to be) easy to reverse as a *conversational* move does not show that it is easy to reverse as a move in broader (extra-conversational) social practices. Whether *those* s-norms are easy to reverse will depend on the relevant g-norms and this, as we have seen, is an open empirical matter.

That said, there are several reasons to think that oppressive s-norms will be especially difficult to reverse. First, who is able to make which sort of move (in a norm-governed activity) is sensitive to one's position (in that activity). In particular, it may be that men are in a privileged position (with respect to the ability to make various sorts of moves) in a social practice governed by g-norms oppressive to women. If this is correct, then it may be especially difficult for women to reverse certain sorts of s-norms enacted by men.

Moreover, it may be that certain sorts of s-norms are especially difficult to reverse independent of who enacts them; oppressive s-norms may well be of this sort.[42] Elsewhere, I have suggested that setting the record straight in response to a sexist remark (or joke) is much akin to trying to un-ring a bell.[43] It seems that there is something complicated and covert going on that is difficult to pinpoint and hence undo. In his "Un-ringing the Bell: McGowan on Oppressive Speech and the Asymmetric Pliability of Conversations," Robert Mark Simpson helpfully develops this suggestion.[44]

Appealing to the growing social psychological literature, Simpson points out that in some contexts it takes very little to activate (sexist) associations.[45] Consequently, there is good reason to believe that sexist comments will sometimes bring to mind and thus make salient a broad set of sexist associations. The sorts of sexist associations I have in mind here connect women with negative characteristics like submissiveness,

[41] See Nielsen 2004.

[42] This seems to be true of even some conversational s-norms. For example, it seems that it is easier to conversationally raise epistemic standards than it is to lower them. For a discussion of this, see Lewis 1983; 1996 and McGowan 2003. Langton (in conversation) appeals to the degradation of American political discourse in order show how easy it is to lower standards.

[43] See my 2009b.

[44] See Simpson 2013.

[45] Simpson (2013) cites Greenberg and Pyszczynski 1985; Steele and Aronson 1995; and Goodman et al. 2008;. Associations are context sensitive and malleable.

stupidity, irrationality, weakness, subservience, and domesticity. Moreover, the evidence demonstrates that these associations affect our ability to reason well and fairly and they are perniciously difficult to shield oneself from.[46] "And this is because comments which aim to discredit an association tend to accidentally reinforce it."[47] Thinking or saying, for example, 'but women are not submissive' tends to reinforce the association between womanhood and submissiveness. In this way, associations are especially difficult to dispel. Thus, once a sexist comment makes such sexist associations salient, it will be quite difficult to make them unsalient. Even attempts to discredit these associations will, unfortunately, tend to further them. These considerations afford good reason to believe that sexist s-norms will in fact be especially difficult to reverse.[48]

Finally, suppose that the s-norms in question are easy to reverse. Does this show that they cannot be oppressive? The answer, I think, is No. So long as the s-norm is followed and actual oppressive harm ensues, the s-norm oppresses even if only for a short period of time. While shorter-lived (or easy to reverse) oppressive s-norms may be "less" oppressive, in some sense, than longer-lived (or harder to reverse) oppressive s-norms, they are oppressive all the same.[49]

5.4.4 *On intentionality and parallel acts*

I have claimed that speech covertly enacts oppressive norms but one might think that a consideration of the role of intentionality in speech acts tells strongly against this claim. There are two forms that this objection might

[46] Simpson (2013) cites Blum 2004 and Kelly and Roeder 2008 but he is careful to point out that not all work on implicit bias appeals to associationistic schemas; there are further questions about how to characterize such schemas, and such schemas may differ between different socially marked groups. See fn. 16 of his 2013.

[47] See Simpson 2013: 571.

[48] That the implicit associations triggered by some sexist utterances are especially difficult or even impossible to reverse certainly does not establish that all harmful score changes enacted by sexist utterances are irreversible. Some clearly are not. We can object to sexist claims, assumptions, or presuppositions, and thereby prevent those claims from becoming part of the common ground or an ongoing and shared component of conversational score. For a discussion of blocking, see Section 2.7.

[49] Simpson doubts this claim on the grounds that such "ephemeral" policies cannot be constitutive of oppression which is "stable, operant over extended periods [and] consistent in its character" but this objection confuses characteristics of the oppressive structure with characteristics of the oppressive s-norm enacted in any particular case. See fn. 13 of his 2013: 568.

take. First, it might seem that oppressive speech requires an intention to oppress. We have already seen, however, that this objection is misplaced but it is worth revisiting the point. Consider the following example. Suppose that the Queen of Schmoo enacts a new law for her realm when she says, "From now on, redheads are not permitted to vote." Suppose further that redheads are unjustly and systematically disadvantaged in this kingdom and they are disadvantaged in this way exactly because they are redheads. In such a case, the queen's utterance oppresses redheads. But now notice this. From the mere fact that the queen intends to enact this law (permissibility fact), it does not follow that she thereby intends to oppress redheads and this is so even though enacting that law in that context oppresses redheads. In short, the Queen may not be fully aware of the social context in which she is speaking. That is, she may not realize that her utterance is oppressive.

Suppose, for example, that the Queen is utterly oblivious to issues of social justice. She firmly (and conveniently) believes that life is a meritocracy and, in her worldview, redheads are at the bottom of the social order because they are naturally inferior, and thus incapable of making informed decisions on important matters. She therefore enacts the law in question in order to protect redheads from themselves. As one can see, one can verbally oppress (as the Queen does) without intending to do so and without being aware of doing so. Furthermore, the absence of the speaker's intention to oppress in no way undermines the oppressive nature of the act. Enacting those particular permissibility facts in that social context is sufficient to oppress (whether the speaker intends to do so and whether the speaker is aware of doing so).

Since the queen's act of oppressing redheads is not dependent on the communication of her intention to do so but is constituted by the performing of a certain illocutionary act (in this case, the standard exercitive of enacting the permissibility fact that redheads are not permitted to vote) in a certain (social) context, it is a parallel act (Section 4.3). The act of oppression is parallel to the illocutionary act of enacting that permissibility fact (or law).

That verbal acts of oppression are parallel acts has several important consequences. First, as we have just seen, one can verbally oppress without intending to do so and without realizing that one is doing so. Second, as with other parallel acts, although the relevant speaker intentions are not necessary, they *can* be present. It is possible, for example, for a speaker, aware of the social conditions, to intend to perform the (parallel act of) oppression. The Queen could intend to oppress in a case where she realizes that the social context is one in which enacting that law would oppress redheads. As we have seen in previous chapters, although the relevant speaker intention is present in such cases, it does not follow from this that the success of the parallel act (of oppression) is dependent in any way on that intention or on the recognition of that intention. Third and finally, all three of the above points apply whether the parallel act of oppression in question involves an oppressor or not.

Oppressive *covert* exercitives are especially interesting because they are *doubly* parallel. First, the enacting of permissibility facts via a covert exercitive is a parallel act. It is an act constituted via the performing of an illocutionary act (of a certain sort in a certain sort of context). Second, the act of oppression thereby constituted is parallel to the (parallel) act of enacting the permissibility fact in question.[50]

Bringing this all back to Steve's utterance, the mere fact that Steve does not intend to oppress women and the mere fact that he is barely aware of enacting permissibility facts at all in no way undermines the claim made here that his remark is in fact an act of oppression. Since Steve's utterance is a move in a norm-governed activity, it is covertly exercitive. Furthermore, because his move abides by an oppressive g-norm of that activity, his remark enacts oppressive s-norms. As such, it is an act of oppression.

5.5 Oppressive speech is widespread

An exercise of speaker authority is not the only way for speech to oppress. Saying things that enact s-norms in broader (non-conversational) social

[50] Moreover, that oppressive covert exercitives are doubly parallel complicates the possibilities with respect to both speaker intention and speaker awareness. A speaker may or may not realize (and may or may not consciously and explicitly intend) that a certain utterance enact particular permissibility facts in a certain context. Typically the relevant intentions and the speaker's awareness will be highly attenuated. Furthermore and independent of these issues, the speaker may or may not realize (or intend) that enacting those permissibility facts will (in that context) also oppress. Finally, although it may seem counter-intuitive, it is possible for the speaker of an oppressive covert exercitive to be an oppressor and to do so without realizing that her utterance oppresses. If she intends to enact the permissibility fact (enacted by her covertly exercitive utterance) and if enacting that permissibility fact is itself unjust and it oppresses without her realizing it, then she is an oppressor who oppresses without realizing it.

structures can do so too. In light of this, we now have good reason to believe that oppressive speech is rather widespread. Consider the Comic-Con attendee who asks a female attendee about her cup size.[51] Consider the TV viewer at a restaurant who loudly complains to his family and friends that the female news anchor's microphone obstructs his view of her chest.[52] Perhaps it comes as no surprise that such *blatantly* sexist remarks oppress, but the mechanism identified here affords reason to believe that considerably less blatant—and perhaps even innocent seeming—comments can also oppress. In fact, evenly kindly intended compliments can oppress: Telling an Asian American that she speaks English very well, for example, can enact harmful s-norms and thus constitute rather than merely cause harm. Sadly such microaggressions are all too common.[53]

5.6 Conclusion

Oppression is a structural phenomenon. Seeing it clearly requires stepping back and recognizing patterns. What may be invisible close up is salient from afar. This much is true. That this is true, however, is compatible with also recognizing the importance of what happens close up. After all, oppressive structures have their effect at the micro-level of personal interaction. This is where the oppressive acts take place; in the realm of the fleeting and localized s-norms enacted by our individual behaviors. The covert mechanism of norm-enactment identified here brings this to light.

[51] Harassment at NYCC 2012, Black cat. http://beautilation.tumblr.com/post/33538802648. Cross-Posted from Mandy Caruso's tumblr, The Grind Haus, October 2012.

[52] I overheard this one myself at Rolling Road Golf Club in Catonsville, Maryland.

[53] I apply the framework of this book to microaggressions in my 2018c.

6

On Pornography

Subordination and Silencing

6.1 Introduction

In Chapter 5, we saw one way that the phenomenon of conversational exercitives generalizes. The phenomenon (of speech covertly enacting permissibility facts) is not limited to the norm-governed activity of conversation; it occurs in all norm-governed activities. Thus, when an utterance constitutes a move in a norm-governed activity other than (but typically in addition to) conversation, that utterance enacts a score change in that other (i.e. non-conversation) norm-governed activity too and therefore it also enacts new permissibility facts for that (non-conversation) norm-governed activity. In Chapter 5, we explored how this covert mechanism highlights how sexist utterances can constitute acts of gender oppression.

In the current chapter, we focus on another way that the phenomenon of conversational exercitives generalizes: the move-constituting action need not be an utterance or even a speech act. In fact, it need not be a communicative act at all. Any action (whether it is communicative or not) that constitutes a move in a norm-governed activity thereby enacts a score change in that activity and thus enacts new permissibility facts in that activity. In this chapter, we do not confine ourselves to moves that are speech or even communicative acts; we consider actions more broadly. In particular, we focus on actions involving pornography and we explore how such actions might (through this covert mechanism of norm-enactment) constitute either acts of subordination or acts of silencing.

The current chapter also further stresses the crucial role of context. We are already familiar with several ways in which context is crucial. What an utterance means and what an utterance does are highly sensitive to context. Saying, "I do" in response to a question can mean that I like chocolate; in another context, it can mean that I plan to attend a party. The illocutionary force of "I do" also varies with context. Saying these words can be an assertion, a promise, or even a marriage and which of these it is depends crucially on the context. Both conversational and covert exercitives are also highly sensitive to context. The very same words uttered in two different conversational contexts will enact different conversational permissibility facts. "My dog is furry" might introduce the presupposition that I have a dog in one conversational context and block my interlocutor's assertion (that furry dogs are unlovable) in a different conversational context. The same is true for covert exercitives. Asking whether someone has a sister is unlikely to contribute to harmful social norms in the vast majority of cases and yet, as we saw in the example of the last chapter, there are cases (e.g. in response to "I banged the bitch") when saying this does do so. In keeping with these observations, we will see further ways in which context is crucial: context determines what is pornographic and it strongly affects which particular permissibility facts are enacted by our actions.

Since our focus in this chapter is on actions involving pornography and since pornography is such a contested category, out first task (Section 6.2) is to characterize what we mean by 'pornography.' Once again, context is crucial. The very same image may be pornography in one context and not in another. In Section 6.3, we consider (MacKinnon's) claim that pornography subordinates and in Section 6.4 we investigate the hypothesis that pornography does so via an exercise of speaker authority. In Section 6.5, we consider an alternative hypothesis (appealing to the covert norm-enactment of norm-governed moves) and then finally in Section 6.6 we consider the phenomenon of silencing and how actions involving pornography might enact norms that silence.

6.2 On pornography

It is notoriously difficult to define pornography. This is, in part, because there are distinct sources of disagreement regarding pornography and its proper definition. One issue concerns which particular objects are instances of pornography. This is a problem about the extension (or referent) of the term 'pornography.' Another issue concerns the definition or defining characteristics of pornography. As is well known, there is no commonly accepted definition of pornography.[1]

One reason for this is that the correctness of a definition depends on the purpose of the definition. The correct way to define prime numbers for a second grader is quite different from the correct way to define them for a graduate student in mathematics specializing in number theory. The same is true for 'pornography.' If my objective were to identify the materials that I do not want my twelve-year-old son to see, I would use one definition. If instead my objective is to identify those materials that are the proper focus of a particular legal argument for regulation, then I would use a quite different definition.

Catharine MacKinnon uses the latter strategy when she defines pornography as the "graphic sexually explicit subordination of women."[2] She is defining pornography so that it targets those very materials that she argues ought to be legally actionable for the particular reasons she offers.[3] This is a prime example of defining something for a particular purpose. In fact, she even says, "For the purposes of this legislation, pornography shall mean . . ."[4]

Since I am here engaged with theorists who offer philosophical precisifications of some of MacKinnon's claims and arguments about pornography, I am here engaged with theorists who use MacKinnon's definition. For this reason, it is important to consider and be clear about that definition. In short, I take MacKinnon to be primarily concerned with materials that present, endorse, and even eroticize a hierarchical sexual relationship.[5] Thus, depictions of mutually respectful and consensual sexual acts (sometimes called 'erotica') would not count as pornography in MacKinnon's special technical sense although such materials would count as pornography in the ordinary sense.[6]

[1] For a helpful discussion of this issue, see Section 1 of West 2013. See also Ogien 2003. There are also many different types of pornography produced for and interpreted by different groups. For a discussion of this complexity, see Green 2000.

[2] See MacKinnon and Dworkin 1998.

[3] See MacKinnon 1987; 1989; 1993; and MacKinnon and Dworkin 1998.

[4] See MacKinnon and Dworkin 1998.

[5] Whether particular BDSM materials satisfy this definition would depend on whether hierarchy is endorsed in those materials. Since such practices are consensual, even though they are sometimes role-played as if they are not, the hierarchy depicted may merely be apparent. How materials function is highly dependent on the context of use.

[6] Gloria Steinem famously distinguished between 'pornography' and 'erotica' in her 1980: 35–9. Some are critical of this distinction. See especially Green 2000. Green is also critical of the gendered and heterosexist nature of MacKinnon's definition of pornography.

Even though I here engage with theorists who are developing MacKinnon's claims and operating with her characterization of pornography, I do not want to limit my consideration of pornography (or actions involving it) to materials that would (or might) satisfy MacKinnon's definition/characterization.

Furthermore, given the context-sensitivity of the pornographic, I will not attempt to "define" pornography. This is because I regard pornography as a kind of function in context. Whether a particular object is pornographic depends on the way that that object functions in a particular context. A photograph of Ellen's mastectomy scars on file in her oncologist's office is not pornography. That same photograph posted on a revenge porn site is pornography.[7] A documentary about the sexual slave trade is not pornography. That same documentary viewed by a man while masturbating is pornography. These examples show that seemingly non-pornographic objects can function as, and thus become pornographic, in certain contexts.[8] Arguably, the reverse is also possible. Seemingly pornographic objects can fail to function as pornography in certain contexts. Pornographic magazines fail to function as such when a stack of them is used as a booster seat for a child at the dining room table. A hard-core pornography video being viewed and discussed at a feminist lecture arguing for the ubiquity of patriarchy would not function in this context as pornography. Such examples suggest that it is misguided to attempt to define pornography in terms of the intrinsic features of the materials themselves. We would do better, it seems, to focus on the function of such objects in particular contexts.

This way of thinking about pornography is similar to the way Nelson Goodman theorizes about the nature of art. Goodman suggests that instead of trying to define art in terms of the intrinsic features of art objects, we reject the 'What is art?' question and focus instead on the more contextually sensitive 'When is art?' question. For Goodman, whether an object is art depends on the context and the complexity

[7] This is a real life example. It is discussed in Laws (2013).

[8] Another widely cited example is Linda Marchiano's book *Ordeal* (Lovelace 1980). Written as a protest of her harrowing experiences in the pornography industry, the book functions as pornography when it is advertised as such. Langton cites this as an example of silencing (because the illocutionary intention to protest goes unrecognized in the context of the pornography catalogue). See Langton 1993: 321.

and density of that object's referential relations in that context.[9] Although I here emphasize the function in context, I will not try to provide a full answer to the 'When is pornography' question. Rather, I will be explicit about the nature of the materials in question and the context in which those materials function.

6.3 MacKinnon's claims

MacKinnon makes many claims about pornography. In this chapter, we shall be concerned with two of her claims. First, we will explore the claim that pornography subordinates women. Later in the chapter (Section 6.6), we will investigate the claim that it silences women.

The subordination claim is actually built into MacKinnon's definition of pornography. She says that pornography is "the graphic sexually explicit subordination of women whether in pictures or in words."[10] This definition may seem question begging. After all, if one defines pornography in this way, then the claim that pornography subordinates is both analytic and true. This is problematic since whether pornography in fact subordinates anyone is an empirical matter. We have two options. We could treat the empirical issue of whether pornography subordinates as settling the empirical question regarding whether anything in the world satisfies MacKinnon's definition (and is thus in the extension of 'pornography' as she defines it). Alternatively, we could re-characterize 'pornography' in order to pinpoint the sorts of materials that concern MacKinnon. For this purpose, we might define pornography as sexually explicit material that eroticizes a gendered hierarchy. Then, the empirical question is whether those sorts of materials subordinate women. In what follows, I employ the latter strategy at least when engaged with MacKinnon's claims and thus with her characterization of pornography.

In order to understand MacKinnon's claim (that pornography subordinates women) more fully, it is useful to first situate our discussion within the context of arguments for the further legal regulation of pornography. I here focus on the legal context of the United States, the

[9] See Goodman 1968. [10] See MacKinnon and Dworkin 1998.

context in which MacKinnon is operating.[11] Although there is some simplification involved, there are roughly three sorts of arguments given. First, some have argued that some (currently protected) pornography ought to be regulated because it violates certain shared community standards of decency and thus constitutes obscenity.[12] Over time, however, what counts as legally obscene has narrowed considerably and currently only so-called "hard-core" pornography can be regulated in this manner.[13] Feminist arguments for the regulation of pornography have typically focused on an alleged connection between pornography and harm. The second argumentative strategy maintains that pornography ought to be regulated because of the harm it *causes*. According to this strategy, pornography ought to be regulated because the harm it causes women outweighs the reasons against regulating it.[14] The third approach maintains that pornography actually *constitutes* harm. According to this "radical" approach, due primarily to MacKinnon, (some) pornography ought to be regulated not because it depicts harm (as it obviously does) and not because it causes harm (as many acknowledge) but because it *is* harm. According to MacKinnon, pornography constitutes the harm of subordinating women.

It is prudent to stress that MacKinnon does not deny that pornography also causes various harms. In fact, she agrees with many of the causal claims made by those implementing the second argumentative strategy. It is just that MacKinnon believes that the correct grounds for justifying the further legal actionability of pornography concerns the constitutive connection between pornography and harm.

[11] Much of what is said here about the U.S. context applies to other jurisdictions. For an overview, see "Introduction and Overview" in Maitra and McGowan 2012: 1–23. Free speech issues are explored in more detail in Chapter 7.

[12] Some pornography is already regulated. The production, purchase, or possession of child pornography is a crime. Since it involves sex with a minor, its production necessarily involves the crime of (child) rape. It is even illegal to buy what one falsely believes is child pornography. Despite this, virtual child pornography is legal (although labels indicating that it is virtual are now required.) Another illegal category of pornography is so-called snuff films that (allegedly) document an actual rape and murder. Some contend that the existence of such films is a complete myth. See Kipnis 1996.

[13] See Greenawalt 1989: 303.

[14] There are further conditions required to justify regulation when a free speech principle is operative. These details are discussed in Chapter 7. For a helpful discussion of the required notion of causation, see Eaton 2007.

6.4 Langton's analysis

Although MacKinnon first made the claim that pornography subordinates women, philosophers have since done considerable work in making sense of it by offering philosophical precisifications of it. Moreover, these analyses (and subsequent debates in the philosophical literature) have since taken on a life of their own. As a result, in what follows, I am less concerned with getting MacKinnon's (extensive and nuanced) views correct than I am with assessing the relative merits of various philosophical reconstructions of this subordination claim.

Our discussion in Chapter 1 (Section 1.7) goes some way towards making sense of the claim that pornography subordinates. We know that speech constitutes harm when it enacts norms that prescribe that harm. So, pornography will subordinate women if it enacts norms that subordinate women.[15] We also know that exercitive speech enacts norms (permissibility facts). Perhaps pornography is a standard exercitive that enacts permissibility facts that subordinate women. Rae Langton advocates this hypothesis and, in illustrating the coherence of subordinating speech, she offers a paradigmatic example of a subordinating speech act:[16]

> Consider this utterance: 'Blacks are not permitted to vote.' Imagine that it is uttered by a legislator in Pretoria in the context of enacting legislation that underpins apartheid. It... makes it the case that blacks are not permitted to vote. It—plausibly—subordinates blacks.[17]

That this utterance subordinates and the extent to which it does is sensitive to context. Not being able to vote in a context where voting does nothing does not subordinate at all. Furthermore, not being able to vote in a context where there are seventeen other perfectly effective ways to participate in the democratic process is considerably less subordinating than not being able to vote in a context where voting is the main way to so participate. Thus, the enacting of these permissibility facts manages to subordinate only because of factors present in the social context of utterance.[18] This act of subordination is therefore a parallel act (Section 4.3). It does not depend on the speaker's

[15] There are other models of subordinating speech. For discussions of subordinating speech as an imperative, see Butler 1997 and Stanley 2015.

[16] See Langton 1993: 305–30. [17] See Langton 1993: 302–3.

[18] Langton offers an analysis of subordination. According to Langton, to subordinate x requires unfairly ranking x as inferior, legitimating discriminatory treatment of x, and depriving x of important powers. See her 1993 at 303.

intention to *subordinate*. Although it depends on the illocutionary intention to enact the permissibility facts (law) in question, enacting this particular law in this particular social context also constitutes the additional (parallel) act of subordinating blacks.[19]

It is also worth pointing out that although they are related phenomena, oppression and subordination are nevertheless distinct. First, individuals qua individuals can be subordinated. A person can only be oppressed, by contrast, in virtue of that person's membership in a social group (Section 5.2). Second and relatedly, oppression requires a systematic and unjust social structure but subordination does not (Section 5.2).

6.4.1 *Challenges for Langton's hypothesis*

This hypothesis that pornography is a subordinating standard exercitive meets with several challenges.[20] Since standard exercitives have specific felicity conditions, this hypothesis will be undermined if pornography fails to satisfy these conditions. Because many of these issues have been discussed in Chapter 5, we will only briefly revisit them here.

Since the producers, distributors, and purveyors (that is, the speakers) of pornography do not seem to intend to be enacting permissibility facts of any kind (legal, moral, or social), the speaker illocutionary intention condition appears to fail.[21] (The main response to this objection is to deny that the speaker illocutionary intention is necessary for illocution.[22]) Standard exercitives also depend on the speaker's locutionary intention. Since standard exercitives express the content of the permissibility fact being enacted, such speech acts are non-ideal if the speaker's locutionary

[19] Langton operates with a broader conception of illocution and she treats subordination as the illocutionary act. See, for example, Langton 1993: 302–3, 307; Langton 1998: 263; and Langton 2009: 350. Doing so makes her vulnerable to the objection that the speaker's failure to intend to subordinate is a failure to intend to perform the illocutionary act in question.

[20] There are other potential problems that are not explored here. If pornography is a speech act, then it must have a speaker and it is unclear who the speaker is. Although this question is important, for present purposes, I simply assume that the producers, distributors, and purveyors of pornography (mostly men) collectively constitute the speaker. In this, I follow Leslie Green. See his 1998: 285–311. Another problem concerns the pictorial elements of pornography. It is unclear that they are appropriately treated as utterances. For this worry, see Bauer 2005: 68–97.

[21] See McGowan 2003. Since Langton treats subordination as an illocutionary act and others follow suit, this objection takes a different form in the literature. The intention to subordinate is treated as the illocutionary intention. See Saul 2006: 61–80.

[22] See Langton 1993 and Langton 2009.

intention fails to match that content. Fully satisfying this condition would require, first, that pornography express the content of the relevant (subordinating) permissibility facts and, second, that the speakers intend to be expressing that content. At first blush anyway, it seems that pornography fails at these conditions too.[23] It is unclear, that is, that pornography says things like 'Women are socially inferior' or 'It is legitimate to rape women' or that the speakers intend to be expressing such things.

In their "Scorekeeping in a Pornographic Language Game," Rae Langton and Caroline West explicitly address this challenge.[24] There, they argue persuasively that (some) pornography expresses, via a complex combination of presupposition and conversational implicature, various hateful messages about women (e.g. 'Women enjoy being raped'). Although 'Women enjoy being raped' (a content Langton and West argue is expressed by some pornography) is not equivalent to 'It is socially legitimate to rape women' (a subordinating content), one can easily see how the latter may be inferred from the former.[25] Therefore, the failure of this particular felicity condition may merely be apparent.

Another collection of challenges to this hypothesis comes from the various hearer recognition conditions.[26] Since pornography is not (at least generally) taken by its hearers (consumers) to be enacting permissibility facts, this hearer recognition condition fails.[27] The consumers of pornography do not take it to be an exercitive speech act. Moreover, since it is not (at least generally) recognized as expressing the content of the (subordinating) permissibility facts in question, the hearer recognition condition (of the alleged actual locutionary content) also fails.[28]

[23] This objection is raised and answered in Langton and West 1999. See also McGowan 2003.

[24] See Langton and West 1999.

[25] One might argue, for instance, that there is a general background assumption in place such that it is socially acceptable to treat a person in ways that that person enjoys. Moreover, with such an assumption in place, the relevant (subordinating) content can be generated. In this way, the general strategy Langton and West employ can be extended to generate the relevant contents.

[26] See McGowan 2003.

[27] This objection also takes a different shape in the literature (again because subordination is (mistakenly) treated as the illocutionary act). See Langton 1993 and 2009.

[28] Langton explores the possibility of privileging some hearers (e.g. those feminists who regard (some) pornography as subordinating women) but abandons this approach on the grounds that it cannot be adequately defended. See Langton 1993: 311.

Far and away the most discussed objection to the current hypothesis concerns the speaker authority condition.[29] Since standard exercitives enact permissibility facts via an exercise of speaker authority, the speaker in question must have, and be exercising, the requisite authority. If (some) pornography is a standard exercitive, then the "speakers" must have the authority to enact permissibility facts in the social world. Arguably, this requirement is doubly problematic. First, it is unclear that the "speakers" have the requisite authority. Second, the nature of this pornographic authority is also unclear.[30]

Plainly, pornography does not have the officially sanctioned and clearly defined powers of public office. So, if pornography enacts permissibility facts in the social world, it must do so via some other sort of authority or social power.[31] But what might this authority or power consist in? One might argue that (some) pornography has derivative but effective authority in virtue of having the entire history of institutionalized sexism behind it.[32] One might argue that pornography has authority through what Maitra calls licensing, a type of omission that confers authority by failing to object.[33] One might argue that, because so many young men learn about the norms of heterosexual sexual relations from pornography, educating the masses about the norms is tantamount to enacting them or one might contend that the perceived expertise of pornography grants it a sort of de facto authority in that realm.[34] Finally, one might argue that since the government protects pornography under the rubric of free speech, pornography thereby has the authority of the government behind it.[35] Of course, each of these lines of response requires much more development than is offered here.[36] Since the authority of the speaker is strictly necessary for standard exercitives,

[29] Many argue against the claim that pornography subordinates on the grounds that it lacks the authority to do so. See, for example, Green 1998: 285–311; Butler 1997; Golding 2000; Sumner 2004; and Bauer 2005; 2015.

[30] See McGowan 2003, 168 and Bauer 2015: 77.

[31] For further discussion of the complex relation between authority, expertise, and standing, see Chapter 3 section 3.4.2.

[32] Matsuda suggests a parallel claim about racist hate speech and racism in her 1993. For a similar suggestion applied to pornography, see Maitra's discussion of derived authority in her 2012.

[33] See Maitra 2012.

[34] See MacKinnon 1987 and Langton 1993: 305–30.

[35] This sort of response is also suggested in Matsuda 1993.

[36] The most direct attempt to deal with this "authority problem" is Ishani Maitra's 2012.

establishing that pornography actually has the requisite authority is crucial work yet undone. For this reason, it poses a serious challenge to the hypothesis that pornography is a (subordinating) standard exercitive. In fact, this challenge is widely regarded as the most important one.[37]

In addition to reasons for doubting that pornography is a standard exercitive (a particular type of speech act), there are reasons to doubt that it is a speech act at all. First, pornography does not appear to work at the conscious level of communicated intentions as speech acts do. Although pornography consumption may well alter beliefs about the social status of women, it seems to have its effect without our conscious awareness. Since speech acts work at the conscious level, it is, however, unclear that the speech act approach can do justice to the sneaky and masked manner in which pornography functions.[38]

An additional reason to think that pornography is not a speech act is that speech acts are contextually embedded but pornography, at least the way it has been discussed thus far in the literature, does not seem to be.[39] To see the contextual embeddedness of speech acts, consider the sentence 'I am tall.' This sentence alone is not a speech act but it can be used in some particular context to perform one. When a particular speaker utters these words on a particular occasion, that totality is a speech act. Moreover, what a speech act does (illocutionarily) and what it expresses (locutionarily) depend on various factors of the context. Suppose that, when teaching a philosophy of language class on indexicals (linguistic expressions, like 'I,' 'here,' 'now,' 'that,' and 'she' whose referent shifts from context to context[40]), a student asks me for an example and I say, "I am tall." In this case, my utterance does not assert that I am tall; it asserts that the sentence 'I am tall' contains at least one indexical. If, by contrast, I am shopping for slacks at a local store and I say, "I am tall,"

[37] Langton herself appears to treat it as such. See Langton 1993; 1998; 2009; and 2011.

[38] Hornsby (1993) explicitly denies that pornography is a speech act. For an exploration of the hypothesis that pornography consumption unconsciously conditions its consumers, see MacKinnon 1987; 1993; and Scoccia 1996. For an argument that a consideration of the felicity conditions of speech act theory undermine Langton's speech act approach, see McGowan 2003.

[39] See Saul 2006: 229–48. Saul goes on to argue that a consideration of the context undermines rather than supports Langton's hypothesis but Saul's argument fails to distinguish between the illocutionary act (of enacting permissibility facts) and the parallel act (of subordinating).

[40] This definition comes from Braun 2012.

the uttering of these words on this occasion asserts the proposition that I am tall. And, of course, when someone else utters these very same words, he or she expresses a different proposition (namely that [the speaker] is tall). As one can see then, a speech act is sensitive to a variety of contextual factors and it makes little sense to try to pinpoint what an utterance does (illocutionarily) or what it expresses (locutionarily) without taking such contextual factors into account.[41]

In light of this, one might think that the current hypothesis (that (some) pornography is a subordinating standard exercitive) is undermined. After all, in the same way that it would be a mistake to say that 'I am tall' has a particular illocutionary force (independent of its use on a particular occasion), so too, it is simply a mistake to say that (even just some) pornography has a particular illocutionary force (independent of its use on a particular occasion). For if pornography really is a speech act, then it too has illocutionary force only on particular occasions of use.[42]

In sum then, the hypothesis that pornography is a subordinating standard exercitive faces several formidable challenges. For these reasons, it makes sense to consider a different hypothesis.

6.5 An alternative hypothesis: norm-governed moves

The second hypothesis appeals to the norm-enacting feature of moves in norm-governed activities. If an action involving pornography constitutes a move in a norm-governed activity, then that action enacts an s-norm (permissibility fact) for that activity. If that enacted s-norm subordinates women, then so does the pornography-involving action that enacts it. In this way, it is possible for actions involving pornography to subordinate women.

[41] Saul makes this point especially forcefully using the example of an 'I do' sign that is used to perform a variety of illocutionary acts in a variety of contexts. See Saul 2006: 229–48.

[42] In response, one might argue that (certain sorts of pornography) have standard uses. Just as the locution 'I am tall' is standardly used to assert the proposition that the speaker is tall, so too, the argument might go, these hierarchy-endorsing types of pornography are standardly used to enact permissibility facts that subordinate women. If this could be established, then it would make sense to talk about the (standard) force of (this subset of) pornography.

Notice first that we are no longer exclusively concerned with speech. We know that speech covertly enacts norms when the utterance in question is a move in a norm-governed activity. Since non-speech actions can be moves in norm-governed activities, non-speech action can enact norms in this covert manner too. To this end, consider the following examples of pornography-involving actions.

Case 1: Joe works at a factory where most of the employees are male. He hangs a pornographic poster in his locker at work.

Case 2: Peter is on a first date and wants to seem manly and able so, after dinner, once he and his date have returned to his apartment and started kissing on the couch, he starts a pornographic film on his DVD player.[43]

Case 3: Patrick is at a philosophy of science conference and he joins two women in conversation. Quickly turning the topic towards the utility of the Internet, Patrick goes on at length about how he is able to access and download all sorts of violent pornography.[44]

Each of these cases is underspecified. Further facts about the context in each example will make a difference with respect to what the pornography-involving actions do or mean. We need to know more about the people and the relationships between them, the background shared assumptions, the broader social context, the nature of the pornographic materials involved, and the intentions and awareness of participants. Notice that each of these things that make a difference will be captured by some aspect of the current framework: their further specification will affect either the score, the g-norms, or the particular move made. Moreover, while these details will affect which particular s-norms are enacted in each case, it is clear that each of the pornography-involving actions in each of the three above cases will enact s-norms of some sort no matter how such contextual details are specified.

This is because each of the above pornography-involving actions is a move in a norm-governed activity. Although each of these actions may well constitute moves in several different norm-governed activities

[43] I thank Anne Eaton for suggesting a slight revision of this example.

[44] This is based on a real case; it happened during the first philosophy conference I ever attended. It is also interesting because it concerns speech about pornography (as opposed to pornography or pornography understood as speech).

simultaneously, I here focus on contributions these actions make to the (rather general) norm-governed activity of social relations. Recall that an action is a move in a norm-governed activity just in case it is governed by the g-norms of that activity. Since these actions are each contributions to a social interaction, they are each thereby governed by the g-norms of social interactions generally and are thus moves in that practice. As such, these actions enact s-norms in the particular token instance of that (norm-governed) activity.[45] Of course, they are each contributions to different sorts of social interactions. Case 1 involves co-worker interaction. Case 2 involves heterosexual dating and case 3 involves interactions at a professional academic conference. These more specific sorts of social interaction will be governed by more specific g-norms.

Recall again that being a move requires only that the action be governed by the relevant g-norms; it does not require that the action abide by those g-norms. Thus, even in cases where an action is clearly out of bounds, it nevertheless constitutes a move so long as it is a contribution to that norm-governed activity. Inappropriate contributions are still contributions and thus moves.

Of course, to say that these actions constitute moves in the norm-governed activity of social interactions shows only that these actions enact s-norms. It does not establish what those s-norms are and thus it does not show both that and how actions involving pornography can subordinate women. To do that, we need to further specify a case. In the following section, we explore various instantiations of Case 1.

6.5.1 *Case 1 explored*

Case 1 could be instantiated in a whole host of different ways. One of the things that matters is Joe's state of mind when he hangs the poster. What was Joe thinking and what was he trying to do when he hung the poster? There are many possibilities and they differ considerably. It could be that Joe is intending to intimidate a female co-worker when he hangs the poster; his action could even be a threat. Suppose that he has been stalking this co-worker for months; she is pretty sure that Joe recently killed her cat, and Joe glares menacingly at her as he hangs the poster while she watches. In a case like this (even if we could not prove it in a

[45] The precise scope of the enacted s-norms is here left open. See Chapter 7 section 7.4.2.1 for a discussion of this issue.

court of law), Joe's action is threatening and it may even be a threat. A very different sort of case involves Joe intending to flirt with his co-worker. Although flirting in the workplace may be misguided and flirting in the workplace via pornography even more so, this is a very different sort of Case 1.

Both of these instances of Case 1 involve Joe having communicative intentions of some sort. In the first case, Joe intends to communicate an intention to intimidate and, in the second, he intends to communicate his sexual-romantic interest. Of course, there are plenty of other communicative intentions Joe could have but it is also possible that he has no such communicative intention. Joe might not *mean* anything at all when he is hanging the pornographic poster in his workplace. It could be that Joe is just an oblivious guy decorating his locker at work. Thus, the action of hanging that poster need not be a communicative act at all. Clearly, differences in Joe's state of mind make a difference to the case.

Facts about the poster matter too. If the poster depicts a violent and degrading sexual image, then hanging it in the workplace is a very different sort of act than hanging a sexually explicit poster that is neither of these things. These are all instances of Case 1 but they each involve different actions of hanging a pornographic poster in a workplace; they are different moves.

Other things matter too. How Joe's action is interpreted by others also makes a difference. His act of hanging the poster might be interpreted as a communicative act when it was not. Or, it could be that Joe was intending to communicate his romantic interest to a certain female co-worker; she took it to be an act of aggression; all the other employees recognized Joe's communicative intentions but they disagreed about whether his attempted communicative act was successful. All of these recognition and interpretation differences potentially make a difference to the case. So do differences in how people react to Joe's act. The reaction could be excitement, offense, fear, indifference, amusement, and or any number of other responses.

Another thing that matters—and it matters quite a lot—is the context in which Joe performs his action. What is this workplace like? What has happened in that work environment prior to Joe's action? In what follows, I describe different workplace environments each involving a (fictional) female employee named Karen; each such description is also based on an actual legal case involving pornography in the workplace.

Work Environment 1: In this workplace, employees "show blatant disrespect for their marital vows" by having non-discreet extra-marital affairs with co-workers; they watch pornography in their offices, use filthy language, tell sexually explicit jokes, and exchange sexually suggestive gifts. Other non-professional behavior includes openly selling Avon products and gambling during work time. Although known to be offensive to an employee named Karen, none of this behavior is directed at Karen. The description of this workplace environment is based loosely on the (U.S.) case *Yuknis v. First Student Inc.*[46]

Work Environment 2: In this workplace, Karen is a receptionist for a supervisor who watches pornography daily for two to three hours in his office and she can see the pornography through a glass partition between their offices. Her supervisor also uses her computer on the weekends to view pornographic sites and her job responsibilities require opening her supervisor's mail, which routinely includes pornographic materials. Although Karen is exposed to pornography in her workplace and although the performance of her job makes that exposure unavoidable, the pornographic materials are not directed at her. This description of a workplace setting is based loosely on the U.S. case *Pakane v. Clart.*[47]

Work Environment 3: Karen is raped by a fellow employee while both are living in a company residential facility and she reports the rape to her supervisors and then to law enforcement. Fellow employees retaliate against Karen by refusing to support her while on the job even in emergency situations, advising her to leave the job, lodging repeated complaints against her, filing unfair evaluations of her performance, excluding her from duties she ought to have been performing, and harassing her with pornography and gendered verbal abuse. This example

[46] See *Yuknis v. First Student Inc.*

[47] See *Patane v. Clark.* This was a hostile work environment suit that was ultimately successful even though the problematic actions (most of them involved pornographic materials) were not directed at the claimant. This case is understood as establishing that the mere presence of pornography in the workplace lowers the status of women and thus can contribute to a hostile working environment. In fact, the official website of the Massachusetts Commission Against Discrimination states: "Employers should specifically prohibit the dissemination of sexually explicit voice mail, e-mail, graphics, downloaded material or websites in the workplace and include these prohibitions in their workplace policies."

is based loosely on the (U.K. case) *Waters v. Commissioner of Police of the Metropolis.*[48]

Clearly, the culture of a particular work environment also makes a difference. This should be no surprise. Since all relevant facts about the work context are tracked by the score, these different work environments have different scores. Moreover, differences in the score at the time of the move typically result in different s-norms being enacted. Thus, even in the simple case where Joe has no communicative intentions whatsoever, hanging the very same pornographic poster in these different workplace environments will likely enact quite different s-norms.

Thus far, I have not said what the enacted s-norms are. Which particular s-norms are enacted in any particular case will depend on the move (in this case, the hanging of the pornographic poster), the score (that is, on what has transpired so far in the norm-governed activity in question) and the g-norms governing the activity in question. Without complete knowledge of these things, one cannot be absolutely certain which particular s-norms are enacted on any particular occasion. That said and without all of the requisite socio-scientific research at hand, one can nevertheless make an educated guess. Let us now return to some instances of Case 1.

Suppose that Joe has no communicative intentions whatsoever when he hangs the poster; the poster is not hard-core and Joe's workplace is similar to Work Environment 1. This may seem to be a fairly innocuous case but we nevertheless have reason to believe that subordinating s-norms are here enacted. To see this, notice first that gender norms inform all other social roles.[49] This means that the g-norms governing co-worker interactions are gendered and they are gendered in a way that tends to disadvantage women relative to men. Second, an action pragmatically presupposes its own appropriateness. This means that hanging a pornographic poster at work pragmatically presupposes that it is appropriate to do so and this appears to require gender-problematic norms. Perhaps the assumption is that there should not be any women in this workplace (because, for example, the work done at this factory requires skill, knowledge, and physical strength and is thus appropriate only for men). Perhaps instead the assumption is that women are and ought to be judged in terms of their appearance and attractiveness to

[48] See *Waters v. Commissioner of Police of the Metropolis.*

[49] See Witt 2011.

men. By operating as if such g-norms are in place, Joe's action thereby enacts those norms (s-norms) and thus brings these broader social practices to bear in the micro-context of this work environment. Although there are various g-norms potentially implicated by Joe's action, at least some of them subordinate women.

Such s-norms may be introduced by Joe's action or they may already be operative in Joe's environment. Even if such s-norms are already operative in Joe's workplace, though, his action nevertheless perpetuates (and in fact re-enacts) those very s-norms. As we know from the previous chapter, since permissibility facts are social constructions, they ontologically depend on a complex form of collective recognition.[50] Because of this, there is an important sense in which permissibility facts must be perpetually re-enacted.[51] Thus, even if the subordinating s-norms are already operative in the context of Joe's action, his act of hanging the poster nevertheless re-enacts those norms by tacitly relying on them. Thus, if the enacted s-norms subordinate women, so does the pornographic-poster-hanging action that enacts those norms. As one can see, actions involving pornography can constitute the subordination of women.

Notice that Joe's action can subordinate women *whether or not participants realize that it does.* Even though Joe does not intend to communicate anything by hanging this poster and even if no one else regards it as an act of subordination, the hypothesis put forward here is that the norm-governed nature of the activity to which he is (perhaps unknowingly) contributing is sufficient to generate the resulting (subordinating) s-norms. Performing that action in that context is tantamount to performing a move in the norm-governed system of co-worker relations and the nature of that move, combined with the context (i.e. score) and the (gendered) g-norms operative in that system are sufficient to enact s-norms that subordinate women. This alternative hypothesis shows not just how pornography can be used to subordinate women, it also shows how this can be both unintentional and unrecognized.

It is not hard to see how other versions of Case 1 might also subordinate women. After all, our reasons for thinking that Joe's action enacts subordinating s-norms are only strengthened in cases where Joe has

[50] See Searle 1995.

[51] This perpetual re-enactment may well be what Judith Butler means by reiteration. See Butler 1997. See also Chapter 5 section 5.4.2.

malevolent intentions towards a particular female co-worker when he hangs the poster, or when the pornographic materials are violent and degrading, or in cases where Joe's workplace is already extremely hostile.

What about a case in which Joe has no communicative intentions when hanging the poster and his workplace is egalitarian and gender just? Even in a case like this, subordinating s-norms are likely to be enacted (although they may not obtain for long). Joe's action still pragmatically presupposes its appropriateness and this requires gender-problematic g-norms. Since Joe's workplace is by hypothesis egalitarian, those s-norms do not obtain prior to Joe's action. Thus, much like the slam poetry case from the previous chapter, his action introduces gender-problematic s-norms to his environment. His action brings broader social g-norms to bear in the micro-context of Joe's workplace. How long these s-norms remain operative will depend on many things (including the nature of the relevant g-norms) but it will also clearly depend on the reaction of others. If others object, their actions also constitute moves that enact s-norms likely to counteract those enacted by Joe's action.

6.5.2 *On the role of intentions*

As argued above, various factors make a difference with respect to which particular s-norms are enacted and one of the things that matter is Joe's intentions when hanging the poster. It makes a difference what Joe is intending to do (e.g. intimidate, flirt, or communicate nothing at all). That this is so may seem to conflict with my earlier claim that intentions do not play a crucial role. After all, I have been stressing that covert exercitives (and this covert mechanism of norm-enactment) do not depend on intentions in the way that standard exercitives do.

This tension is merely apparent. There are different sorts of intentions at play and there are also different respects with which something may matter. The intention to intimidate (or to flirt) is distinct from the intention to enact permissibility facts (or s-norms). I have been stressing that enacting s-norms does not require (a conscious and explicit) intention to do so. It requires only performing an action that is a move in a norm-governed activity.

That this is so is perfectly compatible with other sorts of intentions mattering in various ways. Other sorts of intentions can affect the moral valence of an action and they can thus change the nature of the move constituted by an action. Doing something harmful on purpose is, in an important way, worse than doing it by accident.[52] Thus, the presence of such intentions (especially if they are successfully communicated) rightly affects our moral evaluation of an action. Furthermore, the presence of such intentions can change which move one is making and thus which particular s-norm is enacted. In sum, that actor (/speaker) intention and participant awareness matter in *these* ways, however, in no way undermines the above claim that the enacting of permissibility facts via the performing of a move in norm-governed activity does *not* depend on a conscious and explicit intention to do so.

6.6 Silencing

MacKinnon also claims that pornography *silences* women.[53] This silencing claim is complex and it is situated within an even more complex argumentative framework. It is therefore prudent to first explicitly distinguish some issues. One issue concerns the alleged relationship between pornography and silencing. How exactly does pornography or actions involving it bring such silencing about? On the standard (that is, most discussed) account, pornography consumption *causes* silencing.[54] In what follows, however, I shall focus on the possibility that pornography actually enacts or *constitutes* silencing. If actions involving pornography enact permissibility facts (s-norms) constitutive of some type of silencing, then that pornography-involving action silences.

[52] Strawson stresses this in relation to his discussion of reactive attitudes. See Strawson 1982.

[53] See, for example, MacKinnon 1987 and 1993. MacKinnon also claims that silencing is a violation of the right to free speech but I do not explore that issue here. In so far as silencing constitutes a systematic form of communicative interference, a case can be made that it constitutes a free speech violation. For a helpful discussion of this, see West 2003.

[54] On the standard way of interpreting this, pornography consumption alters consumers' beliefs (about how women behave and ought to behave in sexual contexts) by depicting scenarios allegedly expressive of these descriptive and normative claims about women. So, for example, if one consumes pornography depicting women who enjoy being brutalized during sexual encounters, (some) consumers might come to believe that (all or some) women enjoy (or ought to enjoy) being brutalized during sexual encounters. These altered beliefs then interfere with the consumer's interpretation of women's speech acts during sexual encounters thereby silencing the women in question. There are other (less conscious) ways in which pornography might cause consumers' beliefs to change. Pornography may condition its consumers. See, for example, MacKinnon 1993: 16 and Scoccia 1996. Alternatively, pornography consumption might trigger unconscious imitation mechanisms. For a discussion of this, see Hurley 2004 and Langton 2011. Hurley concentrates on media violence and is not directly concerned with pornography.

Another issue concerns the phenomenon of silencing itself. What exactly is it? In short, it is some kind of interference with, or prevention of, communication.[55] In this chapter, I focus on attempted, but communicatively thwarted, speech acts. I shall identify several different types of communicative impairment. By identifying various ways that a speech act can go wrong, we shall be able to identify various types of interference and hence various types of silencing.

Another issue concerns the relationship between silencing and the free speech right. MacKinnon famously claims that silencing violates that right.[56] This claim is controversial.[57] Here, I am not concerned with the relationship between silencing and the free speech right or with how that relationship feeds into potential arguments for the further regulation of pornographic materials. I am merely exploring how this mechanism of covert norm enactment can highlight constitutive connections between pornography and silencing.

6.6.1 *On refusals*

The silencing literature has thus far focused on the speech act of sexual refusal.[58] The basic idea is that pornography and the practice of producing, distributing, and consuming it somehow interferes with women's

[55] I here focus on attempts to communicate that are thwarted by recognition failures but other phenomena also deserve to be called silencing. Being prevented from even trying to communicate, for example, can also be silencing. For an example of this, see Dotson's (2011) work on testimonial smothering. See also Crenshaw 1991 and Collins 2000. Having one's (successful) communications receive less credibility than is warranted is another potential type of silencing. Some call this testimonial quieting (Dotson 2011). Others call it testimonial injustice (Fricker 2007). Most require that the phenomenon must be systematic in order to count as silencing. One exception to this is Emerick, who regards any instance of communication prevention as an instance of silencing. See his "The Violence of Silencing," an unpublished manuscript. Emerick regards silencing as ubiquitous, not always problematic, and he is primarily concerned with ways that instances of it can constitute violence. Maitra (2009) also has a broad conception of silencing according to which only some instances of it are concerning.

[56] See especially MacKinnon 1993.

[57] For a careful and persuasive defense, see West 2003.

[58] This focus on refusals is problematic. First, it relies on the consent model of sexual communication and this model is widely and rightly criticized. See, for example, Anderson 2005: 101–40. Second, it encourages a false and extremely impoverished understanding of sexual communication. For a discussion of this, See Kukla 2018, unpublished manuscript. Recall that the silencing literature arose out of (some of) MacKinnon's legal arguments and *the law* operates with this consent model. This helps to explain (but does not justify) the current focus on refusals.

ability to successfully perform sexual refusals. Although the various sorts of silencing to be identified here can apply to any sort of speech act, I nevertheless keep with the literature (and simultaneously simplify discussion) by focusing on refusals.

The first order of business therefore is to offer a speech act account of (sexual) refusals.[59] What sort of speech act is it and what are the felicity conditions for its successful performance? Although it may seem that sexual refusal is a mere matter of communicating a certain proposition (namely, that the speaker is not willing to have sex with the addressee), this cannot be correct. To see this, suppose that Sally successfully communicates to Carl that Cindy is not willing to have sex with him. Even supposing that the circumstances are such that Sally's utterance rightly convinces Carl that Cindy is not willing to have sex with him, Sally's utterance is not a sexual refusal.[60] Although Sally's utterance may constitute sufficient evidence that Cindy *would* refuse, nothing that *Sally* communicates to Carl can constitute *Cindy's* refusal.[61] Furthermore, even if Cindy successfully communicates to Carl that she (Cindy) is unwilling to have sex with him (Carl), this communicative act alone is, strictly speaking, insufficient for sexual refusal. More is required.[62]

It is intuitively clear (perhaps even obvious) that refusals concern permission. Since either granting or denying permission requires authority, refusals appear to be authoritative speech acts. In fact, they are (standard) exercitive speech acts.[63] When Cindy says 'No' in response to Carl's sexual advances, Cindy sexually refuses exactly because she

[59] The following discussion borrows from my 2009a. For a critical engagement with that view, see Caponetto 2017. For a response and development of authority silencing, see Mason 2018.

[60] Suppose, for example, that Carl knows that Sally knows what Cindy is willing to do and Carl that knows that Sally is telling the truth. In such a case, Sally's utterance would be sufficient evidence for believing that Cindy is not willing to have sex with Carl.

[61] I do think that it is possible for one person to refuse on behalf of another. Kate may, for example, refuse a party invitation on behalf of her husband Jim. She is able to do so, though, only because she has somehow been authorized to do so. If this is correct (and this speaker authority condition will be motivated in what follows) then Kate's refusal on Jim's behalf also requires her exercise of that transferred authority. I thank Ishani Maitra for raising this worry.

[62] This account is more fully motivated and defended in my 2009a.

[63] Ishani Maitra (2009)disagrees. She says: "All that is needed for a successful performance of refusal is that the audience recognize the speaker's intention to refuse" Maitra 2009: 322. Although Maitra qualifies this claim, she does not require a speaker authority condition.

thereby denies Carl permission to proceed.[64] Having authority over who has sexual access to her body, Cindy is here exercising that authority when she sexually refuses him. Sally cannot refuse on Cindy's behalf exactly because Sally lacks the requisite authority (over who has sexual access to *Cindy's* body).

Now, in the case of sexual refusal, this speaker authority condition may seem somewhat peculiar. After all, it may seem that everyone has (or at least ought to have) the requisite authority and this might make this particular condition seem automatically satisfied and thus trivial. First, even if it is true that everyone has the requisite authority, it is nevertheless important to note that this condition also requires that the speaker is actually *exercising* this authority on the particular occasion in question. As a result, this condition is not automatically satisfied. Second, one might deny that everyone actually has the requisite authority. Suppose, for instance, that all authority is socially constructed. On this view, being recognized (in certain complex ways) as having authority is constitutive of having it. Perhaps, for example, in some contexts, slaves do not have the requisite authority to sexually refuse the slave's owner. If authority requires its recognition, authority is not guaranteed.[65]

6.6.2 *On various types of silencing*

Silencing involves interference with speech acts and their communication and this interference is brought about by (various types of) recognition failure.[66] By looking at different ways that refusals can go wrong, we will be able to identify different types of recognition failure and thus different types of silencing. As standard exercitives, refusals are fairly complex speech acts. Their successful performance requires the satisfaction of a variety of conditions and, as a result, there are several different ways for refusals to be faulty. In what follows, I consider (just) some of those ways.

[64] Again, this consent model of sexuality is problematic. For starters, it seems to presuppose that one person (typically a male) is the initiator or proposer of sexual activity and the other person (typically a female) accepts or declines that proposal. For a discussion of this sort of criticism, see Anderson 2005: 131 and MacKinnon 2005.

[65] A person might have moral, but lack legal, authority.

[66] Again, I am here focusing on attempted but (systematically) thwarted speech acts. Other sorts of phenomena can also be silencing. See note 55.

First, a refusal can go awry if, for whatever reason, the addressee fails to realize that the speaker is intending to refuse. Suppose, for example, that Deirdre says, "May I use your hairdryer" and I say, "No" intending to thereby refuse her request. If Deirdre is so used to getting her own way that it is utterly inconceivable to her that anyone would ever refuse her, then she will fail to recognize my intention to refuse. When this happens, the refusal in question is non-ideal. My uttering of 'No' is a less than ideal refusal (if it is a refusal at all) exactly because the addressee (in this case Deirdre) fails to recognize my intention to refuse.[67]

Second, a refusal will be undermined if the addressee fails to realize that the speaker authority condition is met.[68] In particular, the addressee may fail to realize that the speaker has the requisite authority to refuse. Suppose, for instance, that my department chair tells me that I cannot have a professional leave but I falsely believe that only the dean can do this. In this case, I fail to realize that the speaker is in a position to refuse my leave request. The chair's refusal is non-ideal precisely because I falsely believe that she is unable to refuse.

A third way for refusals to go wrong is for the addressee to fail to recognize that the speaker is sincere. If I say, 'No' sincerely intending to refuse but the addressee, for some reason, falsely believes that I am doing so insincerely, then my refusal will be less than ideal. A sincere refusal that is falsely believed to be insincere is a less than ideal refusal. As one can see, the recognition of the sincerity intention matters too.

Fourth, a refusal will be non-ideal if the addressee falsely believes that the refusal does not accurately reflect the speaker's true feelings.[69] Suppose, for example, that a husband knows (or thinks he knows) that his wife is just confused or that she is soon going to change her mind anyway so although she is refusing (and he realizes that the various conditions for a sincere refusal are met), he nevertheless dismisses her refusal on the grounds that it does not reflect

[67] Austin, Langton, and Hornsby regard uptake (i.e. hearer recognition of the speaker's illocutionary intention) to be a necessary condition for illocution. See Austin 1975: 22, 116, and 139; Langton 1993; Hornsby 1993; 1995; Hornsby and Langton 1998.

[68] There are actually two components to the speaker authority condition (i.e. the speaker must have authority and the speaker must be exercising that authority at the time of utterance) and the recognition of either can fail. I here focus on the first.

[69] I thank Lauren Ashwell for encouraging me to consider this type of case.

what he thinks she really wants. If this happens, then the wife's refusal is non-ideal.[70]

Although I have here identified four distinct ways that refusals can go awry, there are plenty of others. To identify just a few more: A refusal will also be defective if the addressee fails to correctly identify the content of the utterance, if the addressee is wrong about the speaker's perlocutionary intentions or if the addressee is wrong about the speaker's reasons for refusing. We have here but a mere sampling. In the next four subsections I argue that each of these four ways corresponds to a different type of silencing.[71]

6.6.2.1 TYPE 1: FAILURE TO RECOGNIZE THE INTENTION TO REFUSE

Jennifer Hornsby and Rae Langton have offered the first (and the most widely discussed) account of silencing.[72] Silencing, in their sense, is a certain kind of linguistic interference constituted by uptake failure (that is, the addressee's failure to recognize the speaker's intention to refuse).[73] It is important to note that not every instance of uptake failure is

[70] By focusing on this case, I am by no means suggesting that this is the most likely explanation for why someone might fail to respect a refusal. Indeed it is not. Finlayson (2014) seems to assume that the silencing literature is trying to explain why rape happens. This is a misunderstanding; the silencing literature is identifying various speech-related harms along with their free speech impact. See Finlayson 2014. Note also that failing to respect a refusal is a temporally extended action. A refusal can be retracted by consent at any moment and consent can be retracted by refusal at any moment. A refusal at first ignored can coerce and thus cause merely apparent consent. Genuine consent must therefore be distinguished from simply giving up resistance.

[71] These four types are by no means exhaustive. Davies (2014) identifies an interesting silencing phenomenon (overlapping with some of the others) that can occur during the cross-examination of a rape claimant. Wyatt (2009) explores the potential role of second-order meaning conventions in type 1 silencing. Maitra (2009) offers an account of Type 1, focusing on the recognition of communicative, as opposed to illocutionary, intentions. Wieland (2009) focuses on the role of first-order meaning conventions in Type 1. Dotson (2011) explores phenomena the prevent communication and/or prevent it from having an appropriate effect on socially shared knowledge. See also Collins 2000; Fricker 2007. For a discussion of the related phenomenon of gaslighting, see Abramson 2014 and McKinnon 2017. McKinney (2016) explores unjust ways that speech can be forced or extracted.

[72] See Hornsby 1993; 1995; Langton 1993; Hornsby and Langton 1998; and Langton 1998.

[73] Two objections to the Hornsby and Langton account of Type 1 have been prevalent in the literature. For the objection that Hornsby and Langton are wrong about the role of uptake, see Jacobson 1995 and Bird 2002. For my response, see McGowan et al. 2011. See also Mikkola 2011 and Grunberg 2014. For various versions of the objection that Hornsby and Langton's account of silencing undermines the responsibility of rapists, see Bird 2002;

silencing according to Hornsby or Langton. It is silencing only when it is brought about in a systematic manner.[74]

This systematicity condition is underspecified in the literature. It is clear that some such condition is required because one-off idiosyncratic cases of uptake failure should not count as silencing. Suppose, for example, that my son fails to recognize my intention to order him to clean his room because he is distracted by an amazing racecar that happens to drive by. In this case, Shea's failure to recognize my intention to order him does not and should not count as an instance of this type of silencing. Only cases of uptake failure that are brought about in a systematic manner count as silencing. Whether this systematicity condition requires that the recognition failure be widespread, caused by widespread beliefs, likely to be made by others under similar circumstances, brought about by following prescriptive norms, or implicated in oppressive social structures is unclear. I henceforth leave this open but take the systematicity condition to do the requisite work.[75]

Suppose that a woman says, 'No' intending to refuse sex but the addressee fails to realize that she intends to refuse. In such a case, (and so long as the uptake failure is brought about in a systematic manner) the woman is silenced in the manner identified by Hornsby and Langton. This is an instance of Type 1 silencing.

6.6.2.2 TYPE 2: FAILURE TO RECOGNIZE THE SPEAKER AUTHORITY CONDITION

Elsewhere, I have identified a different type of silencing, constituted by systematic interference with the recognition of the speaker authority condition.[76] Suppose that a woman says 'No' intending thereby to refuse sex; the addressee recognizes her intention to refuse, but falsely believes that she does not have the authority to do so.[77] As a result, the addressee

Jacobson 1995; and Wieland 2009. For responses, see Maitra and McGowan 2010 and McGowan et al. 2011. For a different response, see Mikkola 2011.

[74] Maitra offers a similar (Gricean as opposed to Austinian) account of silencing. For Maitra, all cases of uptake failure constitute silencing but she is concerned with only some cases of silencing that meet additional conditions. See Maitra 2009.

[75] For a discussion of this under-discussed systematicity condition, see McGowan et al. 2016. See also Maitra 2004. See also note 55.

[76] See my 2009a.

[77] Caponetto (2017) argues that there is an internal tension on my account. For Caponetto, refusals are a negative response to a certain kind of (open call) request for

falsely believes that the attempted refusal fails. When this happens for systematic reasons, the woman is silenced in a different sense. She is silenced because her refusal is not communicated; it is mistaken as a failed refusal.[78] This recognition failure is caused by the addressee's false belief that she does not have authority over who has sexual access to her body. Since type 2 also involves communicative failure, it too is a type of silencing.

Since the recognition failure with type 2 silencing is different from the recognition failure with type 1 silencing, the communicative failure is also different. Distinct communicative failures mean distinct types of silencing. With type 1, the speech act is not even taken as an attempted refusal. With type 2, by contrast, it is taken as an attempted but failed refusal.

Notice that type 2 silencing can occur when the distribution of social power is extremely unjust. Suppose, for example, that a female slave tries to sexually refuse her male master. Although the master may recognize her intention to refuse him, she will be silenced in this second way if he nevertheless fails to realize that she has the authority to refuse him. (When the law failed to recognize marital rape, for instance, a wife lacked the *legal* authority to refuse her husband.) If the master believes, for example, that his female slave is his property, then he may well also believe that it is he (and not she) who has authority over who has sexual access to her body. Similar silencing can occur when a husband, for example, believes that his wife cannot refuse him or when a paying customer believes that sex workers cannot refuse.[79]

6.6.2.3 TYPE 3: FAILURE TO RECOGNIZE THE SINCERITY CONDITION

Elsewhere I have argued for a third type of silencing that is constituted by systematic interference with the recognition of the sincerity condition.[80] Consider a case in which a woman says 'No' intending to refuse sex but, although the addressee recognizes her intention to refuse, he mistakenly

permission and that request pragmatically presupposes the speaker's recognition of the requisite authority. See Mason (2018) for a response.

[78] This is a departure from my earlier view (2009a) when I denied that authority silencing is communicative failure.

[79] Type 2 silencing is likely to undermine other sorts of authoritative speech acts (besides refusal) and may well affect persons in virtue of membership in other socially marked groups.

[80] This type of silencing is developed and defended in McGowan 2014.

believes that she is doing so insincerely.[81] Since the addressee recognizes her intention to refuse, there is no uptake failure in this case. As a result, she is not type 1 silenced. The problem here is that the addressee mistakenly believes that she is refusing insincerely. In cases where the speaker intends to communicate her sincerity (as is the case with most refusals), the addressee's failure to recognize the speaker's sincerity means that the speaker has failed to communicate her sincerity (even if she manages to communicate her refusal). Since type 3 involves a distinct communicative failure, it too is a distinct type of silencing.

6.6.2.4 TYPE 4: FAILING TO RECOGNIZE THE SPEAKER'S TRUE FEELINGS

A fourth type of silencing involves the addressee failing to recognize that a refusal reflects the speaker's true feelings. Suppose that a woman says 'No,' sincerely intending to refuse sex, but although the addressee recognizes her sincere refusal, the addressee nevertheless falsely believes that refusing is not what the speaker's "deep self" really wants. Suppose, for example, that the addressee believes that the woman will change her mind as soon as she realizes how amazing he is or as soon as he talks her out of her Catholic guilt. In a case like this, the addressee realizes that the speaker sincerely intends to refuse when she says 'No' but the addressee falsely believes that the speaker is herself mistaken about her true and innermost desires. If the addressee's mistake about the speaker's true feelings is brought about systematically, then this is yet another type of silencing. Since the illocutionary intention to refuse is recognized in this case, it is not type 1 silencing. Since the speaker's exercise of authority is recognized in this case, it is not an instance of type 2 silencing. Finally, since the speaker's sincerity is recognized, it is not an example of type 3 silencing. As one can see, the recognition failure in this case is distinct from the recognition failures involved in each of the other three types of silencing.

This recognition failure also constitutes communicative failure. After all, speech acts pragmatically presuppose that speakers are credible testifiers about their own internal states. Thus, if a speaker intends to communicate that her refusal reflects her true feelings (as speakers who

[81] West (2003: 400) considers this case, distinguishes it from Hornsby and Langton (1998) silencing, but does not treat it as a type of silencing.

refuse typically do), then the addressee's failure to recognize this constitutes a communicative failure. Since the recognition failure and hence the communicative failure is distinct, this constitutes a fourth type of silencing.[82]

6.6.3 *On constitutive connection to pornography*

Let us now consider how pornography or actions involving it might potentially constitute these types of silencing. Recall that constituting the harm of silencing is really just a very specific way of causing it; it would involve causing that type of silencing by enacting a norm such that the type of silencing in question results from adhering to (or following) that norm. In other words, the enacted permissibility facts (s-norms) govern the silencing practice in question. Thus, if a pornography-involving action enacts s-norms that prescribe some type of silencing, then that pornography-involving action enacts or constitutes that type of silencing.

Since there are two ways to enact norms (via an exercise of speaker authority and by contributing to norm-governed activities), there are two ways to enact norms that silence. I consider each in turn.

6.6.3.1 EXERCISE OF AUTHORITY

One way for pornography to silence via an exercise of authority is for pornography to be a standard exercitive (that enacts norms that silence). This hypothesis requires treating pornography as a speech act and, in particular, as a standard exercitive speech. We have already (in Section 5.3.1) seen how this hypothesis fares. Pornography does not seem to have the requisite authority; it does not seem to intend to enact norms and it is not generally taken as doing so. It also does not seem to function at the conscious level of communicated intentions as speech acts do. These are all reasons to doubt that pornography is a standard exercitive speech act.

There is another way for pornography to be (or to be involved in) a standard exercitive speech act. Instead of treating pornography en masse as a speech act, one might instead consider particular actions involving pornography. It is certainly possible for a person with authority to use pornography when communicating an intention to exercise his or her

[82] Again, I am not claiming that this explains why rape happens. See note 70.

authority over someone in order to enact certain permissibility facts. Moreover, if the enacted permissibility facts silence, then so would the pornography-involving action that enacts those permissibility facts. Although pornography *could be* used in communicative acts that silence in this way, such cases would be relatively rare. After all, several fairly specific conditions would be required. The agent would need to have and be exercising the requisite authority; the agent would need to intend to enact the permissibility facts in question; those permissibility facts would need to silence; and hearers would need to recognize the agent's intention to enact those very permissibility facts. So although it is *possible* for actions involving pornography to silence via this mechanism, it seems that actual cases will be few and far between.

6.6.3.2 MOVES IN NORM-GOVERNED ACTIVITIES

Of course, there is another way for pornography (or actions involving it) to silence: Pornography-involving actions can enact silencing permissibility facts (s-norms) by making moves in norm-governed activities. If a certain action involving pornography (say, the action of viewing a particular piece of pornography on a particular occasion or the action of hanging a pornographic poster at work) is a move in some norm-governed activity, then that action will trigger the g-norms of that activity thereby enacting s-norms (permissibility facts). Now, if it turns out that some such actions involving pornography enact s-norms that silence, then so does the pornography involving action that enacts those s-norms.

6.6.3.3 NORMS THAT SILENCE

Thus far we have considered how pornography or people performing speech acts with pornography or actions involving pornography might enact norms. I turn now to a consideration of which norms might constitute the different types of silencing and which types of pornography might be associated with those norms.

Consider a pornographic scenario in which the uttering of 'No' counts merely as a way to sexually excite the addressee. In such scenarios, the perlocutionary effect of sexually exciting the addressee is portrayed as all that matters. (Any illocutionary or communicative intentions are presented as utterly beside the point.) Consider now an action (non-incidentally) involving this type of pornography. As a move in a norm-governed activity, we know that this action enacts s-norms. Perhaps, in some contexts, this action would enact an s-norm to the effect that uttering 'No' counts merely as an attempt to sexually excite the addressee (but it does not count as a refusal). If this action were to enact this s-norm, then it would enact s-norms constitutive of type 1 silencing. For if the illocutionary intention to refuse is made irrelevant in this way, then abiding by this s-norm will involve systematic failure to recognize the intention to refuse thereby constituting type 1 silencing. This is one way that an action involving pornography could enact type 1 silencing.

Consider now type 2 silencing, which is constituted by systematic interference with the recognition of the speaker authority condition. Some pornography depicts women as sexual objects to be used and not as autonomous agents with wills to be respected. An action (non-incidentally) involving this sort of pornography might, in some contexts, enact an s-norm to the effect that (some) women (or some women sometimes) do not have the authority to sexually refuse. If such an s-norm were in place, this would bring about systematic interference with the recognition of the speaker authority condition thereby constituting this second type of silencing. Since the pornographic-involving action enacts this s-norm, it thereby constitutes type 2 silencing.

Recall that type 3 silencing is constituted by systematic interference with the recognition of the speaker sincerity condition. With an eye towards identifying a sort of pornography that might enact this sort of silencing, consider a pornographic scenario where the woman says 'No' but in which she is depicted as clearly communicating her sexual consent. Actions involving this type of pornography might, in some contexts, enact an s-norm to the effect that saying 'No' counts as an insincere refusal (and cannot count as a sincere one). Since abiding by this s-norm would systematically bring about interference with the recognition of the speaker sincerity condition, the enacting of this s-norm constitutes this third type of silencing. Therefore any action enacting such an s-norm would also constitute the parallel act of (type 3) silencing.

Finally, consider type 4 silencing. This type of silencing is constituted by systematic failure to recognize the speaker's true feelings of refusal. What sort of pornography might constitute this type of silencing? Consider rape myth pornography. It depicts women who sincerely refuse but who then enjoy being raped. Perhaps rape myth pornography (or actions involving it) enacts an s-norm to the effect that one ought to operate on the assumption that women want sex even when the women think they don't. Abiding by this s-norm will systematically prevent the recognition of the speaker's true feelings of refusal thus constituting type 4 silencing.

As one can see, there are certainly candidate norms for each of the four types of silencing. Moreover, there are probably plenty of other norms that prescribe each of the four types. Thus, if pornography (or actions involving it) enacts any one of these s-norms and if following them results in some type of silencing, then the pornography-involving action constitutes, rather than merely causes, that type of silencing.

6.7 Conclusion

In this chapter, we have explored two provocative claims about what (some) pornography does. In particular, we have explored the claim that it subordinates women and that it silences women. As we have seen, these claims do not fare well when understanding pornography as a standard exercitive speech act. They do considerably better, however, when we understand pornography as (non-incidentally) involved in actions that constitute moves in norm-governed activities. Since pornography use is rampant, so is the covert enactment of s-norms involved with that use. It is certainly possible therefore that at least some of the time the enacted s-norms either subordinate or silence in one of the four ways.

7

Race, Speech, and Free Speech Law

> Imagine that an African American man boards a public bus on which all the other passengers are white. Unhappy with the newcomer, an elderly white man, turns to the African American man and says, "Just so you know, because I realize that you're not very bright, we don't like your kind around here, . . . boy. So, go back to Africa!"[1]

What the elderly white man said is a lot of things. It is outrageous, insulting, scary, intimidating, hateful, rude, and so socially inappropriate to be unnerving on solely those grounds. It is also harmful. Despite the recognized harms of utterances like this, such speech acts are nevertheless legally protected under current U.S. free speech law. As the courts see it, the elderly white man is merely exercising his right to free speech; his utterance is an expression of his opinion about an issue of public concern. It is therefore political expression and thus highly protected by the First Amendment of the U.S. Constitution. According to the standard liberal defense of such speech, any associated harms are merely the price we pay for freedom of expression. Furthermore, any attempt to regulate such utterances would amount to illegitimate state intervention and a slippery slope to thought control.

The epigraph at the beginning of this chapter originally appeared in M. K. McGowan, 'On "Whites Only" Signs and Racist Hate Speech: Verbal Acts of Racial Discrimination', in I. Maitra and M. K. McGowan (eds.), *Speech and Harm: Controversies Over Free Speech*, 2012, p. 121, and has been reprinted by permission of Oxford University Press.

[1] Elsewhere I used a similar example to make a similar argument (McGowan 2012). I changed the example primarily by removing the word 'nigger'. This word is so powerful that it overpowered the example. Some took me to be working on the semantics of slurs or on acts of slurring instead of the related set of issues concerning the harms of racist (hate) speech. For a fascinating discussion of the history of the term 'boy', see Brooks, *The Law of Address*, an unpublished manuscript.

In this chapter, I argue that this standard defense of public racist speech is insupportable.[2] A clear understanding of both U.S. free speech doctrine and the linguistic and normative functioning of public racist utterances shows that some racist speech in public spaces ought to be legally actionable even under the strict free speech protections of U.S. law. To say that it ought to be actionable is to say that there are sufficient grounds (in terms of harm prevention) to justify legal intervention. What precise form that intervention should take is a separate question that is not pursued here.

The chapter proceeds as follows. In Section 7.1, the philosophical background of a free speech principle is introduced thereby clarifying precisely what such a principle involves. In Section 7.2, the nature of discrimination is explored. Then, in Section 7.3, I present two strategies for arguing for further speech regulation and offer reasons to prefer one of them. In Section 7.4, I implement that strategy, which I call a parity argument, to argue that the elderly white man's utterance ought to be actionable even under U.S. free speech law. In Section 7.5, I situate my particular argument within the broader (speech act) free speech literature and emphasize why I depart from others in the ways that I do.

7.1 Philosophical foundations of free speech

There is considerable confusion about the nature and scope of a free speech principle. A commitment to free speech does not mean that speech cannot be regulated. Plenty of speech is and should be regulated. Consider, for example, speech used to enact contracts, criminal solicitation, insider trading, and false advertising. Clearly, freedom of expression is compatible with various types of speech regulation.

What a principle of free speech does, by contrast, is make it harder (but not impossible) to regulate speech. In short, freedom of speech is a legal right that protects speech against unwarranted state regulation.[3]

[2] In so doing, I join a long line of theorists. To name just a few: Crenshaw 1993; Delgado 1993; Lawrence 1993; MacKinnon 1993; Matsuda 1993; Delgado and Stefancic 1991; Brison 1998a; 1998b. As I see it, my contribution is the identification of the sneaky mechanism of norm enactment that supports arguments based on a constitutive connection to harm. For an introduction to various philosophical issues on race and language, see Anderson et al. 2012.

[3] I am here focusing on the legal (as opposed to a moral or political) principle of free speech.

It involves a presumption against the regulation of speech that makes it more difficult (but not impossible) for the state to regulate speech. The idea here is that because speech is so valuable, there have to be especially compelling reasons to regulate it. Consequently, it takes more to justify the regulation of speech than it does to justify the regulation of actions that are not speech.

Despite such protections, some speech is nevertheless regulable. Suppose, for example, that I declare, in a very public way, that John Jones is a pedophile. Suppose further that I know this to be false; I do it out of malice and I succeed in harming his reputation in provable ways. (Suppose, for example, that he loses his job as a direct and demonstrable result of what I say.) In such a case, my defamatory utterance is harmful and it is harmful enough for Jones to succeed in seeking damages against me and this is so despite my defamatory utterance being (valuable) speech. Defamation is actionable under tort law as is speech constitutive of harassment and utterances that constitute an intentional infliction of emotional distress.

Other categories of speech are regulable under criminal law. True threats, price fixing, criminal conspiracy, criminal solicitation, asking for a bribe, accepting a bribe, offering a bribe, extortion, and insider trading are all examples of verbal crimes that are regulable despite being (merely) verbal.

Still other categories of speech are actionable under civil rights law. Speech that constitutes discrimination is one such example. In this chapter, I focus on speech constitutive of discrimination. In particular, I argue that the elderly white man's utterance enacts discriminatory norms in a public space and it therefore constitutes (rather than merely causes) an act of discrimination. Moreover, this is sufficient to justify its legal actionability under anti-discrimination law.

Before turning to that argument, further information regarding the philosophical foundations of free speech is required. There are several related but distinct justificatory questions and we need to distinguish them.

7.1.1 Why is speech so valuable?

Why exactly should it be more difficult to regulate speech than it is to regulate other actions? What is it about speech that warrants these special protections? One possibility is that nothing does. Free speech skepticism maintains that this practice of treating speech as more difficult to regulate is ultimately without adequate justification. There are important unresolved issues here but I shall henceforth operate on the assumption that a free speech principle is justified and I do this because I here aim to argue that *even in the face* of special free speech protections, there are nevertheless compelling reasons to treat the elderly white man's utterance as an actionable act of discrimination. I shall therefore assume—at least for the sake of argument—that *something* justifies the free speech principle and thus the special protections afforded by it.

Most justifications for a free speech principle offer one (or a combination of) the following three general sorts (each of which can be instantiated in distinct ways).[4] One proposed sort of justification maintains that speech ought to be protected because the free flow of ideas is the best (or only) way to access the truth (or knowledge). By saying what we think and by attending to the opinions and reactions of others, we, as a society, are more likely to form better justified and hence true beliefs. This proposed justification is sometimes called the argument from truth and it is often attributed to J. S. Mill.[5]

Another proposed sort of justification maintains that freedom of expression is required in order for a democracy to function well. A society will be genuinely democratic only if we are free to criticize the government, tell our representatives what we want them to do, and freely discuss matters of public concern. Meiklejohn's careful articulation of this position is often cited, but this sort of justification has earlier roots.[6] It is sometimes called the argument from democracy.

A third sort of justification focuses less on social benefits and more on the individual. This justification of free speech protections maintains that speech must be free in order for persons to be genuinely autonomous by deciding for themselves what to think and do. If the state limits expression, then we are prevented from even considering some possibilities. In

[4] Speech might be valuable intrinsically (that is, in itself) or it might be valuable instrumentally (that is, as a means to something else of value). If the special protections extended to speech are justified in virtue of speech being a means to something else of value, then the justification in question is said to be consequentialist. Otherwise, it is said to be non-consequentialist.

[5] See Mill 1978.

[6] See Meiklejohn 1960. Schauer (1982: 36) identifes this sort of justification in the work of Hume, Kant, and Spinoza.

this way then, the free expression of ideas is a requirement of autonomy. Scanlon is credited with the origins of this sort of justification.[7] It is often called the autonomy defense of free speech.

7.1.2 The scope of a free speech principle

Another important question concerns what counts as speech for the purposes of a free speech principle. To exactly which class of actions will the special protections be extended? One might think that the answer to this question is simple: Everything that is speech in the ordinary sense. Although this answer is simple and intuitive, it is not correct.

To see this, notice that neither burning a flag nor wearing an armband are speech in the ordinary sense but such actions count as speech for the purposes of a free speech principle. Moreover, plenty of speech in the ordinary sense (e.g. "I hereby hire you to kill my boss" or "It is henceforth against company policy to hire women") is regulated without raising any free speech concerns at all. Justifying these regulations does not require meeting the raised standards relevant to a free speech principle. Consequently, it seems that such utterances are entirely outside the scope of such a principle. When it comes to free speech then, the word 'speech' is being used in a special technical sense and this raises some questions about precisely what this special technical sense is.[8]

Whether a particular action counts as speech in this technical sense matters since it determines how difficult it is to justify the regulation of that action. Following Schauer, I shall say that actions that are outside the scope of a free speech principle (including some actions that are speech in the ordinary sense) are *uncovered* by that free speech principle.[9] Uncovered actions include insider-trading, speech that is used to enact contracts, criminal solicitation, and much non-expressive action (e.g. scratching one's nose in private).

That said, plenty of ordinary speech (and some non-linguistic but expressive actions like wearing an armband in political protest) does fall within the scope of a free speech principle and is thus covered by that principle. As a result, proposed regulations of such covered (speech)

[7] See Scanlon 1972.

[8] See Schauer 1972; 1982; Greenawalt 1989; Maitra and McGowan 2007; 2009 and Simpson 2016.

[9] See Schauer 1982.

actions must meet heightened standards of scrutiny. When those heightened standards are met, the speech in question is regulated even though it is covered by a free speech principle. Defamation is an example of covered but actionable speech. When the heightened standards are unmet, the speech in question is not regulated. So-called political speech falls into this category.

There are several distinct questions regarding what counts as speech in this technical (coverage) sense. First, one might distinguish between the *descriptive* question regarding what *actually* counts as speech in a particular system (and thus has extended to it as a matter of fact the special protections of the free speech principle in question) and the *normative* question regarding what *ought* to count as speech in that system.[10] Furthermore, this normative question comes in two forms. The *narrow normative coverage question* concerns what ought to count as speech in the actual system in question and the *broad normative coverage question* concerns what ought to count as speech in the free speech system we ought to have.[11] This broad normative coverage question is doubly normative: it is concerned both with which free speech principle we ought to have and with what ought to count as speech with respect to that principle.

Notice also that these questions about the scope of a free speech principle are related to the above question about what makes speech so valuable in the first place. In particular, it seems that what ought to count as speech should have the property (or properties) that make speech valuable in the first place.

7.1.3 *Conditions for regulation*

As we have seen, some utterances (e.g. verbally hiring an assassin) are uncovered and thus do not count as speech for the purposes of a free speech principle. As a result, regulating such utterances raises no free speech concerns. Other categories of speech, by contrast, are regulated even though they do count as speech in the free speech sense. What conditions must be met for the legitimate regulation of such speech?

[10] See Maitra and McGowan 2007; 2009.
[11] See Maitra and McGowan 2007; 2009.

First, it is widely agreed that the prevention of harm is the only legitimate justification for state interference with individual liberty. As a result, justifications for speech regulation must involve the prevention of harm. Therefore, it is a necessary condition of legitimate speech regulation that the harms associated with failing to regulate the speech in question outweigh any harms that would be associated with regulating it. Although this "balancing of harms" condition is necessary for justified speech regulation, it is not sufficient. That is, it is not enough to show that some category of speech is, on balance, harmful. To justify regulating it, it has to be especially harmful. To say that the regulation of speech must meet heightened standards of justification just means that the (amount and type of) harm (prevention) required to justify the regulation of some category of covered speech must be *greater* than the (amount and type of) harm (prevention) required to justify the regulation of an uncovered action. As a result, there will be cases where it is not permissible to regulate covered speech even when the same (amount and type of) harm (prevention) would warrant the regulation of an uncovered action. A second necessary condition of legitimate regulation, therefore, is that the speech in question be harmful enough to meet the relevant raised standards.

Note that, depending on the system of free speech in question, there may be various levels of protection. It may be that some categories of speech (e.g. political speech) are more valuable, and hence more difficult to regulate, than other categories of speech (e.g. commercial speech). In other words, it might take a lesser showing of harm (prevention) to justify the regulation of commercial speech than it does to justify the regulation of political speech. Finally, the regulations themselves must meet certain conditions.[12]

A third important condition for legitimate regulation is that other remedies (remedies that do not involve the regulation of covered speech) are somehow inadequate. Such remedies might be inadequate because they are ineffective (at preventing or reversing the harms in question),

[12] The regulations must be precise enough to pinpoint the class of speech actions to be regulated. The degree of precision required varies. Strict scrutiny requires "narrow tailoring" whereas rational basis review requires only "rational relation." In addition to such breadth concerns, regulations must also be non-vague and content/viewpoint neutral. For a discussion of these complexities, see Volokh 1996a.

too costly, or harmful themselves. This condition treats the regulation of harmful covered speech as a remedy of last resort.

7.2 Two argumentative strategies

With this framework in place, I now identify two different strategies for arguing for further speech regulation. Using one of those strategies, I then argue that the elderly white man's utterance ought to be legally actionable. Again, I am here concerned with the theoretical question concerning whether some speech is harmful enough to warrant legal intervention. This justificatory question is prior to the more practical question regarding *how* to regulate it. I here leave this practical question open.

7.2.1 Strategy one: the value of speech strategy

The first strategy settles on a particular answer to the question regarding what makes speech valuable (and thus justifies the extending of special free speech protections to it) and then argues that the category of speech in question is not valuable in this way. Consequently, that category of speech should not be afforded the special protections of a free speech principle and is thus regulable on a lesser showing of harm.

This is a widespread argumentative strategy especially in the philosophical free speech literature. Sunstein, for example, uses this strategy when he argues that further government regulation of the press is warranted because such regulation would enhance the value of speech (which for him is the quality of political deliberation).[13] Shiffrin employs a value of speech strategy when she argues that lies should not be afforded any free speech protection.[14] Brison turns this strategy on its head by arguing that the very same autonomy considerations used by others to justify the free speech protection of racist hate speech actually tell *against* its free speech protection.[15]

7.2.2 Strategy two: parity argument

The second strategy identifies an uncontroversially regulable category of speech, specifies precisely what justifies the regulation of that category of

[13] See Sunstein 1993a. [14] See Shiffrin 2014. [15] See Brison 1998a.

speech, and then argues that the utterance (or category of speech) in question is regulable for exactly the same reasons. This strategy is based on the simple idea that like cases should be treated alike.[16] After all, it simply stands to reason that if category of speech Q is regulable in manner z because of X and X is also true of some utterance y, then y should be regulable in manner z too.

The guiding principle that like cases should be treated alike pervades the law. It underscores reliance on precedents; it also underscores the setting of new precedents by extending the law in novel but justified ways. Consider, for example, the justification for hostile environment sexual harassment law. Although hostile environment is technically a form of harassment, this form of harassment is harmful because it is discriminatory. Thus, recognizing a hostile environment as a form of workplace harassment is essentially an extension of anti-discrimination law. This extension is justified because a hostile work environment does the very same thing that other acts of gender discrimination do: it systematically and unfairly harms and it does so on the basis of membership in a legally protected class (in this case gender). Clearly, this justification relies on parity considerations.

This sort of parity argument appears in various forms in the free speech literature. Both Matsuda and Brison argue that racist hate speech is akin to a physical assault and thus ought to be treated accordingly by the law.[17] Elsewhere, I have argued that some instances of racist hate speech uttered in public places ought to be regulable for exactly the same reasons that the hanging of a 'Whites Only' sign is regulable; they each enact discriminatory norms in public spaces.[18] Others explore the possibility that (some) racist hate speech constitutes group defamation thereby arguing for a parity-based extension of defamation law.[19] The idea here is that just as defamation law recognizes the harm that some

[16] These two argumentative strategies (each implemented in the free speech literature) may mirror argumentative strategies elsewhere in the philosophy of law regarding the justification of particular laws. See Dworkin 1986 and Shapiro 2011. I thank Chris Essert for bringing this to my attention.

[17] See Matsuda 1993; Brison 1998b. Since assault is not a category of speech, this argumentative strategy is not technically an instance of the parity strategy in the narrow way that I have defined it here.

[18] See McGowan 2012.

[19] See Lasson 1985; Delgado 1993; Brison 2000; Waldron 2012.

speech does to the reputation of individuals, these theorists argue that (some) racist hate speech harms the reputation (and social standing) of social groups.[20]

7.2.3 Parity strategy preferred

Each of the two argumentative strategies relies on a particular answer to an underlying justificatory question but the two strategies rely on answers to *different* underlying justificatory questions. The value of speech strategy relies on a particular answer to the basic justificatory question regarding what makes speech valuable enough to warrant the special protections of a free speech principle. The parity strategy, by contrast, relies on a different justificatory question regarding what justifies the regulation of the clearly regulable category of speech. Although related, these two justificatory questions are not the same.

For my purposes, a parity argument is preferable. After all, I am here concerned with speech that constitutes (rather than merely causes) discrimination and we have perfect clarity with respect to why such discriminatory speech is actionable. Since the parity strategy relies on an answer to *that* justificatory question and since we have an answer to that justificatory question, the parity strategy is preferable for my purposes.

I aim to argue that the elderly white man's utterance ought to be actionable for the very same reasons that (already actionable) verbal acts of discrimination are actionable. Consequently, the requisite parity argument must first identify the justification for the actionability of such verbal acts of discrimination and then demonstrate that the elderly white man's utterance satisfies those very justificatory conditions. Before turning to the particulars of this parity argument, however, it is prudent first to be clear on the nature of discrimination.

[20] Waldron regards this as an oversimplification. He is interested in enduring written speech (libel) as opposed to verbal utterances (slander). He seems to think that the former have a much more significant impact on social conditions. He also stresses that individual defamation concerns harm to "appraisal respect," but group defamation (as Waldron understands it) concerns harm to "recognition respect." See Darwall 1977; Waldron 2012. In my estimation, Waldron underestimates the normative impact of verbal speech.

7.3 On discrimination

Although the concept of discrimination is widely used in everyday conversation and in the law, it is rarely actually defined.[21] Moreover, it is considerably more complex than it may at first appear.[22] In what follows, I shall explore the concept of discrimination, distinguish between several different senses of the term, and pinpoint which sense of the term concerns us here.

Although discrimination is normally thought to be a morally bad thing, there is a sense of the term that is morally neutral. To discriminate in this neutral sense is just to make a distinction. I might discriminate between trees that are deciduous from trees that are not but, by so doing, I merely track a difference in their objective properties and there is nothing morally wrong with doing so.

Discrimination, in the morally loaded sense, concerns an unjust way of treating people. To discriminate in this sense involves differential treatment of persons based on morally irrelevant characteristics of those persons. If I were to refuse to befriend people with floppy earlobes, for example, I would be discriminating in this morally loaded sense. Since having floppy earlobes is not a morally relevant property and thus not a good reason to refuse to befriend someone, my refusing to befriend such persons is an instance of discrimination in this sense.

Another conception of discrimination, one that dominates the philosophical literature, further ties the concept of discrimination to membership in social groups.[23] On this characterization of discrimination, it would be impossible to discriminate against floppy-earlobed persons in our society exactly because floppy-earlobed persons do not constitute a social group in our society. Discrimination, on this account, involves

[21] Instead, anti-discrimination legislation typically uses the term without defining it. Such legislation is typically explicit, however, regarding the prohibited grounds of discrimination (e.g. age, race, and gender). For an example of this, see Article 14 of the *European Convention for the Protection of Human Rights and Fundamental Freedoms.*

[22] There are controversies concerning how to define discrimination, how to understand what precisely is morally bad about it, and how to distinguish it from related notions like oppression. For a discussion of these, see Altman 2011.

[23] Andrew Altman treats this as the core concept of discrimination in his Stanford Encyclopedia entry on it. See Altman 2011. Others who do so include: Young 1990; Sunstein 1993a.

disadvantaging persons in virtue of their group membership.[24] Who can be discriminated against will vary from society to society and from time to time depending on which groups are socially marked in that society and at that time.

In addition to these senses of discrimination, there is also the legal notion of discrimination. Without getting too bogged down in legal complexities, it is sufficient for current purposes to note two important differences between the above morally loaded senses of the term and the legal notions.[25] (I here focus on the U.S. context.) First, only some socially marked groups are protected by current U.S. anti-discrimination law. Thus, while it is morally problematic to refuse to rent apartments to obese persons and although obese persons are a socially marked group in our society, doing so will not count as discrimination in the legal sense since obese persons are not a protected class under current anti-discrimination law.[26] Second, only certain sorts of disadvantageous treatment count as discrimination in this legal sense. While it may be morally reprehensible for me to prohibit non-white people from entering my house and although doing so may be harmful and/or disadvantageous, it does not constitute discrimination in the legal sense since my house is a private residence. This disadvantage or harm is not a legally recognized one. Were I the proprietor of a public accommodation, by contrast, and were I to prohibit non-white people from entering my inn, then my practice would constitute discrimination in the legal sense.

Now that we are clearer on the relevant notion of discrimination, it is worth pointing out that it is conceptually distinct from the related (and often overlapping) phenomenon of oppression. To see this, recall that oppression requires a structure. If a person is harmed or disadvantaged

[24] As Altman (2011) rightly stresses, a disadvantage is a relative harm with an implicit comparison class. To say that non-whites are discriminated against in the United States today, for example, is to say that they are disadvantaged *relative to whites* in the United States today.

[25] There are several legal notions since there is variation across jurisdictions.

[26] This is beginning to change. Some states treat (some instances of) obesity as a disability. How disabilities are defined varies between states. In California, for example, obesity qualifies as a disability only if it is the result of an underlying physiological condition (e.g. endocrine malfunction). See *Cassista v. Community Foods, Inc.* Rhode Island, by contrast, can recognize obesity as a disability without establishing an underlying physiological cause of that obesity. See *Cook v. State of Rhode Island.* I thank Ann Garry for bringing these developments to my attention. For an important intersectional criticism of antidiscrimination law, see Crenshaw 1989.

in virtue of her membership in a social group but this happens in a social context in which members of that group are not systematically disadvantaged in virtue of that group membership, then the person in question is unjustly harmed but she is not oppressed per se. This is what it means for oppression to require a structure. Of course, the law is most likely to legally protect only those social groups it recognizes as systematically disadvantaged and thus deserving of further legal protections. Furthermore, discrimination in the legal sense requires that the social group in question be singled out by anti-discrimination law but oppression requires no such thing. As one can see then, although these notions are highly related, they are nevertheless distinct (at least as they are being used here).[27]

7.4 The parity argument

Consider again the case of the elderly white man's utterance on the public bus:

> Imagine that an African American man boards a public bus on which all the other passengers are white. Unhappy with the newcomer, an elderly white man, turns to the African American man and says, "Just so you know, because I realize that you're not very bright, we don't like you're your kind around here, . . . boy. So, go back to Africa!"

I aim to present a parity argument for the legal actionability of the elderly white man's utterance. In particular, I aim to show that the elderly white man's utterance satisfies the same conditions sufficient for the actionability of an uncontroversially actionable category of speech: verbal acts of discrimination. Treating like cases alike therefore requires that the elderly white man's utterance be actionable too.

Because this parity argument requires identifying the justification for the actionability of the uncontroversially regulable type of speech (in this case, verbal acts of discrimination), the first order of business is to pinpoint the precise justification for the actionability of verbal acts of discrimination. To this task, I now turn.

[27] Young (1990), for example, is concerned to distinguish oppression from the non-legal philosophically dominant morally loaded sense of discrimination.

7.4.1 The justification for the actionability of verbal acts of discrimination

In what follows, I consider two paradigmatic examples of verbal acts of discrimination: the hanging of a 'Whites Only' sign and the verbal enacting of a discriminatory hiring policy. Verbal acts of discrimination are actionable and the justification for their actionability is clear: Such acts are actionable precisely because they *enact* norms (or permissibility facts) that are *discriminatory* in the legal sense.

7.4.1.1 'WHITES ONLY' SIGNS

The hanging of a 'Whites Only' sign is actionable when hanging that sign enacts a discriminatory policy in a public place governed by anti-discrimination law. Suppose, for example, that a restaurant proprietor in the segregated U.S. South of 1952 hangs a sign in his restaurant that reads: 'Whites Only.' In this case, the hanging of this sign enacts a policy (permissibility fact) for this restaurant such that non-white persons are prohibited service.[28]

Of course, precisely what the posting of a 'Whites Only' sign does on any particular occasion will depend heavily on the context in which this action takes place. Posting such a sign in a laundromat, for example, may well enact permissibility facts for the establishment in question (i.e. the laundromat), but if it merely renders it impermissible (or inadvisable) for patrons to wash non-white clothes, in a washing machine with an automatic bleach cycle, then the enacted permissibility facts would not be discriminatory in the relevant (legal) sense. As we have seen again and again, context matters.

In the above case, though, the proprietor's act of posting the sign is an actionable act of discrimination and this is because the policy enacted by his hanging of the sign is discriminatory in the legal sense. The restaurant policy enacted by this action disadvantages a class of persons (i.e. non-whites) who are protected by current U.S. anti-discrimination law and the disadvantage in question (i.e. denial of service at a public accommodation) is a legally recognized harm under current U.S. anti-discrimination law. As one can see then, this restaurant policy is discriminatory in the

[28] A successful discrimination claim does not require that service be denied; it could instead involve disparate treatment based on group membership.

legal sense. Moreover, since the proprietor's action enacts this policy, the discriminatory practice that ensues is brought about via adherence to the policy (norm or permissibility fact) enacted. Consequently, the proprietor's action constitutes (and does not merely cause) discrimination.

Notice that although it is a communicative act, the proprietor's hanging of the sign is not speech in the ordinary sense. Strictly speaking, the act of hanging the sign does not include the proprietor actually saying anything. Despite this, because the proprietor has the communicative intention to enact the policy stated on the sign (and because this intention is recognized and because the proprietor has the authority to enact that policy and this is recognized and because several further conditions are met), the proprietor's act of hanging the sign constitutes the (standard exercitive) speech act of enacting that policy.[29] Indeed, the law regards the hanging of such a sign as the enacting of an unlawful and discriminatory policy. 'Whites Only' signs are widely cited as an example of discriminatory speech.[30]

7.4.1.2 VERBALLY ENACTING DISCRIMINATORY HIRING POLICY

Speech in the ordinary sense can also constitute an act of discrimination. Suppose, for example, that John is the Chief Executive Officer of Macho Co. and during the course of a company meeting, the purpose of which is to revise the company's hiring policies, John says, "From now on, we only hire men. Women are too distracting and only men need to work anyway." Supposing that John intends to be enacting a new hiring policy when he says this and that he is recognized as doing so (and that further conditions are met), this utterance enacts a hiring policy for Macho Co. It makes it against company policy to hire women.[31] Because the discriminatory hiring practice that would ensue results from adherence to the policy enacted by the utterance, the utterance constitutes (and does not merely cause) discrimination.

[29] Recall (from Chapter 1 section 1.3) that not all speech acts are speech in the ordinary sense of uttering words. There are many ways, for example, that I could perform the speech act of asserting that 2 + 2 = 4. I could say '2 + 2 = 4'; I could write down '2 + 2 = 4' or I could pick up a piece of paper on which '2 + 2 = 4' is already inscribed and hold it up in way that signals my commitment to it.

[30] See, for example, MacKinnon 1987: 163–97; Lawrence 1993; and McGowan 2012.

[31] Note that this utterance does not make it illegal to hire women and it does not make it immoral to hire women. The sort of permissibility involved regards the policies of the company. Again, the permissibility facts enacted are neither legal nor moral.

This hiring policy is discriminatory in the legal sense. The group of persons disadvantaged (in this case, people gendered as women) are a protected class under current U.S. anti-discrimination law. Discrimination based on sex or gender is explicitly prohibited. Moreover, the disadvantage in question (not being hired) counts as the sort of public disadvantage that anti-discrimination law protects against. For these reasons, this policy is discriminatory in the legal sense. Since John's utterance enacts this policy, his utterance *constitutes* an act of discrimination and is thus actionable.

7.4.2 Parity considerations and the elderly white man's utterance

A consideration of two paradigmatic examples of verbal acts of discrimination suggests that enacting a discriminatory norm in a public place is sufficient for constituting an actionable act of discrimination.[32] I now aim to show that the elderly white man's utterance ought to be actionable precisely because it too enacts discriminatory norms in a public place.

The elderly white man's utterance is a conversational contribution and thus it dependently enacts various s-norms for the conversation to which he is contributing. By directly enacting changes to the conversational score, his utterance dependently enacts changes to the conversation-specific s-norms operative in the conversation in question and it does so via the g-norms governing (all) conversation as a norm-governed activity. Such conversational permissibility facts (s-norms), however, are not my focus.

In addition to constituting a move in the norm-governed activity of conversation, the elderly white man's utterance is also a move in broader (non-conversational) social activities that are also norm-governed. Since there are social norms governing how to treat strangers in public spaces, public space social interaction is a norm-governed practice. Moreover, the elderly white man's utterance is a move in this norm-governed practice, so it directly enacts score changes and thus dependently enacts s-norms to this particular instance of this activity. In other words, the elderly white man's utterance dependently enacts s-norms for the social interaction among the people on that bus. Before attempting to specify

[32] I assume that the discriminatory norm enacted is followed so that a discriminatory practice ensues. See Chapter 1 section 1.7.

which particular s-norms are dependently enacted (and determining whether any of them are discriminatory in a legal sense), the under-described case of the elderly white man's utterance requires additional contextual detail.

After all, there are a variety of unspecified further details that make a difference and they need to be made explicit. First, I assume that the other passengers hear and appear to agree with what the elderly white man said; they do not object or attempt to block his (outrageous) remark. Were someone to object, the conversational move of objecting would enact score changes of its own and so there is a chance that the potentially problematic s-norms enacted by the elderly white man's utterance would be terminated (or altered) by such an objection.[33] I further assume that the other passengers are subsequently unfriendly towards and wary of the African American man addressed. Suppose for example that some women draw their possessions and their children closer to them; some young men glare at the African American man in defiance and other passengers stare and snicker. With these further contextual details specified, I turn now to a consideration of which particular s-norms are enacted by the elderly white man's utterance.

7.4.2.1 WHAT A 'WHITES ONLY' SIGN DOES

Elsewhere I have argued that the elderly white man's utterance enacts the same discriminatory norms for the public bus that the hanging of a 'Whites Only' sign would enact.[34] I argued that the s-norms enacted by the elderly white man's utterance discriminate against persons of color at that time and place just as a 'Whites Only' policy would.

Clearly, the enacted s-norms are not the same in *every* respect. As Brown rightly points out, the scope of those norms is different.[35] The policy enacted by a 'Whites Only' sign governs a variety of bus-related activities outside of the particular bus on which it hangs but we know that the scope of the s-norms enacted by the elderly white man's

[33] Recall that, on my view, moves immediately enact score changes (Chapter 4 section 4.2). If a move is (soon) questioned, that questioning move enacts score changes of it own and may change some components of the score back to what it was before the blocked move. In the common ground framework, by contrast, blocked moves never become a part of the common ground because they are never shared.

[34] See McGowan 2012.

[35] See Brown 2015: 89–90. Again, the example has been modified. See note 1.

utterance is significantly more limited. S-norms govern only the particular instance of the norm governed activity to which the move in question contributes. This means that the s-norms enacted by the elderly white man's utterance govern only this particular public space social interaction and so they do not extend outside of this particular public bus.[36] There are other differences too. The mechanisms of enacting these norms are importantly different. The hanging of the 'Whites Only' sign is a standard exercitive that relies on an exercise of speaker authority; the elderly white man's utterance is a covert exercitive that relies on the g-norms of the norm-governed activity to which that utterance contributes.

It is sufficient for my parity argument, however, to show that the 'Whites Only' policy and the enacted s-norms are the same in virtue of both being discriminatory. A 'Whites Only' policy on a public bus is discriminatory because it denies non-white persons equal access to a public accommodation and it does so based on that person's race. Might the elderly white man's utterance do the same? That is, might it enact an s-norm for that public bus that denies that African American man equal access to that public accommodation at that time and might it do so because of his race?

One might doubt that the elderly white man, who is after all a mere passenger on the bus, has the power to enact an s-norm strong enough to deny anyone equal access to the bus. This possibility is bolstered, however, by the following two realizations. First, we know that the elderly white man's utterance is a covert exercitive that enacts at least one s-norm and we know that it does so by triggering the g-norms governing public space social interactions. Second, we know that at least some of those g-norms systematically disadvantage non-whites (relative to white persons). After all, racism is not a mere matter of white supremacist beliefs located in individual minds. It is also in the world; it is a complex set of social practices and norms that systematically disadvantage some in virtue of their race and hence systematically advantage others in virtue of theirs.[37]

[36] Of course, if the public space social interaction moves outside the bus (say the elderly white man follows the African America man off the bus) then the s-norms would govern social space outside of that bus.

[37] For discussion of the structural aspects of racism, see Lichtenberg 1992; Young 1992; Garcia 1996; Shelby 2003; Haslanger 2004.

What this means is that some of the g-norms governing our social interactions are racist and this lends support to the hypothesis that the s-norms enacted by the elderly white man's utterance are both racially problematic and powerful.

Notice that the power of the elderly white man's utterance resides in the norm-governed (and racist) nature of the broader social practices to which his utterance contributes. The particular s-norms enacted by his utterance are not merely the result of him exercising his individual power and they are not brought about by his intention to bring them about. Rather, the s-norms enacted result from his action contributing to a larger practice (i.e. norm-governed activity); his utterance enables the normative force of that social practice to come to bear in the micro-context of that public bus.

Even with these structural considerations in mind and with the consequent power that broader social practices of racism impart to the situation, it may nevertheless seem that there is an important difference between the norms enacted by the 'Whites Only' sign and those enacted by the elderly white man's utterance. After all, the 'Whites Only' policy *prohibits* non-white persons from some parts of that pubic bus, but it may seem that the elderly white man's utterance merely renders non-white persons *unwelcome* on that bus.

7.4.2.2 DISCRIMINATION, EQUAL ACCESS, AND HOSTILE ENVIRONMENT

Merely making non-white persons unwelcome (without also prohibiting their presence and/or denying them service) in a public accommodation is also discriminatory in the legal sense. In Delaware, for example, it is unlawful to have an explicit policy that renders some persons—on account of "race, age, marital status, creed, color, sex, disability or national origin"—more (or less) welcome or desirable as patrons.[38] Thus, in Delaware, a 'Whites Preferred' policy or a 'Non-whites unwelcome' policy would be discriminatory and thus unlawful and actionable. Moreover, such anti-discrimination law is neither limited to explicit policy nor to the state of Delaware.

[38] Del. Code § 4504.

Hostile environment is a legally recognized form of discrimination and it does not require that the hostility be explicit. Thus, if the elderly white man's utterance enacts s-norms for that public bus that render non-white persons less welcome than white persons, then a hostile environment discrimination claim is viable. Hostile environments deny persons equal access and they are discriminatory in the legal sense when they do so based on membership in a legally recognized social group.

Hostile environment anti-discrimination law got its start in the 1980s with developments in workplace sexual harassment law. The U.S. Supreme Court first endorsed hostile environment workplace sexual harassment in *Meritor Savings Bank v. Vinson* in 1986.[39] Prior to those developments which were instigated by the EEOC in 1980, only so called "quid pro quo" sexual harassment (propositions like "sleep with me or you're fired") were legally recognized as discriminatory gender-based workplace harassment.[40] Since a hostile environment towards women denies women equal access to employment and workplace, it is discriminatory. By acknowledging hostile environment as a form of workplace sexual harassment, the law essentially extended what counts as discriminatory conduct.

Even if one doubts that the elderly white man's utterance enacts s-norms strong enough to prohibit non-whites from that bus, there is ample reason to believe that at least some of the enacted s-norms act against, and are thus hostile towards, persons of color. Moreover, since these s-norms operate in a space governed by anti-discrimination law (e.g. a public bus is a public accommodation), the utterance that enacts those s-norms constitutes an act of discrimination.[41] After all, what matters for the actionability of the utterance in question is the discriminatory nature of the norm enacted and not the particular mechanism of enacting that norm.[42]

[39] 477 U.S. 59 (1986). Lower courts recognized it earlier. See *Bundy v. Jackson.*

[40] Prior to that, even so called "quid pro quo" sexual harassment went unrecognized as a form of gender discrimination. "Employers have argued, and courts have held, that firing a female employee for refusing to submit to sexual demands did not constitute a Title VII violation because the class discriminated against was defined by willingness to perform sexual favors, rather than by gender" Bartels 2015: 576.

[41] For the harm of discrimination to obtain, the discriminatory norms must be followed (Chapter 1 section 1.7) and what is required for this is different with public accommodation hostile environment. I take the other passengers' reaction to meet this condition.

[42] One might think that the mechanism of norm enactment matters when discriminatory intent is required. Standard exercitives are in an important way intentional while

My bold proposal is that just as women should not be subject to catcalls and sexist jokes in the workplace, so too persons of color should not be subject to racist remarks and hate speech in our public spaces.[43] To think otherwise is to deny persons of color equal access to public accommodations and thus to deny persons of color equal protection under the law. If hostile environment is discriminatory in a workplace, it ought to be legally recognized as discriminatory in other spaces *already* legally recognized as governed by anti-discrimination law.

The claim is not merely that the racist utterances sometimes *cause* people of color to feel unwelcome. This is no doubt true but such subjective perceptions are intractable and insufficiently objective to ground legal intervention. After all, as many who are reluctant to embrace further speech regulations are prone to point out, just about anything can be offensive to someone or other. Rather, the claim is that racist utterances sometimes *constitute* the legally actionable *harm* of discrimination.[44] When an utterance enacts an s-norm in a public accommodation that is hostile towards of persons of color and it does so because that person is a person of color, then the utterance that enacts that s-norm is an act of discrimination. It constitutes rather than merely causes the discriminatory hostile environment.

covert exercitives are not. This reasoning, however, is a mistake. First, the illocutionary intention to enact a norm (required for standard exercitives) is distinct from an intention to perform (the parallel act of) discrimination. Discriminatory standard exercitives thus do not require an intention to discriminate. Furthermore and even more to the point, the *legal* notion of discriminatory intent is a technical legal one and it is *not* the same as this ordinary notion (i.e. of an intention to perform an act one knows is discriminatory). Again, the legal notion is complex and controversial but it requires something like an intention to perform an act (or practice) that is discriminatory and the claimant's group membership is one motive for performing that action (or practice) or a reasonable person could forsee that it would have a disparate impact on persons belonging to the claimant's protected social group or the respondent ought to realize that doing so constitutes disparate treatment of the claimant qua member of that protected social group. Thus, the legal notion of discriminatory intent does not require that the respondent be aware of and intend to bring about the discriminatory act or conduct in question.

[43] Similarly, Citron (2014) argues that hostile environment anti-discrimination law ought to be extended to the internet.

[44] Koppelman rejects an earlier version of this argument (McGowan 2012) by saying that "speech can't be deemed unprotected whenever it has bad effects on the opportuntities of minorities" (Koppelman 2013: 771). I reject "bad effects" as an adequate gloss. I also reject much of what else he says in his 2013.

Although my proposal that racist utterances in public places ought to be legally actionable may seem extreme, it really isn't. Given that racist speech enacts s-norms, it simply stands to reason that these s-norms are sometimes hostile towards the persons targeted by that hateful speech. If women should be legally protected from gender-based hostility in the workplace, then it simply stands to reason that persons of color should be protected from race-based hostility on their way to work and in restaurants and other public accommodations. Finally, the suggestion that hostile environment anti-discrimination law should also apply to public accommodations is not just a mere possibility from the philosopher's armchair. There are a few successful actual cases of it and they also happen to involve speech.[45]

7.4.2.3 REAL U.S. CASES

Consider *Bond v. Michael's Family Restaurant*. Mischeral Bond, a black woman, and her six-year-old daughter, Pairresh, are enjoying a meal at Michael's Family Restaurant in Milwaukee, Wisconsin. They overhear a customer, Ozzie Balistreri, complaining about panhandlers; Balistreri also said that a "nigger" asked him for money just before entering the restaurant. The owner Marge Christodoulakis responds with, "Those god damn niggers". A few minutes later, two black men take money from a table that had been left by an elderly patron. Christodoulakis then loudly complains that "two niggers" just stole money; Christodoulakis uses the phrase "god damn niggers" several times and a customer seated near Balistreri says, "those niggers wonder why we hate them so much." Upon hearing all of this, Mischeral Bond informed Christodoulakis that she and her daughter had overheard the remarks and found the use of the word 'nigger' disturbing. Christodoulakis responded, "Honey, if you don't like it, then you can just leave." Finally, as Bond and her daughter were packing up to go, Christodoulakis asked Bond if she knew what the word 'nigger' meant and suggested that she look it up in the dictionary when she got home. Mischeral and Pairresh Bond then leave the restaurant.

[45] These cases are extremely rare but I regard them as a step in the right direction. Ironically, others cite these cases as a reductio of hostile environment law in general. See Volokh 1996b. Volokh regards all public accommodation and much of the workplace hostile environment cases as unconstitutional but thinks that some "directed" harassing workplace speech can be permissibly regulated. See Volokh 1992.

The State of Wisconsin Labor and Industry Review Commission found in favor of the Bonds and I wholeheartedly agree.[46] The utterances described, much like the elderly white man's utterance, enact racially hostile s-norms in a public accommodation. This constitutes a racially hostile environment and is thus discriminatory. The Wisconsin Labor and Industry Review Commission ordered the restaurant owner to pay $5,546.49 in attorney's fees and costs.[47]

Such hostile environment claims are not limited to the speech of proprietors. They can also apply to the speech of employees. Consider the case of *Craig v. New Crystal Restaurant*.[48] In this case, Daniel Craig, a homosexual man, went to New Crystal Restaurant for breakfast. After taking his order, the waitress Sandy DeLucio got into an argument with the cook. Another waitress Gloria Matteson noticed that DeLucio was not attending Craig, so Matteson served Craig his breakfast. As Craig was eating, four waitresses (including Delucio and Matteson) sat at a booth in the dining room. After finishing his breakfast, Craig walked over to the booth of waitresses to request his check and one of the waitresses gave it to him. Craig told the waitresses that he was displeased with the service and that if it were his restaurant he would fire them all. As he turned and walked toward the cashier, he heard Matteson say to the other waitresses, "I don't know who he thinks he is, that holier than thou damn faggot!"

The Chicago Commission on Human Relations determined that Craig was discriminated against; this constituted a hostile environment in a public accommodation, and Craig was thereby denied equal access to that accommodation. The Chicago Commission on Human Relations ordered the owner of the restaurant to pay attorney's fees and associated costs, compensatory damages for emotional distress, a sanction for failing to appear at a hearing, and a fine for violating the relevant code.

There are several interesting things about this particular case. First, this successful discrimination claim is based on a single utterance. According to the facts of the case, "[a]t the time of the alleged violation, the New Crystal Restaurant had a relatively large percentage of customers whom the owners

[46] Others disagree. Interestingly, they also under-describe the case. See Volokh 1996b; Koontz 2008. Koontz favors the actionability of hostile speech only when *directed at* unwilling listeners (where unwilling appears to mean not at all open to potential persuasion). In this, he follows Volokh 1992, 1996b.

[47] See *Bond v. Michael's Family Restaurant*.

[48] See *Craig v. New Crystal Restaurant*.

and employees of New Crystal Restaurant believed to be gay" and "[t]here is no evidence that New Crystal Restaurant's owners or its employees discouraged any of these customers from patronizing New Crystal Restaurant or otherwise discriminated against them."[49] The Commission thus based the discrimination finding on this *single* utterance.[50]

The utterance in question was determined to constitute a discriminatory hostile environment even though that utterance was made by an employee. Moreover, the owners were not even on the premises at the time of the incident and Matteson "admitted that she knew that the owners of New Crystal Restaurant expected her to be pleasant to all customers and not to discriminate based on sexual orientation."[51] The Chicago Commission on Human Relations nevertheless determined that "owners of public accommodations should be held liable for the acts of their non-managerial and non-supervisory agents if done during the course of serving a member of the public whether or not the owners knew about or authorized the alleged discrimination."[52] This holds owners of public accommodations to a higher standard than employers are held in workplace hostile environment cases.[53]

There are even cases where the speech of *patrons* is taken to constitute a hostile environment. Consider the case of *Neldaughter v. Dickeyville Athletic Club*.[54] This case involved homophobic speech (as well as throwing of dirt and rocks and obscene gestures) aimed at homosexual softball players during softball games. The Wisconsin Labor and Industry Review Commission found that the ball field is a public accommodation; the actions of the bystanders and other players constituted a hostile environment in that public accommodation, but did not hold the respondents

[49] See *Craig v. New Crystal Restaurant*, p. 2.

[50] Craig did overhear Matteson call him a faggot later that day (when he returned to the restaurant to discuss the incident with an employee who was not present at the time of the incident) while Matteson was describing the incident to others. Because Craig was not a customer at the time, because Matteson did not direct the comment at him, and because her use of the term faggot was not intended to insult him, it was no part of the finding. See *Craig v. New Crystal Restaurant*. Clearly the Commission distinguished between intended and unintended overhearers.

[51] See *Craig v. New Crystal Restaurant*.

[52] See *Craig v. New Crystal Restaurant*, p. 14.

[53] Workplace hostile environment typically requires a pattern of hostility and employers are liable only if they knew or should have known about the harassment and failed to take corrective action.

[54] See *Neldaughter v. Dickeyville Athletic Club*.

(the Dickeyville Athletic Club) accountable since it was not demonstrated that the Dickeyville Athletic Club had the authority to remove or stop the harassing attendees. The Commission suggested, however, that had the Dickeyville Athletic Club owned that land (or had a certain sort of agreement with the owners), they would have been legally responsible for the discriminatory environment.

Given all of this, it is not such a stretch to think that the elderly white man's utterance is discriminatory in the legal sense. After all, we know that his utterance enacts s-norms for that public bus. We also know that that public bus is a public accommodation. Moreover, it stands to reason that the enacted s-norms are racially hostile. What remains open is whether the enacted s-norms are hostile enough to constitute a violation of the relevant code and this question is best left to the appropriate agencies in the relevant jurisdictions. A genuine commitment to anti-discrimination and equal access requires the law to both recognize and seek to remedy all instances of group-based discrimination in public accommodations.

7.5 Situating my argument

There are several ways in which my approach differs from other theorists who also argue for further speech regulation. In order to better situate my work and to forestall potential misunderstandings, I will briefly describe some of the differences between my approach and that of others.

First, most theorists working in the philosophical free speech literature who argue for the further regulation of racist speech and who appeal to speech act theory in doing so rely on the model of the standard exercitive.[55] I, by contrast, rely on the covert exercitive. Reliance on the standard exercitive to show that racist speech constitutes harm requires demonstrating that the racist speech in question satisfies the various felicity conditions of standard exercitives (i.e. the speaker has and is exercising authority over the realm over which the enacted norms preside, participants recognize that the speaker has and is exercising that authority, the speaker intends to enact the harmful norm in question, participants recognize that intention, the utterance communicates the content of that

[55] Philosophical speech act approaches include: Langton 2011: 72–93 and Maitra 2012. Matsuda's classic work also assumes that authority is required. See Matsuda 1993.

norm, and so on). Elsewhere I have argued that it is far from clear that any of these conditions are met.[56] In this chapter, however, I have argued that the conditions required for the elderly white man's utterance to be a covert exercitive are definitely met. Furthermore, I have argued that the s-norm enacted is harmful in a legally actionable way.

Second, many who argue for the further regulation of racist speech aim to justify the regulation of a new *category* of speech: racist hate speech. I, by contrast, aim to show that some instances of racist speech fall into an already recognized-as-regulable category of speech: verbal acts of discrimination. This approach affords several advantages. First, there is no need to show that every instance of racist hate speech is regulable and that it is regulable for the same reasons. Second, there is no need to define the notoriously difficult-to-define category of racist hate speech. All that is required is a recognition that more speech than previously recognized is in fact discriminatory.[57]

Third and finally, I work within an actual free speech system (that of the U.S.) rather than argue for a new one. Other theorists argue for the free speech system we ought to have and it is at least more complex determining how their ideal theory would or should apply to actual free speech systems.[58]

7.6 Conclusion

I have here argued that some public racist utterances meet the relevant harm-prevention standards required to show that it is legitimate to regulate such utterances despite a commitment to free speech. This theoretical-justificatory question is distinct from practical questions about how (and even whether) to regulate such utterances. I leave it to others to contend with the more hands on practical questions regarding the details of real world regulation.

That said, I recognize that regulation would raise substantial practical challenges. In particular, concerns about vicarious liability (that is,

[56] See McGowan 2012.

[57] This strategy generalizes. Some instances of racist speech fall under other already recognized-as-regulable categories (e.g. intentional infliction of emotional distress, true threat, harassment, and defamation).

[58] Examples include: Scanlon 1972; Sunstein 1993b; Shiffrin 2014.

holding one person, in these cases, the proprietor, legally responsible for the actions of others) would only be compounded by the potentially one-off nature of hostile public accommodation environment harassment. Recall the case of *Craig v. New Crystal Restaurant*, in which the claimant, Daniel Craig, was determined to have been discriminated against because a single comment on a single occasion constituted a hostile environment for him as a patron at that time. Hostile environment in a public accommodation is thus importantly different from hostile environment in a workplace. After all, a workplace involves the same people over time and can thus have a reporting system for harassment, an investigation procedure, an adjudication process, and corrective measures, all of which alleviate concerns about vicarious liability.

Either these practical issues can be solved or they cannot. If they can, then we should do the difficult work involved. The mere fact that something is difficult is not a decisive reason against doing it. It is extremely difficult, for example, to distinguish between a wife venting about her husband and the verbal crime of hiring an assassin but this no reason to fail to regulate criminal solicitation. It can be extremely difficult to distinguish between a mere prediction and a true threat. Again, this is not a reason to refrain from regulating the verbal crime of issuing true threats. We routinely do what is difficult. Racist remarks in public places are discriminatory and, if possible, the law should afford a remedy. Equal protection under the law and genuine equality require it.

If, however, the practical issues cannot be solved, then this means that there are routinely cases of discrimination that the law cannot remedy. Moreover, since the harm is discrimination, those harmed are already recognized by the law as in special need of legal protection. If this is the situation and we care at all about equality and justice, we had better find a different solution. If the law is too blunt an instrument, perhaps we should look elsewhere for a remedy.[59]

Either way, we should all be more pro-active about the climate in our public spaces. "If everyone in the pool is a trained lifeguard, no one is going to drown."[60] If everyone one of us is involved in the remedy by

[59] For a discussion of how social meaning can undermine the efficacy of law, see Lessig 1995.

[60] Michael Francis McNally (2017), in arguing for international safety codes while C.E.O of the U.S. Division of Skanska International.

being informed about the appropriate standards, inclined to notice violations, and empowered to respond in positive ways, then the climate of our public spaces will be significantly more egalitarian. Moving in a more positive direction, I turn now to consider how this covert mechanism of norm enactment might bring about more positive change. How might individual actions enact more egalitarian s-norms and thereby transform social spaces for the better?

Conclusion

The phenomenon of covert exercitives sheds light on various kinds of harmful speech. Sexist comments can oppress (Chapter 5). What may seem to be an offhand remark, and thus merely a minor irritant, may nevertheless enact local norms that oppress. Actions involving certain kinds of pornography can constitute harm even in cases where the agent has no intention to do so, even in cases where the agent does not have authority, and even in cases where the pornography-involving actions are not communicative acts (Chapter 6). There are also potential legal consequences of the covert norm-enacting nature of speech. When racist speech in public places enacts racially hostile s-norms, there are sufficient legal grounds for treating such utterances as actionable acts of discrimination (Chapter 7).

Other applications

The particular applications explored in the second half of this book do not come close to exhausting the possibilities. Covert norm enactment is ubiquitous and it should thus come as no surprise that the phenomenon identified here can illuminate the (norm-enacting) role that speech plays in plenty of other sorts of cases.

It is not hard to see, for example, that the phenomenon of covert exercitives also helps to explain various otherwise perplexing features of microaggressions.[1] One might think that microaggressions are mere symptoms of a social problem that obtains elsewhere. On this (rather widespread) view, microaggressions signal that there is an unjust social hierarchy; they are evidence of that hierarchy, but they play no real part in

[1] These points are further developed in McGowan 2018b and 2018c.

enacting or perpetuating that hierarchy. That microaggressions routinely enact s-norms, however, demonstrates that they both trigger and extend broader (unjust) social structures. Moreover, by enacting s-norms, microaggressions actually add to the social structure (since such structures are merely compositions of social norms and practices).

The phenomenon of covert exercitives also shows how microaggressions can be harmful even in cases where the perpetrator neither intends nor foresees that harm. As we have seen repeatedly, (speech) actions can be genuinely harmful even though those harms are invisible to the speaker/actor.

Others theorists have also applied the phenomenon to additional and interesting cases. Sorial, for example, uses covert exercitives to justify sedition law.[2] Saul explores the phenomenon as a potential account of racial figleaves[3] and political dog whistles.[4] Several theorists have used the framework to account for acts of slurring;[5] Ayela and Vasilyeva use it to explore the harms of homophonic speech and to argue for the moral responsibility of overhearers;[6] Gelber appeals to covert exercitives to define a regulable class of hate speech;[7] and Aas uses it to investigate issues in disability studies.[8] Given the ubiquity of the phenomenon, the possibilities seem endless.

Positive potential

Thus far, we have focused exclusively on harm but how might this pervasive yet hidden mechanism of norm enactment make positive contributions to our social world? Recall that, in Chapter 7, we considered legal intervention in the case of racist speech in our public places. There, I suggested that if the law cannot or will not remedy those harms, we should all be more proactive about the norms operative in our social interactions. How might we do this and what role might covert exercitives play?

It is possible for our words and actions to tap into more egalitarian social practices and thereby facilitate their governance in a micro-context. Again, what we say does not just enact conversational s-norms; it also changes the

[2] See Sorial 2010 and 2015. [3] See Saul 2017. [4] See Saul 2018.

[5] See Bianchi 2014; Cousens 2014; Lenehan 2014; Soon, "On Slurring," unpublished manuscript; Popa-Wyatt and Wyatt 2017.

[6] See Ayala and Vasilyeva 2016. [7] See Gelber 2017. [8] See Aas 2016.

s-norms of the social space in which that conversation is taking place. I shall now show how it is possible to say things that enact more egalitarian norms in our social spaces.

In order to do this, I will analyze a conversation that takes place during a philosophy department meeting.[9] This department is professional and collegial but it is also somewhat hierarchical. There is a clear ranking amongst the faculty members. The full professors are above the associate professors who are above the assistant professors who are above the instructors who are above the adjunct faculty members. This ranking is institutionalized in a variety of ways (e.g. via salary, benefits, job responsibilities, and possibilities for advancement) but it is also reflected in the culture of the department. Adjunct faculty members are not included in the running of the department and, although instructors do attend department meetings and join in the discussion, they have no say in what and when they teach. This arrangement is fairly typical in American academia.

To set the scene, Peter is a full professor and the chair. Ralph is a longtime permanent instructor and the only person of color in the department; Jane is the only junior faculty member and the only woman. Being chair is a mere chore to the senior men and its associated stipend negligible. To Ralph, however, being chair would be a much valued signal of professional recognition and inclusion and the associated stipend would be a real windfall for him and his family.

Peter: "We really need to figure this out. I am stepping down as chair at the end of this year and someone really needs to step up. Nobody wants to do it but someone has to."

[Awkward silence.]

Jane: "Well, I know that I am not eligible to be chair. I just got here and I don't have tenure but is Ralph eligible?"

[Long awkward silence.]

Jane: [with her hands in the air] "I am just trying to be clear on the eligibility conditions so we can be sure that we are considering all of our options. I am not sure that this would be of interest [turns to Ralph sitting along side wall] to you, Ralph, but if it does and we could

[9] This example is also discussed in McGowan 2018a.

make it happen, it would be good for everyone—especially given that no one else seems to want to do it!"

[Many slightly reluctant nods in the room]

Peter: Ahh, well, we'll come back to this.

Let's focus on Jane's contributions. Jane's comments enact many changes to the conversational score but the primary change of interest is that she expands the scope of the relevant quantifier in order to include Ralph. By raising the possibility of Ralph being chair, Jane made it subsequently conversationally inappropriate for others to continue to just ignore that possibility. Jane rendered Ralph conversationally relevant.

Of course, Jane did more than that.[10] After all, her comments are not just moves in a conversation, they are also moves in a social interaction. One of the many things Jane did was to operate on the assumption that Ralph is a valued and equal member of the department. She acted as if the department was not hierarchical and she did so in the hope that her doing so would come to make the department less so.

Suppose it works. Suppose, for example, that the senior faculty only needed to see someone treat Ralph like a valued colleague in order to realize that they really hadn't been. Suppose that going forward they invite Ralph to lunch; they consult him in the hallways about pedagogy, and they advocate for him with the administration. In such a case, Jane's comments rely on egalitarian norms being operative in the department and doing so sets in motion a process that results in egalitarian norms being operative in the department.

Several points are worth highlighting. First, acting as if something is the case is one way to make it the case. This is so with socially constructed facts. Acting as if I am confident can cause people to treat me in ways that actually make me confident. As Maitra has stressed, acting as if I have authority can, so long as the relevant others play along, come to make it the case that I actually have authority in a certain realm.[11] Acting as if you are my friend will help to make it the case that you are my friend.[12]

[10] Elsewhere, I have argued that Jane's utterances constitute a different (and better kind of) counter-speech. See McGowan 2018a.

[11] Maitra calls this licensing. See Maitra 2012. The phenomenon was identified earlier in Thomason (1990: 342–3).

[12] James argues that faith in a fact can help to make that fact obtain (or open one up to otherwise unavailable evidence of that fact). James uses the friendship example. See William 1979.

Second, Jane manages to enact egalitarian s-norms for this social interaction even though Jane is a junior woman with relatively little power. Enacting norms does not require authority. When one's utterances are moves in norm-governed activities, one enacts score changes and thus s-norms for the activity in question. Because Jane's remarks abide by egalitarian g-norms, she brings those egalitarian social norms to bear in that micro-context and she does this despite her relative lack of power. Moreover, she sets in motion a process whereby more egalitarian *g*-norms come to govern the department.

Third, Jane's actions are risky.[13] A positive outcome is by no means guaranteed; it could have turned out horribly for all involved. Jane might have managed to merely anger her senior colleagues and thereby make the department culture an acrimonious one. Ralph might resent her intervention and further withdraw from department life. Unfavorable consequences are real possibilities; Jane's actions are genuinely perilous.

Fourth, indirection is one mechanism for reducing this risk. Jane was strategic when she chose to indirectly challenge the culture of the department. Feigning ignorance of the import of her comments allowed herself and others to act as if her remarks were really only about the requirements for being chair.[14] Being indirect in this way allows participants, Jane included, to save face.[15]

Fifth, this example demonstrates that it is possible to reshape social norms.[16] It is even possible for relatively powerless individuals to do so in micro-contexts. As Bicchieri and Mercier stress, changing social norms is greatly facilitated when participants are mutually aware of alternatives.[17] Similarly, according to Tankard and Paluck, individuals can shape norms (and the perception of those norms) "when their public behavior

[13] Reclaiming slurs is another risky form of linguistic reform. See Herbert 2015.

[14] It is also possible for Jane to unwittingly enact more egalitarian norms if, for example, she was naively assuming that the department is egalitarian.

[15] Suppose, instead, that Jane had said, "You all think you are so decent but actually you are really crappy and you perpetually step on our only instructor and our only person of color! Get a grip!" Had she said this, it is unlikely to have gone well for anyone. I recognize, however, that sometimes being direct and confrontational is the best option, all things considered.

[16] It can sometimes seem like social norms cannot be changed at least by individual action. After all, violating the norms can trigger their enforcement thereby strengthening them. This grim and hopeless picture of our social world is sometimes attributed to Butler. See, for example, Nussbaum (1999).

[17] See Bicchieri and Mercier 2014.

calls attention to existing norms".[18] In Jane's case, she acted as if norms of teamwork were operative and these norms are already familiar to those involved. That they are already familiar to all department members greatly facilitates the process of reshaping the department's g-norms.

When in the company of others, our words and our actions more generally are contributions to broader social practices and thus enact norms. Consequently, we are perpetually shaping the normative landscape. Whatever we do (even if we do nothing), we are making moves and thus enacting s-norms. There is just no way to avoid the normative impact of being socially-situated. In every social moment, we are therefore each faced with an unavoidable choice: We can participate in business as usual and behave in ways that allow extant norms to go unchallenged or we can behave in ways that shape our social world for the better. What will you do?

[18] See Tankard and Paluck 2016; 187.

Bibliography

Aas, Sean. 2016. "Disabled—Therefore Unhealthy?" *Ethical Theory and Moral Practice* 19 (5): 1259–74.

Abramson, Kate. 2014. "Turning Up the Lights on Gaslighting," *Philosophical Perspectives* 28(1): 1–30.

Altman, Andrew. 2011. "Discrimination," in Edward N. Zalta (ed.), *The Stanford Encyclopedia of Philosophy* (Spring 2011 Edition). http://plato.stanford.edu/archives/spr2011/entries/discrimination/.

Anderson, Luvell, Sally Haslanger, and Rae Langton. 2012. "Language and Race," In Gillian Russell and Delia Graff Fara (eds.), *Routledge Companion to the Philosophy of Language*. Routledge.

Anderson, Michelle. 1995. "Silencing Women's Speech," in Laura Lederer and Richard Delgado (eds.), *The Price We Pay*. New York: Hill and Wang: 122–30.

Anderson, Michelle. 2005. "Negotiating Sex," *Southern California Law Review* 41: 101–40.

Article 14. *European Convention for the Protection of Human Rights and Fundamental Freedoms*. http://conventions.coe.int/Treaty/en/Treaties/Html/005.html.

Austin, J. L. 1975. *How to Do Things With Words*. Cambridge, MA: Harvard University Press: 14–152.

Ayala, Saray, and Nadya Vasilyeva. 2016. "Responsibility for Silence," *Journal of Social Philosophy* 47 (3): 256–72.

Bach, Kent, and Harnish, Robert M. 1979. *Linguistic Communication and Speech Acts*. Cambridge, MA: MIT Press.

Bartels, Victoria T. 2015. "Meritor Savings Bank v. Vinson: The Supreme Court's Recognition of the Hostile Environment in Sexual Harassment Claims," *Akron Law Review* 20 (3): 575–89.

Bauer, Nancy. 2005. "How To Do Things With Pornography," in S. Shieh and A. Crary (eds.), *Reading Cavell*. London: Routledge: 68–97.

Bauer, Nancy. 2015. *How to Do Things With Pornography*. Cambridge, MA: Harvard University Press.

Beaver, David I., and Bart Geurts. 2011. "Presupposition," in Edward N. Zalta (ed.), *The Stanford Encyclopedia of Philosophy* (Summer 2011 Edition), http://plato.stanford.edu/archives/sum2011/entries/presupposition/.

Bertolet, Rod. 1994. "Are There Indirect Speech Acts?" in S. Tsohatzidis (ed.), *Foundations of Speech Act Theory*. London: Routledge: 335–49.

Bianchi, Claudia. 2014. "The Speech Act Account of Derogatory Epithets: Some Critical Notes," in J. Dutant, D. Fassio, and A. Meylan (eds.), *Liber Pascal Engel*, University of Geneva: 465–80. http://www.unige.ch/lettres/philo/publications/engel/liberamicorum.

Bicchieri, Cristina. 2006. *The Grammar of Society: The Nature and Dynamics of Social Norms*. Cambridge: Cambridge University Press.

Bicchieri, Christine and Hugo Mercier. 2014. "Norms and Beliefs: How Change Occurs," in Maria Xenitidiou and Bruce Edmonds (eds.), *The Complexity of Social Norms*. Heidelberg:Springer: 37–54. https://doi.org/10.1007/978-3-319-05308-0_3

Bird, Alexander. 2002. "Illocutionary Silencing," *Pacific Philosophical Quarterly* 83 (1): 1–15.

Black cat. 2012. "Harassment at NYCC 2012," http://beautilation.tumblr.com/post/33538802648. Cross-Posted from Mandy Caruso's tumblr, *The Grind Haus*, October 2012.

Blum, Lawrence. 2004. "Stereotypes and Stereotyping: A Moral Analysis," *Philosophical Papers* 33 (3): 251–89.

Bond v. Michael's Family Restaurant. 1994. Wisc. Labor & Indus. Rev. Comm'n, Case Nos. 9150755, 9151204 (March 30, 1994).

Brandom, Robert. 1994. *Making it Explicit: Reasoning, Representing, and Discursive Commitment*. Cambridge, MA: Harvard University Press.

Braun, David. 2012. "Indexicals," in Edward N. Zalta (ed.), *The Stanford Encyclopedia of Philosophy* (Summer 2012 Edition), http://plato.stanford.edu/archives/sum2012/entries/indexicals/.

Brison, Susan. 1998a. "The Autonomy Defense of Free Speech," *Ethics* 108 (2): 312–39.

Brison, Susan. 1998b. "Speech, Harm, and the Mind-Body Problem in First Amendment Jurisprudence," *Legal Theory* 4 (1): 39–61.

Brison, Susan. 2000. "Relational Autonomy and Freedom of Expression," in C. MacKenzie and S. Natalie (eds.), *Relational Autonomy: Feminist Perspectives on Autonomy, Agency, and the Social Self*. Oxford: Oxford University Press: 280–99.

Brooks, Robert. *The Law of Address*, unpublished manuscript.

Brown, Alexander. 2015. *Hate Speech Law: A Philosophical Investigation*. New York: Routledge.

Bundy v. Jackson. Bundy 641 F. 2d 934. 1981.

Butler, Judith. 1997. *Excitable Speech: A Politics of the Performative*. New York: Routledge.

Camp, Elisabeth. 2018. "Insinuation, Indirection, and the Conversational Score," in D. Fogal, M. Moss, and D. W. Harris (eds.), *New Work on Speech Acts*. Oxford: Oxford University Press.

Caponetto, Laura. 2017. "On Silencing, Authority, and the Act of Refusal," *Rivista di Estetica* 63: 35–52.

Carston, Robyn. 2002. *Thought and Utterances: The Pragmatics of Explicit Communication*: Appendix 1: 376, 378. Oxford: Blackwell.

Cassista v. Community Foods, Inc., 856 P.2d 1143 (Cal. 1993).

Citron, Danielle. 2014. *Hate Crimes in Cyberspace*. Cambridge, MA: Harvard University Press.

Clark, Herbert. 1996. *Using Language*. Cambridge: Cambridge University Press: 62–70.

Codatos, M., I. Testoni, and S. Ronzani. 2012. "Analysis of a Meeting of Sociodrama on the Representation of the Ideal Woman," *Interdisciplinary Journal of Family Studies* 42 (2): 146–62.

Collins, Patricia Hill. 2000. *Black Feminist Thought: Knowledge, Consciousness, and the Politics of Empowerment*, second edition. New York. Routledge.

Cook v. State of RI, Dept. of MHRH, 783 F. Supp. 1569 (D.R.I. 1992)

Cousens, Chris. 2014. "Who Said That?: A Contextualist Extension to McGowan's Scorekeeping Model," *Philosophy Honours Thesis*, University of Melbourne. https://mupcunimelb.files.wordpress.com/2015/03/chris-cousens-who-said-that-a-contextualist-extension-to-mcgowans-scorekeeping-model.pdf.

Craig v. New Crystal Restaurant. 1995. Chicago Commission on Human Relations Case No 92-PA-40 (October 18, 1995). 2,14.

Crenshaw, Kimberlé. 1989. "Demarginalizing the Intersection of Race and Sex: A Black Feminist Critique of Antidiscrimination Doctrine, Feminist Theory and Antiracist Politics," *University of Chicago Legal Forum* 1 (8). Available at: https://chicagounbound.uchicago.edu/uclf/vol1989/iss1/8

Crenshaw, Kimberlé. 1991. "Mapping the Margins: Intersectionality, Identity Politics, and Violence Against Women of Color," *Stanford Law Review* 43 (6): 1241–99.

Crenshaw, Kimberlé. 1993. "Beyond Racism and Misogyny: Black Feminism and 2 Live Crew," in Mari J. Matsuda, Charles R. Lawrence III, Richard Delgado, and Kimberlé Williams Crenshaw (eds.), *Words that Wound: Critical Race Theory, Assaultive Speech, and the First Amendment*. Boulder, CO. Westview.

Crenshaw, Kimberlé. 2012. "From Private Violence to Mass Incarceration: Thinking Intersectionally About Women, Race, and Social Control," *UCLA Law Review* 59: 1418–72.

Darwall, Stephen. 1977. "Two Kinds of Respect," *Ethics* 88 (1): 36–49.

Davidson, Donald. 1963. "Actions, Reasons, and Causes," *Journal of Philosophy* 60 (23): 686–7.

Davies, Alex. 2014. "How To Silence Content with Porn, Context, and Loaded Questions," *European Journal of Philosophy* 24 (2): 498–522.

Davis, Wayne. 1992. "Speaker Meaning," *Linguistics and Philosophy* 15: 223–53.

Delaware Code Title 6 § 4504. 6 DE Code § 4504 (2015)https://law.justia.com/codes/delaware/2015/title-6/chapter-45/section-4504/

Delgado, Richard. 1993. "Words that Wound: A Tory Action for Racial Insults, Epithets and Name Calling," in M. Matsuda, C. Lawrence, R. Delgado, and K. Crenshaw (eds.), *Words that Wound: Critical Race Theory, Assaultive Speech, and the First Amendment*. Boulder, CO: Westview Press: 89–110.

Delgado, Richard and Jean Stefancic. 1991. *Critical Race Theory: An Introduction*. New York: NYU Press.

Dotson, Kristie. 2011. "Tracking Epistemic Violence, Tracking Practices of Silencing," *Hypatia* 26 (2): 236–57.

Dworkin, Ronald. 1986. *Law's Empire*. Cambridge, MA: Harvard University Press.

Eaton, Anne. 2007. "A Sensible Antiporn Feminism," *Ethics* 117 (4): 674–715.

Elgin, Catherine. 1996. *Considered Judgment*. Princeton, NJ: Princeton University Press, 1996.

Elgin, Catherine and Nelson Goodman. 1988. *Reconceptions in Philosophy and Other Arts and Sciences*. Indianapolis, IN: Hackett.

Emerick, Barrett. 2017. "The Violence of Silencing," forthcoming in Jennifer Kling (ed.), *Pacifism, Politics, and Feminism*. Leiden: Brill .

Finlayson, Lorna. 2014. "How To Screw Things With Pornography," *Hypatia* 29 (4): 774–89.

Fricker, Miranda. 2007. *Epistemic Injustice: Power and the Ethics of Knowing*. Oxford: Oxford University Press.

Frye, Marilyn. 1983a. "Oppression," in Marilyn Frye, *The Politics of Reality*. Freedom, CA: The Crossing Press: 1–16.

Frye, Marilyn. 1983b. "Sexism," in Marilyn Frye, *The Politics of Reality*. Freedom, CA: The Crossing Press: 17–40.

Garcia, Jorge. 1996. "The Heart of Racism," *Journal of Social Philosophy* 27 (1): 5–46.

Gates, Henry Louis. 1993. "Let Them Talk: Why Civil Liberties Pose No Threat to Civil Rights," *The New Republic*: 37–49. September 20 & 27, 1993.

Gelber, Katherine. 2002. *Speaking Back: The Free Speech versus Hate Speech Debate*. Amsterdam: John Benjamins Ltd.

Gelber, Katherine. 2017. "A Principle for Regulating Hate Speech: A Systematically- and Authority-derived (SAD) Approach," draft presented at the workshop 'Free Speech and its Discontents', Princeton University Center for Human Values, December.

Golding, Martin. 2000. *Free Speech on Campus*. Landham, MD: Rowman & Littlefield.

Goodman, Nelson. 1968. *Languages of Art: An Approach to a Theory of Symbols*. Indianapolis: Bobbs-Merill.

Goodman, Nelson. 1978. *Ways of Worldmaking*. Indianapolis: Hackett Publishing.

Goodman, Jeffery A., Jonathan Schell, Michelle G. Alexander, and Scott Eidelman. 2008. "The Impact of a Derogatory Remark on Prejudice Toward a Gay Male," *Journal of Applied Social Psychology* 38 (2): 542–55.

Green, Leslie. 1998. "Pornographizing, Subordinating and Silencing," in Robert Post (ed.), *Censorship and Silencing: Practices of Cultural Regulation*. Los Angeles, CA: Getty Research Institute: 285–311.

Green, Leslie. 2000. "Pornographies," *The Journal of Political Philosophy* 8 (1): 27–52.

Green, Mitchell. 2017a. "Speech Acts," in Edward N. Zalta (ed.), *The Stanford Encyclopedia of Philosophy* (Winter 2017 Edition), URL = <https://plato.stanford.edu/archives/win2017/entries/speech-acts/>.

Green, Mitchell. 2017b. "Conversation and Common Ground," *Philosophical Studies* 174 (6): 1587–604.

Greenawalt, Kent. 1989. *Speech, Crime and the Uses of Language*. Oxford: Oxford University Press: 303.

Greenberg, Jeff and Tom Pyszczynski. 1985. "The Effect of an Overheard Slur on Evaluations of the Target: How to Spread a Social Disease," *Journal of Experimental Social Psychology* 21 (1): 61–71.

Grice, H. P. 1989. *Studies in the Way of Words*. Cambridge, MA: Harvard University Press.

Grunberg, Angela. 2014. "Saying and Doing: Speech Actions, Speech Acts and Related Events," *European Journal of Philosophy* 22 (2): 173–99.

Habermas, Jurgen. 1984. *The Theory of Communicative Action, Volume I: Reason and the Rationalization of Society*. London: Heinemann.

Haslanger, Sally. 2000. "Race and Gender: (What) Are They? (What) Do We Want Them To Be?" *Nous* 34 (1): 31–55.

Haslanger, Sally. 2004. "Oppressions: Racial and Other," in Michael Levine and Tamas Pataki (eds.), *Racism in Mind*. Ithaca, NY: Cornell University Press: 97–123.

Haslanger, Sally. 2010. "Ideology, Generics, and Common Ground," in Charlotte Witt (ed.), *Feminist Metaphysics: Essays on the Ontology of Sex, Gender, and the Self*. Dordrecht. Spring: 179–207.

Haslanger, Sally. 2012. *Resisting Reality: Social Construction and Social Critique*. Oxford: Oxford University Press.

Herbert, Cassie. 2015. "Precarious Projects: the Performative Structure of Reclamation," *Language Sciences* 52: 131–8.

Herbert, Cassie and Rebecca Kukla. 2016. "Ingrouping, Outgrouping, and the Pragmatics of Peripheral Speech," *Journal of the American Philosophical Association* 2 (4): 576–96.

Horisk, Claire. Manuscript. *The Pragmatics of Demeaning Jokes*.

Hornsby, Jennifer. 1993. "Speech Acts and Pornography," *Women's Philosophy Review* 10: 38–45.

Hornsby, Jennifer. 1995. "Disempowered Speech," in Haslanger (ed.), *Philosophical Topics* 23 (2): 127–47.

Hornsby, Jennifer and Rae Langton. 1998. "Free Speech and Illocution," *Legal Theory* 4: 21–37.

Hurley, Susan. 2004. "Imitation, Media Violence, and Freedom of Speech," *Philosophical Studies* 117 (1–2): 165–218.

Ignatiev, Noel. 1995. *How the Irish Became White*. New York: Routledge.

Jacobson, Daniel. 1995. "Freedom of Speech Acts? A Response to Langton," *Philosophy and Public Affairs* 24: 64–79.

Jacobson, Matthew. 1998. *Whiteness of a Different Color*. Cambridge, MA: Harvard University Press.

Johnson, Casey. 2018. "Just Say 'No': Obligations to Voice Disagreement," in Casey Johnson (ed.), *Voicing Dissent: The Ethics and Epistemology of Making Disagreement Public*. New York: Routledge.

Kelly, Daniel and Erica Roeder. 2008. "Racial Cognition and the Ethics of Implicit Bias," *Philosophy Compass* 3(3): 522–40.

Kipnis, Laura. 1996. *Bound and Gagged: Pornography and the Politics of Fantasy in America*. New York: Grove Press.

Koontz, Daniel. 2008."Hostile Public Accommodations Laws and the First Amendment," *NYU Journal of Law and Liberty* 3: 197–266.

Koppelman, Andrew. 2013. "Review of Speech and Harm: Controversies over Free Speech," *Ethics* 123 (4): 768–71.

Kukla, Rebecca. 2018. *Ethics* 129: 70–97.

Kukla, Rebecca and Mark Lance. 2009. *Yo! and Lo!: The Pragmatic Topography of the Space of Reasons*. Cambridge, MA: Harvard University Press.

Kukla, Rebecca and Mark Lance. 2013. "Leave the Gun: Take the Canoli! The Pragmatic Topography of Person Calls," *Ethics* 123 (3): 456–78.

Langton, Rae. 1993. "Speech Acts and Unspeakable Acts," *Philosophy and Public Affairs* 22 (4): 293–330.

Langton, Rae. 1998. "Subordination, Silence and Pornography's Authority," in Robert C. Post (ed.), *Censorship and Silencing: Practices of Cultural Regulation*. Los Angeles, CA: Getty Research Institute for the History of Art and the Humanities: 261–83.

Langton, Rae. 2009. *Sexual Solipsism: Philosophical Essays on Pornography and Objectification*. Oxford: Oxford University Press: 103–350.

Langton, Rae. 2011. "Beyond Belief: Pragmatics in Hate Speech and Pornography," in Ishani Maitra and Mary Kate McGowan (eds.), *Speech and Harm: Controversies Over Free Speech*. Oxford: Oxford University Press: 72–93.

Langton, Rae. 2018. "Blocking as Counter-speech," in D. Fogal, M. Moss, and D. W. Harris (eds.), *New Work on Speech Acts*. Oxford: Oxford University Press.

Langton, Rae and Caroline West. 1999. "Scorekeeping in a Pornographic Language Game," *Australasian Journal of Philosophy* 77 (3): 303–19.

Lasson, Kenneth. 1985. "In Defense of Group Libel Laws or Why the First Amendment Should Not Protect Nazis," *Human Rights Annual* 2, 1985.

Lawrence, Charles R. 1993. III, "If He Hollers, Let Him Go: Regulating Racist Speech on Campus," in M. Matsuda, C. R. Lawrence, R. Delgado, and K. Crenshaw (eds.), *Words that Wound: Critical Race Theory, Assaultive Speech, and the First Amendment*. Boulder, CO: Westview Press: 53–88.

Laws, Charlotte. 2013. "I've Been Called the 'Erin Brockovich' of Revenge Porn, and For the First Time Ever, Here is My Entire Uncensored Story of Death Threats, Anonymous and the FBI," *xoJane*, November 21, 2013. http://www.xojane.com/it-happened-to-me/charlotte-laws-hunter-moore-erin-brockovich-revenge-porn.

Lenehan, Rose. 2014. "Beyond Slurs: Communicating Evaluative Perspectives," MA Thesis, MIT, 2014; https://dspace.mit.edu/handle/1721.1/101526.

Lepore, Ernest and Herman Cappellen. 2005. *Insensitive Semantics: A Defense of Semantic Minimalism*. Malden, MA: Blackwell.

Lepore, Ernest and Matthew Stone. 2015. *Imagination and Convention: Distinguishing Grammar and Inference in Language*. Oxford: Oxford University Press.

Lessig, Lawrence. 1995. "The Regulation of Social Meaning," *The University of Chicago Law Review* 62 (3): 943–1045 at 1001.

Lewis, David. (1969) 2002. *Convention: A Philosophical Study*. Reprint, Oxford: Blackwell Publishers.

Lewis, David. 1983. "Scorekeeping in a Language Game," *Philosophical Papers Volume I*. New York: Oxford University Press: 233–49.

Lewis, David. 1996. "Elusive Knowledge," *Australasian Journal of Philosophy* 74 (4): 549–67.

Lichtenberg, Judith. 1992. "Racism in the Head, Racism in the World," *Philosophy and Public Policy Quarterly* 12 (1/2): 3–5.

Lovelace, Linda with Mike McGrady. 1980. *Ordeal: The Truth Behind Deep Throat*. New York: Citadel Press Books.

Lycan, William. 1986. *Logical Form in Natural Language*. Cambridge, MA: The MIT Press: 73–186.

Lycan, William. 2000. *Philosophy of Language: A Contemporary Introduction*. London and New York: Routledge: 24–5.

MacBride, Fraser. 2014. "Truthmakers," in Edward N. Zalta (ed.), *The Stanford Encyclopedia of Philosophy* (Spring 2014 Edition), http://plato.stanford.edu/archives/spr2014/entries/truthmakers/.

MacFarlane, John. 2009. "Nonindexical Contextualism," *Synthese* 166, 231–50.

MacKinnon, Catharine. 1987. *Feminism Unmodified: Discourses on Life and Law*. Cambridge, MA: Harvard University Press.

MacKinnon, Catharine. 1989. *Towards a Feminist Theory of the State*. Cambridge, MA: Harvard University Press.

MacKinnon, Catharine. 1993. *Only Words*. Cambridge, MA: Harvard University Press.

MacKinnon, Catharine. 2005. *Women's Lives, Men's Laws*. Cambridge, MA: Harvard University Press. 243.

MacKinnon, Catharine and Andrea Dworkin. 1998. *In Harm's Way: The Pornography Civil Rights Hearings*. Cambridge, MA: Harvard University Press: 444.

Maitra, Ishani. 2004. "Silence and Responsibility," *Philosophical Perspectives* 18 (1): 189–208.

Maitra, Ishani. 2009. "Silencing Speech," *Canadian Journal of Philosophy* 39 (2): 309–38.

Maitra, Ishani. 2012. "Subordinating Speech," in I. Maitra and M. K. McGowan (eds.), *Speech and Harm: Controversies Over Free Speech*. Oxford: Oxford University Press: 94–120.

Maitra, Ishani and Mary Kate McGowan. 2007. "The Limits of Free Speech: Pornography and the Question of Coverage," *Legal Theory* 13 (1): 41–68.

Maitra, Ishani and Mary Kate McGowan. 2009. "On Racist Hate Speech and the Scope of a Free Speech Principle," *Canadian Journal of Law and Jurisprudence* 23 (2): 343–72.

Maitra, Ishani and Mary Kate McGowan. 2010. "On Silencing, Rape and Responsibility," *Australasian Journal of Philosophy* 88 (1): 167–72.

Maitra, Ishani and Mary Kate McGowan. 2012. "Introduction and Overview," in Ishani Maitra and Mary Kate McGowan (eds.), *Speech and Harm: Controversies Over Free Speech*. Oxford: Oxford University Press: 1–23.

Mallon, Ron. 2004. "Passing, Traveling and Reality: Social Constructionism and the Metaphysics of Race," *Nous* 38 (4): 644–73.

Manne, Kate. 2018. *Down Girl: The Logic of Misogyny*. New York: Oxford University Press.

Mason, Elinor. 2018. "Rape, Harassment, and the Silencing of Sexual Refusal." Unpublished manuscript.

Massachusetts Commission Against Discrimination. www.mass.gov/mcad/resources/employers-businesses/emp-guidelines-harassment-gen.html.

Matsuda, Mari. 1993. "Public Response to Racist Speech: Considering the Victim's Story," in Matsuda, Lawrence, Delgado, and Crenshaw (eds.), *Words that Wound*. Boulder, CO: Westview Press: 17–51.

McGowan, Mary Kate. 2003. "On Conversational Exercitives and the Force of Pornography," *Philosophy & Public Affairs* 31 (2): 155–89.

McGowan, Mary Kate. 2004. "Conversational Exercitives: Something Else We Do With Our Words," *Linguistics and Philosophy*, 27 (1): 93–111.

McGowan, Mary Kate. 2005. "On Pornography: MacKinnon, Speech Acts and 'False' Construction,", *Hypatia* 20 (3): 22–49.

McGowan, Mary Kate. 2009a. "On Silencing and Sexual Refusal," *Journal of Political Philosophy* 17 (4): 487–94.

McGowan, Mary Kate. 2009b. "Oppressive Speech," *Australasian Journal of Philosophy* 87 (3): 389–407.

McGowan, Mary Kate. 2012. "On 'Whites Only' Signs and Racist Hate Speech: Verbal Acts of Racial Discrimination," in Ishani Maitra and Mary Kate McGowan (eds.), *Speech and Harm: Controversies Over Free Speech*. Oxford: Oxford University Press: 121–47.

McGowan, Mary Kate. 2014. "Sincerity Silencing," *Hypatia* 29 (2): 458–73.

McGowan, Mary Kate. 2018a. "Responding to Harmful Speech: More Speech, Counter Speech, and the Complexity of Language Use," in Casey Johnson (ed.), *Voicing Dissent: The Ethics and Epistemology of Making Disagreement Public*. New York: Routledge.

McGowan, Mary Kate. 2018b. "Speech, Permissibility and the Social World," in D. Fogal, M. Moss, and D. W. Harris (eds.), *New Work on Speech Acts*. Oxford: Oxford University Press.

McGowan, Mary Kate. 2018c. "On Political Correctness, Microaggressions, and Silencing in the Academy," in Jennifer Lackey (ed.), *Essays on Academic Freedom*. Oxford: Oxford University Press.

McGowan, Mary Kate, Margaret Hall, and Shan Shan Tam. 2009. "On Indirect Speech Acts and Linguistic Communication: A Response to Bertolet," *Philosophy* 84 (330): 495–513.

McGowan, Helmers, Stolzenberg, and Adelman. 2011. "A Partial Defense of Illocutionary Silencing," *Hypatia* 26 (1): 132–49.

McGowan, Mary Kate, Ilana Walder-Biesanz, Morvareed Rezaian, and Chloe Emerson. 2016. "On Silencing and Systematicity: The Challenge of the Drowning Case," *Hypatia* 31 (1): 74–90.

McKinney, Rachel. 2016. "Extracted Speech," *Social Theory and Practice* 42 (2): 258–84.

McKinnon, Rachel. 2017. "Allies Behaving Badly: Gaslighting as Epistemic Injustice," in Ian James Kidd, Jose Medina, and Gaile Poulhouse (eds.), New York: Routledge.

McNally, Michael Francis. 2017. https://www.youtube.com/watch?v=8608ngM2aXY&feature=youtu.be&app=desktop at 8:00–8:07.

Meiklejohn, Alexander. 1960. "Free Speech and its Relation to Self-Government," in Alexander Meiklejohn, *Political Freedom: The Constitutional Powers of the People*. New York: Harper Press: 3–89.

Meritor Savings Bank v. Vinson. 477 U.S. 59. 1986.

Mikkola, Mari. 2011. "Illocution, Silencing, and the Speech Acts of Refusal," *Pacific Philosophical Quarterly* 92 (3): 415–37.

Mill, J. S. 1978. *On Liberty*, ed. Elizabeth Rappaport. Indianapolis: Hackett Publishing Company.

Neale, Stephen. 1990. *Descriptions*. Cambridge, MA: MIT Press.

Neldaughter v. Dickeyville Athletic Club. 1994. Wisconsin Labor and Industry Review Commission, Case no. 9132522 (May 24, 1994). http://lirc.wisconsin.gov/erdecsns/17.html.

Nielsen, Laura Beth. 2004. *License to Harass: Law, Hierarchy and Offensive Public Speech*. Princeton, NJ: Princeton University Press.

Nussbaum, Martha. 1999. "The Professor of Parody," *The New Republic Online*. February 1999. Posted November 2000. https://philpapers.org/rec/NUSTPO-3

Ogien, Ruwen. 2003. *Penser la Pornographie*. Paris: Presses Universitaires de France: 23–35.

Patane v. Clark, 508 F. 3d 106 (2nd Circuit, 2007).

Popa-Wyatt, Mihaela, and Jeremy Wyatt. 2017. "Slurs, Roles and Power," in *Philosophical Studies*: 1–28. https://doi.org/10.1007/s11098-017-0986-2

Priske, Rusty. 2015. "My Night at the Slam/ Reacting to Oppressive Speech," https://rustythepoet.wordpress.com/2014/03/16/my-night-at-the-slam-reacting-to-oppressive-speech/.

Putnam, Hilary. 1987. *The Multiple Faces of Realism*. LaSalle, IL: Open Court.

Roberts, Craige. 2012. "Information Structure: Towards an Integrated Formal Theory of Pragmatics," in J. Yoon and A. Kathol (eds.), *Ohio State University Working Papers in Linguistics No. 49*, Papers in Pragmatics. https://www.researchgate.net/publication/239057993_Information_Structure_in_Discourse_Towards_an_Integrated_Formal_Theory_of_Pragmatics.

Russell, Bertrand. 1905. "On Denoting," *Mind* 14 (56): 479–93.

Russell, Bertrand. (1918) 1956. "The Philosophy of Logical Atomism," in R. Marsh (ed.), Logic and Knowledge. London: Allen and Unwin: 29.

Saul, Jennifer. 2006. "Pornography, Speech Acts, and Context," *Proceedings of the Aristotelian Society* 106 (2): 61–248.

Saul, Jennifer. 2017. "Racial Figleaves, the Shifting Boundaries of Permissibility, and the Rise of Donald Trump," *Philosophical Topics* 45 (2): 91–116.

Saul, Jennifer. 2018. "Dogwhistles, Political Manipulation, and the Philosophy of Language," in D. Fogal, M. Moss, and D. W. Harris (eds.), *New Work on Speech Acts*. Oxford: Oxford University Press.

Scanlon, Thomas. 1972. "A Theory of Freedom of Expression," *Philosophy and Public Affairs* 1 (2): 204–26.

Schauer, Frederick. 1972. "The Boundaries of the First Amendment: A Preliminary Explanation of Constitutional Salience," *Harvard Law Review* 117 (6): 1765–809.

Schauer, Frederick. 1982. *Free Speech: A Philosophical Enquiry*. Cambridge: Cambridge University Press.

Schauer, Frederick. 2014. "Review of Speech and Harm: Controversies over Free Speech," *Notre Dame Philosophical Reviews*. Available at https://ndpr.nd.edu/news/speech-and-harm-controversies-over-free-speech/

Scoccia, Daniel. 1996. "Can Liberals Support a Ban on Violent Pornography?" *Ethics* 106 (4): 776–99.

Searle, John. 1969. *Speech Acts: An Essay in the Philosophy of Language*. Cambridge: Cambridge University Press.

Searle, John. 1979a. "Indirect Speech Acts," in John Searle, *Expression and Meaning*. Cambridge: Cambridge University Press: 30–57.

Searle, John. 1979b. "A Taxonomy of Illocutionary Acts," in John Searle, *Expression and Meaning*. Cambridge: Cambridge University Press: 1–29.

Searle, John. 1995. *The Construction of Social Reality*. New York: The Free Press.

Searle, John and Daniel Vanderveken. 1985. *Foundations of Illocutionary Logic*. Cambridge: Cambridge University Press.

Shapiro, Scott. 2011. *Legality*. Cambridge, MA: Harvard University Press.

Shelby, Tommie. 2003. "Ideology, Racism, and Critical Social Theory," *The Philosophical Forum* 34 (2): 153–88.

Shiffrin, Seana. 2014. *Speech Matters: On Lying, Morality, and the Law*. Princeton, NJ: Princeton University Press.

Simpson, Robert Mark. 2013. "Un-ringing the Bell: McGowan on Oppressive Speech and the Asymmetric Pliability of Conversation," *Australasian Journal of Philosophy* 91 (3): 555–75.

Simpson, Robert Mark. 2016. "Defining 'Speech': Subtraction, Addition, and Division," *Journal of Law and Jurisprudence* 29 (2): 457–94.

Soon, Valerie. "On Slurring," unpublished manuscript.

Sorial, Sarah. 2010. "Can Saying Something Make It So? The Nature of Seditious Harm," *Law and Philosophy* 29 (3): 273–305.

Sorial, Sarah. 2015. *Sedition and the Advocacy of Violence: Free Speech and Counter Terrorism*. London and New York: Routledge.

Sperber, Dan and Deirdre Wilson. 1986. *Relevance: Communication and Cognition*. Cambridge, MA: Harvard University Press.

Stalnaker, Robert. 1973. "Presupposition," *Journal of Philosophical Logic* 2: 77–96.

Stalnaker, Robert. 1974. "Pragmatic Presupposition," in M. Munitz and P. Uner (eds.), *Semantics and Philosophy*. New York: New York University Press: 197–213.

Stalnaker, Robert. 1978. "Assertion," in P. Cole, (ed.), *Syntax and Semantics, Volume 3: Speech Acts*. New York: Academic Press: 315–22.

Stalnaker, Robert. 1998. "On the Representation of Context," *Journal of Logic, Language, and Information* 7: 3–19.

Stalnaker, Robert. 1999. "Assertion," in R. Stalnaker (ed.), *Context and Content: Essays on Intentionality in Speech and Thought*. Oxford: Oxford University Press:78–95.

Stalnaker, Robert. 2002. "Common Ground," *Linguistics and Philosophy* 25: 701–21.

Stanley, Jason. 2000. "Context and Logical Form," *Linguistics and Philosophy* 23 (4): 391–434.

Stanley, Jason. 2015. *How Propaganda Works*. Princeton, NJ: Princeton University Press.

Stanley, Jason and Zoltan Gendler Szabo. 2000. "On Quantifier Domain Restriction," *Mind and Language* 15: 219–61.

Strawson, Peter. 1964. "Intention and Convention in Speech Acts," *The Philosophical Review* 73: 439–60.

Strawson, Peter. 1982. "Freedom and Resentment," in Gary Watson (ed.), *Free Will: Oxford Readings in Philosophy*. Oxford: Oxford University Press: 58–80.

Steele, Claude M. and Joshua Aronson. 1995. "Stereotype Threat and the Intellectual Test Performance of African Americans," *Journal of Personality and Social Psychology* 69 (5): 797–811.

Steinem, Gloria. 1980. "Erotica and Pornography: A Clear and Present Difference," in Laura Lederer (ed.), *Take Back The Night: Women on Pornography*. New York: Morrow : 35–9.

Sumner, Wayne. 2004. *The Hateful and the Obscene: Studies in the Limits of Free Speech*. Toronto: Toronto University Press.

Sumner, Wayne. 2013. "Review of Speech and Harm: Controversies over Free Speech," *Social Theory and Practice* 39 (4): 710–18.

Sunstein, Cass. 1993a. "The Anti-Caste Principle," *Michigan Law Review*, 92: 2410–55.

Sunstein, Cass. 1993b. *Democracy and the Problem of Free Speech*. New York: The Free Press.

Sveinsdottir, Asta. 2017. *Categories We Live By: The Construction of Sex, Gender, Race, and Other Social Catgeories*. Oxford: Oxford University Press.

Szabo, Zoltan G. 2000. "Descriptions and Uniqueness," *Philosophical Studies* 101: 29–57.

Tankard, Margaret E. and Elizabeth Levy Paluck. 2016. "Norm Perception as a Vehicle for Social Change," *Social Issues and Policy Review* 10 (1): 181–211.

Thomason, Rich. 1990. "Accommodation, Meaning, and Implicature," in P. Cohen, J. Morgan, and M. Pollack (eds.), *Intentions in Communication*. Cambridge, MA: MIT Press: 325–63.

Tirrell, Lynne. 2012. "Genocidal Language Games," in Ishani Maitra and Mary Kate McGowan (eds.), *Speech and Harm: Controversies Over Free Speech*. Oxford: Oxford University Press: 174–221.

Tirrell, Lynne. n.d. "Authority and Gender: Flipping the F-Switch," unpublished manuscript.

Van Fraassen, Bas. 1968. "Presupposition, Implication, and Self-reference," *The Journal of Philosophy* 65 (5): 136–52.

Volokh, Eugene. 1992. "Comment: Freedom of Speech and Workplace Harassment" *UCLA Law Review* 39: 1832–43.

Volokh, Eugene. 1996a. "Freedom of Speech, Permissible Tailoring, and Transcending Strict Scrutiny," *University of Pennsylvania Law Review* 144 (6): 2417–22.

Volokh, Eugene. 1996b. "Freedom of Speech in Cyberspace from the Listener's Perspective," *University of Chicago Legal Forum* 377, 414–21.

Von Fintel, Kai. 2008. "What is Presupposition Accommodation Again?" *Philosophical Perspectives* 22 (1): 137–70.

Waldron, Jeremy. 2012. *The Harm in Hate Speech*. Cambridge, MA: Harvard University Press.

Waters v. Commissioner of Police of the Metropolis [2000] IRLR 720.

West, Caroline. 2003. "The Free Speech Argument Against Pornography," *Canadian Journal of Philosophy* 33 (3): 391–422.

West, Caroline. 2013. Section 1. "Pornography and Censorship," in Edward N. Zalta (ed.), *The Stanford Encyclopedia of Philosophy* (Fall 2013 Edition), http://plato.stanford.edu/archives/fall2013/entries/pornography-censorship/

Wieland, Nellie. 2009. "Linguistic Authority and Convention in a Speech Act Analysis of Pornography," *Australasian Journal of Philosophy* 85 (3): 435–56.

William, James. 1979. "The Will to Believe," in James William, *The Will to Believe and Other Essays in Popular Philosophy*, Cambridge, MA and London: Harvard University Press; first published in 1897.

Williamson, Timothy. 1996. "Knowing and Asserting," *The Philosophical Review* 105 (4): 489–523.

Wilson, George and, Samuel Shpall. "Action," in Edward N. Zalta (ed.), *The Stanford Encyclopedia of Philosophy* (Summer 2012 Edition), http://plato.stanford.edu/archives/sum2012/entries/action/.

Witek, Maciej. 2016. "Mechanisms of Illocutionary Games," *Language and Communication* 42 (2006): 11–22.

Witt, Charlotte. 2011. *The Metaphysics of Gender*. Oxford: Oxford University Press: 29.

Wyatt, Nicole. 2009. "Failing to do Things With Words," *Southwest Philosophy Review* 25 (1): 135–42.

Young, Iris Marion. 1990. *Justice and the Politics of Difference*. Princeton, NJ: Princeton University Press.

Young, Iris Marion. 1992. "Five Faces of Oppression," in Thomas Wartenberg (ed.), *Rethinking Power*. New York: SUNY Press: 175–195.

Yuknis v. First Student Inc. 481 F3d 552. No. 06-3479. United States Court of Appeals, Seventh Circuit. Submitted February, 21, 2007. Decided March 28, 2007.

Index